Copyright © 1969
Philippine Copyright 1969

By South-Western Publishing Company

All Rights Reserved

The text of this publication, or any part thereof, may not be reproduced or transmitted in any form or by any means, electronic or
mechanical, including photocopying, recording, storage in an information retrieval system, or otherwise, without the prior written permission
of the publisher.

Library of Congress Catalog Card Number: 69-20125

T78—   3 4 5 6 7 8 H 5 4 3 2 1

Printed in U.S.A.

8TH EDITION
COLLEGE
TYPEWRITING

D. D. LESSENBERRY *Professor of Education, Emeritus
University of Pittsburgh*

S. J. WANOUS *Professor of Education, School of
Education, UCLA (Los Angeles)*

C. H. DUNCAN *Head, Business Education Department
Eastern Michigan University*

T78
INTERMEDIATE
COURSE

SOUTH-WESTERN PUBLISHING CO.

Cincinnati   •   Chicago   •   Dallas
Burlingame, Calif.   •   New Rochelle, N.Y.

CONTENTS  INTERMEDIATE TYPEWRITTEN COMMUNICATION

 # PREFACE

Office typists must have sufficient basic skill to enable them to type with confidence for extended periods. They must be able to use that skill in typing a wide variety of business papers consisting of letters, memorandums, reports, tables, outlines, invoices, statements, agenda, minutes, and other similar documents. Office typists must also be expert in handling the fine points of style relating to these papers, such as the typing of titles, attention lines, and reply reference and carbon copy notations in letters, footnotes in reports, and braced headings in tables.

Job know-how and good work habits are also essential. Office typists must know how to use the various scales and other devices on their typewriters. They must be able to proofread. They must know how to arrange their materials for quick use. Generally, they must be able to work with a minimum of supervision. This means that they will need to make many decisions about their work without help from someone else.

COLLEGE TYPEWRITING, Intermediate Course, Eighth Edition, was especially designed to help students meet the foregoing specifications of an office job.

ORGANIZATION OF THE BOOK

This book is conveniently organized into 75 well-balanced lessons, 4 end-of-book typing projects, and a Reference Guide of useful typewriting information.

The 75 lessons are organized into 12 sections. Each section includes a developing series of related problems, information on typing these problems, model illustrations, copy that first builds and then measures problem-solving skill, as well as copy that builds and measures basic skill. In addition, the first 4 lessons of the book provide for a quick review of the material covered in the first typewriting course. These lessons confirm a student's background training as well as his ability to tackle the new problems in the intermediate course.

Midway through the book and again at the end, there are two short sections which focus on the measurement of achievement in basic skill and production power. Two opportunities are thus provided to evaluate, intensively, each student's overall growth in skill, work habits, production know-how, proofreading, and other attributes of an office typist.

SPECIAL FEATURES OF THIS BOOK

1. The teaching experiences of more than 2,000 typewriting instructors have been woven into the pattern of this book. Before the revision got under way, college instructors across the country were asked to describe their classroom practices and preferences. These responses provided the background against which the lessons were revised.

2. Realistic, scientifically controlled copy is provided for basic skill measurement. The findings of classroom studies of copy difficulty, which were conducted by Dr. Jerry W. Robinson, established the difficulty levels of copy used for basic skill comparison and measurement. As a result, these materials are typical in difficulty of those used in offices. Moreover, the three factors having a high bearing on copy difficulty—syllable intensity, average strokes per word, and·percentage of high-frequency words—were held constant in the growth indexes throughout the 75 lessons, thus providing a consistent measure of student progress.

3. Clear, succinct, uniform directions are given for the first problems of each new group. Model illustrations are provided. Thereafter, the directions are gradually diminished until the student makes most of the decisions on matters of procedure, based on his past experience in typing similar problems.

4. Emphasis is placed on integrating spelling, punctuating, and capitalizing with typewriting, not only to make these skills more useful in an office setting but also to lay the foundation for careful proofreading.

5. Composing skill is developed through drills and uniquely devised problems. Office typists frequently compose short responses to incoming letters. Composing skill is developed in a similar setting in the 75 lessons and especially in one of the end-of-book projects, which is devoted completely to this type of learning.

Many other features which proved to be useful and desirable in former editions of the book have been further refined and retained.

ACKNOWLEDGMENTS

The authors express their grateful thanks to the instructors, students, and business workers who have contributed so generously of their ideas for the content and organization of this book. They have helped to make this book an effective aid to those who wish to learn to type with maximum skill and to those who teach typewriting at the college level.

Lessenberry • Wanous • Duncan

Problem 3: Minutes of Meeting (Partial)

2" top margin; leftbound with SS; 5-space ¶ indentions

	Words
ANNUAL MEETING OF THE STOCKHOLDERS	7

The annual meeting of Weaver Chemical Company shareholders was held June 30, 19--, at the Company's principal office, Weaver Building, 50 Washington Place, Providence, Rhode Island, at twelve o'clock noon, EDT, with Karl Warner, President and Chief Executive Officer, presiding.

Present on behalf of management were Louise Kramer, Vice-President; Kermit Fellows, Treasurer; and John Baldwin, General Counsel and Secretary.

Represented in person or by proxy were 25,000 shares of the Company's common stock, approximately 83½ percent of the total shares outstanding and entitled to vote.

Among the actions taken were the following:

1. Election of two directors for a term expiring in 1975. They are R. R. Irvine and G. C. Walker.

2. Approval of a resolution to amend the Certificate of Organization to provide for a two-for-one split of the common stock and to double the number of shares of common stock.

   For--15,112   Against--8,421   Not voting--1,467

3. Approval of a resolution to amend the Certificate of Organization and Bylaws in stated respects as to the price restriction on sales of stock to employees.

   For--19,077   Against--3,797   Not voting--2,126

In his opening statement, the Chairman said that the year just passed was a good year for the Company and that he believed the coming year would be another good year for it. The earnings for the first quarter look very satisfactory. The Chairman also referred to the Board's action which authorized an increase in the regular quarterly dividend from 50 cents to 55 cents a share, payable September 1 to holders of record July 16.

The meeting was adjourned at 1:30 p.m.

John Baldwin, Secretary

Words column:
7, 17, 29, 41, 53, 63, 73, 86, 92, 103, 115, 125, 134, 144, 154, 165, 174, 184, 189, 198, 209, 219, 229, 231, 240, 250, 263, 275, 287, 298, 310, 323, 327, 335, 339, 344

SECTION  BASIC AND PROBLEM SKILLS CHECKUP

LESSONS 76–79

Purpose. This section checks on your ability to operate a typewriter and to type samples of the problems covered in earlier lessons.

Machine Adjustments. Unless otherwise directed, use a 70-space line and single spacing for the drills. Follow the other directions carefully.

LESSON 76

76A Preparatory Practice ⑤ *each line three or more times*

Alphabet   The missile, its jets blazing, flew unswervingly; it exploded quickly.

Figure-symbol   Model #7006, marked $528.11, is selling for $435.99––a loss of $92.12.

Capitals   Senator John Poe visited the United States Naval Academy in Annapolis.

Fluency   No problem that we tackle is ever so big as the problem that we dodge.

   | 1 | 2 | 3 | 4 | 5 | 6 | 7 | 8 | 9 | 10 | 11 | 12 | 13 | 14 |

76B Typewriter Operation Checkup ⑩ *perform each operation as directed below*

1. **Paper Guide.** Set the paper guide at 0 (or whatever setting is appropriate for the typewriter you are using). See page iii if your typewriter needs a different setting.

2. **Margins.** Set the margin stops for a 50-space line; then a 60-space line; then a 70-space line.

3. **Paper Bail and Card Holders.** Have the card holders in "up" position. Raise the paper bail; twirl a sheet of paper into the typewriter; replace the paper bail. Work quickly.

4. **Line-Space Regulator.** Set the line-space regulator for double spacing.

5. **Touch Regulator.** (a) Set the touch regulator at its lowest setting; then type the following sentence:

    A sheet of paper that is 11 inches long will hold 66 horizontal lines.

   (b) Set the regulator at a medium setting and retype the sentence. (c) Set the regulator at its highest setting. Type the sentence again. (d) Set the regulator at the point you prefer.

6. **Paper Release.** Operate the paper release and remove the paper from the typewriter. Return the release to its normal position. Practice inserting and removing the paper several times.

76C Problem Checkup: Manuscripts; Word Division ㉟ *25′ timing; circle errors; figure g-pram*

$$\text{G-PRAM (gross production rate a minute)} = \frac{\text{Gross (total) words typed}}{\text{Length (in minutes) of writing}}$$

Problem 1: Unbound Manuscript

Margins: 2″ top; 1″ side; DS; 5-space ¶ indention

	Words
CHANGING TYPEWRITERS	4

• Triple-space

(¶ 1) Sometime during your training you may   12
be assigned to a make of typewriter you have   21
not used before. While each make has its indi-   30
vidual characteristics, basic skill requirements   40
are the same for all of them; and you should   49
be able to change from one make to another   58
with a minimum of difficulty. (¶ 2) Changing   66
from a nonelectric to an electric typewriter   76
can provide a different kind of experience.   84
The basic skill needed is still the same, but   93
you must adapt techniques to the instant   101

2" top margin; unbound report form; SS body of report as illustrated

	Words
May 20, 19--	3

WEAVER CHEMICAL COMPANY | 7

DS

Notice of Annual Meeting of Common Stockholders | 17

TS

To the Common Stockholders of | 23
Weaver Chemical Company | 28

The annual meeting of the common stockholders of this Company | 40
will be held at the principal office of the Company, Weaver Build- | 54
ing, 50 Washington Place, Providence, Rhode Island, on Tuesday, | 67
June 30, 19--, at twelve o'clock noon, EDT, for the following | 79
purposes: | 82

1. To elect two directors for a term expiring in 1975. | 93

2. To consider a resolution to amend the Employees' | 103
Profit-Sharing Plan. | 108

3. To consider a resolution to amend Article II of the | 119
Bylaws to provide that the annual meeting of stock- | 130
holders of the Company shall be held on the last | 140
Tuesday of March in each and every year, or on such | 151
other day as a majority of the directors shall set | 161
from time to time. | 165

4. To consider a resolution amending the Certificate of | 177
Organization to provide for a two-for-one split of | 187
the common stock and to double the authorized shares | 198
of common stock. | 202

5. To consider a resolution ratifying the appointment | 213
of Haskins & Sells as the Company's auditors. | 222

Only common stockholders of record at the close of business | 234
May 15, 19--, will be entitled to vote at the meeting or any ad- | 247
journment thereof. | 251

Regardless of whether or not you now plan to attend the meet- | 263
ing, please execute the enclosed proxy and return it promptly in | 277
the envelope which is provided. If you are present at the meeting, | 290
you may, if you wish, revoke your proxy and vote in person. | 303

TS

John Baldwin	Karl Warner	308
Secretary	President	311

response of the electric machine. You may be   110
startled to find a number of extra characters   119
popping up in unexpected places, the machine   128
may "run away" from you once or twice, or   137
strange things may happen as you use the   145
wrong keys; but these mishaps usually right   154
themselves in a few days. (¶ 3) Remember   161
that it is the way of human nature to resist   170
any kind of change. Adjustments to new   178
situations require much time and patience. If   187
you work more slowly at first, however, think-   197
ing carefully about the location of new keys   206
and parts and trying to develop stroking   214
power to match that required by the new   222
machine, you will be back in top form in a   230
few days. But keep in mind that it is up to   240
you to adapt to the new machine—the ma-   248
chine cannot adapt to you.   253

Problem 2: Unbound Manuscript with Footnote

Margins: 2″ top; 1″ side; DS; SS and indent quo-
tation 5 spaces from both margins; SS footnote;
leave extra space between body and footnote
divider line to maintain a 1″ bottom margin

Words

TIME-SHARING   3

TS

(¶ 1) One of the most important develop-   9
ments since the computer was introduced is   18
time-sharing. It makes instant data processing   27
available to companies of all sizes at low cost.   37
(¶ 2) Lewis E. Lachter writes as follows: 45

    (¶ 3) There are time-sharing sys-   50
    tems today where as many as 100 per-   57
    sons are using a single computer at   64
    one time. Each individual feels he   71
    has exclusive use of the computer,   78
    and with the tremendous capacity of   86
    the hardware involved, he essentially   93
    does.[1]   95

(¶ 4) Banks and large industrial and engineer-   103
ing companies are the big users of time-   111

Words

sharing. More medium and small firms will   119
be using time-sharing as costs go down and   128
additional computers become available.   135

———————————   139

    [1]Lewis E. Lachter, "Closer Manager/   146
EDP Interaction," Administrative Manage-   158
ment (January, 1968), p. 21.   165

Problem 3: Numbered Items

Margins: 2″ top; 1″ side; SS; DS between num-
bered items; indent them 5 spaces from left margin

Words

WORD DIVISION   3

Divide—   5

  1. Words between syllables only.   11
  2. Hyphenated words and compounds at   19
    hyphens only.   22
  3. Words by putting as much as possible   30
    of the word on the first line to suggest   38
    the completed word.   42
  4. A word of three or more syllables at a   51
    one-letter syllable. Type the one-letter   59
    syllable on the first line unless it is part   68
    of such terminations as ible, able, or   78
    ical, in which case carry it to the sec-   86
    ond line. If a one-letter syllable pre-   94
    cedes a second one-letter syllable,   101
    divide between them.   105

Do not—   107

  5. Separate a one-letter syllable at the   116
    beginning or end of a word.   121
  6. Separate a two-letter syllable at the   130
    end of a word.   133
  7. Divide the last word on a page.   140

Avoid if possible—   144

  8. Separating a two-letter syllable at the   153
    beginning of a word.   157
  9. Dividing words at the ends of two or   165
    more consecutive lines or a word at   172
    the end of the last complete line of a   180
    paragraph.   182

Project 4: Administrative Reports

Use full sheets of paper. Prepare original copies only. Erase and correct your errors.

Vertical spacing as illustrated.
Arrange attractively on page.

Problem 1: Agenda for Meeting

	Words
WEAVER CHEMICAL COMPANY	5
Agenda for Meeting of the Board of Directors	14
April 12, 19––	17
1. Call to Order	20
2. Reading and Approval of Minutes	28
3. Reports of Officers	32
President's Report . . . . Karl Warner	45
Vice-President's Report . . . . Louise Kramer	58
Treasurer's Report . . . . Kermit Fellows	71
4. Reports of Standing Committees	78
Report on Branch Operations . . . . Anthony Mosich	92
Report on Production Activities . . . . David Jackey	104
Report on Research and Development . . . . Jeno Gabor	117
Report on Dividend Declaration . . . . Kermit Fellows	130
5. Reports of Special Committees	137
Report on Training Programs . . . . Oscar Noonan	150
Report on Changes in Pricing Policy . . . . . Xavier Kimball	163
Report on Change to Centrix System . . . . . John Baldwin	176
6. Resolutions	179
Resolution on Increasing Number of	186
Directors . . . . Louise Kramer	199
Resolution on Employing Salyer & Justiz,	207
Management Consultants . . . . Felix Cousens	220
Resolution on Increasing Salaries of	228
Officers . . . . Anthony Mosich	241
7. Announcement of Next Meeting	248
8. Adjournment	251

77A Preparatory Practice ⑤ *each line three or more times*

Alphabet   Brazilian Judge Frank Wavo is quietly confirming the risk of smallpox.

Figure-symbol   Mark Invoice 118299 "350 sets @ 67¢ a set, less 2 4/5% cash discount."

Direct reaches   Myron Trumble tried to unlock the gate in front of the deserted house.

Fluency   The future is not with the job; it is with the one who holds that job.

| 1 | 2 | 3 | 4 | 5 | 6 | 7 | 8 | 9 | 10 | 11 | 12 | 13 | 14 |

77B Typewriter Operation Checkup ⑩ *perform each operation; then type four 1' writings on the lines in No. 3*

Full sheet; 1½" top margin; DS; DS twice between writings

1. **Carriage-Release Levers and Tab Clear Key.** Locate these parts on your typewriter. Use them to clear any tabulator stops now set on your machine.

2. **Tab Set Key.** Set a tabulator stop at the center of the paper.

3. **Tabulator and Backspace Key.** Tabulate to the center of the paper; use the backspace key to center each of the following titles horizontally:

The Development of Young Data Processors
A Plan to Stop the Gold Drain
Look What's Happening to Glass!
GENERAL PREDICTIONS ABOUT COMPUTER USES

77C Problem Checkup: Memorandum; Announcement; Postal Card ㉟ *25' timing; circle errors; figure g-pram*

Proofreader's Marks

Mark	Meaning	Example
∧	insert	for my ∧car (new)
ℬ	delete	us ~~all~~ to go
∪ or tr	transpose	to (quickly go)
lc	lower-case letters	the Manager
⌒	close up space	could see h⌒er
ital	change to italic	the Journal of
#	add space	in#the house
⌐	move to left	⌐A man earns
⌐	move to right	Learn the names
≡	capitalize	south; South; South
ds	double spacing	ds → 1/2
ss	single spacing	ss → 1/2
⁋	paragraph	

Problem 1: Rough Draft of a Memorandum

Half sheet; 1" top margin; 1" side margins; current date; block style

	Words
Current date *(September 26, 1972, line 6; 3 blank lines here)*	3
Subject: Office copiers	8
The ideal copier would produce dry copies in less than a ~~minute~~ second	21
at less than a penny a copy. It would be compact, use uncoated	34
paper, and reproduces all colors. In addition, it would be simple,	47
silent, odorless, and durable. Even if such a copier were available,	61
many managers would not buy it. They would recognize that, while	74
they only needed some of its features, they would have to pay for	87
all of them.	90

Braced Headings. A braced heading is a title that applies to two or more columns. In typing the table, leave room for the braced heading; then insert it after typing the column heads. To center the braced heading, proceed as follows: (1) Move the carriage to the first space in the area to be bracketed; note the number on the scale. (2) Move the carriage to the last space in the area to be bracketed; note the number on the scale. (3) Add the two numbers; divide by 2 to get the number on which to center the heading.

Exact center
DS body
Decide spaces be-
tween columns

Note. *Use a ruler and pen to draw the vertical rulings.*

Words

EMPLOYEES AND SALARIES BY DEPARTMENTS

←—DS

December 31, 1968

←—DS
←—DS

Department	Average Weekly Salary		
	All	Male	Female
Data Processing	$280	$300	$225
Accounting	240	250	225
Collections	280	310	250
Billing	192	190	195
Payroll	220	250	200
Training	330	320	350
Administrative	280	275	300
Mail	170	180	165

←—SS
←—DS
←—SS
←—DS
←—SS

8
11
33
37
47
50
61
68
73
77
81
85
90
95
98
109

Exact center
DS body
Decide spaces
between columns

Words

SALARIES PAID PER EMPLOYEE AND PERCENT OF TOTAL SALES

Division	Per Employee		Percent of Sales	
	1960	1968	1960	1968
Northwest	$8,496	$10,400	49%	49%
Pacific	8,312	10,600	47	50
Rocky Mountain	8,100	9,900	45	46
Southwest	7,920	9,300	42	43
Midwest	8,200	9,250	48	49
South	7,680	8,900	42	44
Overseas	8,050	10,400	45	45

6
11
35
41
51
55
67
74
80
86
92
97
102
108
120

Problem 2: Centered Announcement

Half sheet; DS; center problem vertically and each line horizontally

Line 11 long way up   Words

THE WAGNER-PERKINS PUBLISHING COMPANY   8

invites you to a   11

CONTINENTAL BRUNCH   15

served continuously from 11 a.m. to 1 p.m.   23

CABANA ROOM OF THE HOTEL EL DORADO   30

(use next Wednesday's date) October 4, 1972 33

Problem 3: Centered Announcement

Full sheet; center Problem 2 in reading position (2 lines higher than if it were centered exactly); TS

Problem 4: Postal Card

48-space line; SS; block style; current date; address the card to yourself; use your surname in salutation

September 26, 1972   Words

We were very much pleased to receive your   16

subscription to TRAVEL. We look forward to   24

having you as a regular reader for many years 33

to come.   35

If you have any questions about your subscrip- 44

tion, please write us. Again, thanks.   52

TRAVEL Magazine   55/67

LESSON 78

78A Preparatory Practice ⑤ *each line three or more times*

Alphabet   This capital, Byzantium, was subjected to six very frightening quakes.

Figure-symbol He said, "Ship 14 #872 lamps, listed at $39.50 less 6% cash discount."

Long reaches   My uncle, Jimmy Bricklin, mumbled sadly, "My TV must be broken again."

Fluency   One step a day takes me on the way to the place I want to be some day.

| 1 | 2 | 3 | 4 | 5 | 6 | 7 | 8 | 9 | 10 | 11 | 12 | 13 | 14 |

78B Typewriter Operation Checkup ⑩ *perform each operation as directed below*

Full sheet; 70-space line; DS; 1½" top margin

1. **Margin-Release Key.** Type Sentence 1 below. Turn the cylinder forward about five lines; depress the margin-release key; move the carriage to the extreme left. Erase *may*. Return to original typing position; type *can* in the erased space.

2. **Ratchet Release.** Type Sentence 2. Operate the ratchet release; turn the cylinder forward about three inches. Disengage the ratchet release and turn the cylinder back to the line of writing. Type over the sentence.

3. **Variable Line Spacer.** Type Sentence 2. Operate the variable line spacer and turn the cylinder forward about three inches. With the variable line spacer still depressed, return as accurately as you can to the writing line and release the variable line spacer. Type over the sentence.

4. **Bell and Margin Lock.** Space forward 20 spaces from where you have set the left margin. Type Sentence 3 until you hear the bell ring. Count the number of spaces between the ringing of the bell and the locking of the machine. Consider this number when you set your right margin stop.

Sentence 1   Both pica and elite type may be measured six lines to a vertical inch.

Sentence 2   A sheet of paper 8½ inches wide will hold 102 elite or 85 pica spaces.

Sentence 3   For a 1-inch top margin on a page, you should begin to type on Line 7.

| 1 | 2 | 3 | 4 | 5 | 6 | 7 | 8 | 9 | 10 | 11 | 12 | 13 | 14 |

Problem 5: Table with Horizontal Rulings

Exact center; DS body; decide spaces between columns

LABOR FORCE WITH PROJECTIONS

Male Only

Age Group	1960	1970	1980
14 to 19 years	3,792,000	5,164,000	5,744,000
20 to 24 years	4,939,000	7,466,000	9,064,000
25 to 34 years	10,940,000	12,063,000	17,590,000
35 to 44 years	11,454,000	10,930,000	12,084,000
45 to 54 years	9,568,000	10,725,000	10,219,000
55 to 64 years	6,445,000	7,388,000	8,184,000
65 years and over	2,425,000	2,108,000	2,096,000
Total	49,563,000	55,844,000	64,981,000

Source: Statistical Abstract of the United States, 1966, p 219.

Words
6
8
34
39
52
62
71
81
91
100
110
120
126
134
147
169

Problem 6: Table with Horizontal Rulings

Exact center; DS body; decide spaces between columns; add horizontal rulings as in Problem 5

COMPARISON OF SALES TO QUOTA

For 1968

Salesman	Quota	Sales	Percentage
Caldwell, Robert A.	$75,000	$70,000	93%
Draughn, William	82,000	85,000	104
Elbertson, George	66,000	66,000	100
Fleming, Burton	90,000	82,000	91
Gamble, Theodore	82,000	83,000	101
Henderson, T. E.	75,000	70,000	93
Jackson, Charles	85,000	90,000	106
Kinsey, F. Norbert	78,000	85,000	109
Longway, Myron F.	60,000	55,000	92

Words
6
8
30
37
48
57
64
71
78
85
92
99
106
113
125

Problem 1: Personal Business Letter in Modified Block Style with Open Punctuation

Full sheet; 65-space line; open punctuation; date on Line 14 from top; address on 4th line below date

	Words
4201 Broadway | Portland, Oregon 97232 |	8
April 15, 19–– | London & Bond Insurance	15
Co., Ltd. | 515 West Sixth Street | Los	23
Angeles, California* 90014 | Gentlemen	30
(¶ 1) Thank you for your comments about	37
the article I wrote for The Office. My origi-	48
nal manuscript contained answers to your	56
questions about typing envelopes, but limita-	65
tions of space did not permit them to be	73
included. I can, however, summarize my rec-	82
ommendations for you. (¶ 2) On a small en-	89
velope type the address (blocked and single-	98

*Always leave 2 spaces between the state name or abbreviation and the zip Code.

	Words
spaced) 2 inches from the top and 2 1/2 inches	107
from the left edge of the envelope. On a	116
large envelope type the address in this style	125
2 1/2 inches from the top and 4 inches from	134
the left edge of the envelope. (¶ 3) Type	141
mailing notations (such as AIRMAIL) below	149
the stamp and at least 3 line spaces above the	159
envelope address. Type the return address	167
(blocked and single-spaced) on Line 2 from	176
the top of the envelope and 3 spaces from the	185
left edge. Type addressee notations (such as	194
Please Forward) a triple space below the re-	203
turn address and 3 spaces from the left edge	212
of the envelope. (¶ 4) I hope the guides are	220
helpful. Please write to me again if there is	229
any further information I can provide. | Very	238
truly yours | Henry S. Baxter	244

Problem 2: Business Letter in Modified Block Style with Mixed Punctuation

Letterhead (or full sheet); 60-space line; mixed punctuation; date on Line 18 from top; address on 4th line below date*

	Words
Current date | Dr. William Biel | 3420 Viola	9
Street | Danville, IL 61832 | Dear Dr.	16
Biel (¶ 1) Will you take just a minute or	24
two to do us a favor? We need your answers	32
to a few questions about the banks in your	41
area. This is one way that banking services	50
can be improved to serve you better. (¶ 2)	58
The enclosed questionnaire is very short––it	67
will take less than five minutes of your time.	76
Please fill it out and return it to us in the	85
envelope provided. (¶ 3) Gibbs Associates is	93
a public opinion polling firm and is the Mid-	102
west affiliate of Elmo Popper in New York.	111
We are members of the Chicago Better Busi-	119
ness Bureau and have been serving clients in	128
this area for a number of years. (¶ 4) Thank	136
you for your help. | Sincerely yours | William	145
F. Gibbs | President | (*Your initials*) Enclosures	152

*Insert the necessary punctuation when mixed punctuation is specified even though it does not appear in the copy.

GIBBS ASSOCIATES

330 N. Michigan Avenue
Chicago, IL 60601

Midwest Affiliate of Elmo Popper, New York

Current date

Dr. William Biel
3420 Viola Street
Danville, IL 61832

Dear Dr. Biel:

Will you take just a minute or two to do us a favor? We need
your answers to a few questions about the banks in your area.
This is one way that banking services can be improved to serve
you better.

The enclosed questionnaire is very short--it will take less
than five minutes of your time. Please fill it out and return
it to us in the envelope provided.

Gibbs Associates is a public opinion polling firm and is the
Midwest affiliate of Elmo Popper in New York. We are members
of the Chicago Better Business Bureau and have been serving
clients in this area for a number of years.

Thank you for your help.

Sincerely yours,

William F. Gibbs

William F. Gibbs
President

bdf

Enclosures

Modified Block Style with Mixed Punctuation

Problem 3: Table with Leaders

Typing Leaders. Strike the period and the space bar alternately, using the first finger of each hand. Type the first leader in the second space after the last letter of the first item. Leave three or four spaces between the last leader and the largest number in the next (figure) column. To align the periods, note on the front of the cylinder scale whether you are typing on odd or even numbers for the first line. Use this pattern to type the periods in the remaining lines.

Reading position
SS body
Decide spaces
*   between columns*

CIRCULATION OF LEADING U.S. MAGAZINES*

Top 11

Magazine	Circulation	Words
		8
		9
		17
Reader's Digest	17,336,168	27
TV Guide	12,718,141	37
McCall's	8,545,839	46
Look	7,756,351	56
Family Circle	7,386,700	65
Life	7,354,615	75
Better Homes & Gardens	7,274,726	84
Woman's Day	7,225,073	93
Ladies' Home Journal	6,779,059	103
Good Housekeeping	5,618,738	112
National Geographic	5,607,457	122
		125

Source: The World Almanac, 1969, p. 352.   137

*Based on average circulation per issue during the six months prior to January 1, 1968.   148 / 155

Problem 4: Table with Leaders

Half sheet
Exact center
DS body
Decide spaces
*   between columns*

TYPE OF TRAINING GIVEN TO GRADUATES

Figures Are Number of Employers

Before-Job Assignment	High School	College	Words
			7
			14
			30
Training by Supervisor	14	13	39
General Trainee Orientation	14	13	49
Informal Training	11	9	58
Special School	3	3	67
			71

Source: "84% of Surveyed Companies Supplement Formal Education," Administrative Management (August, 1968), p. 59.   82 / 97 / 99

Problem 3: Outline

Full sheet; 40-space line; 2" top margin

	Words
THE OFFICE OF 1984	4
TS	

I. SHORTAGE OF ADMINISTRATIVE MANAGERS — 12

DS

A. Four Times as Many Needed — 18
B. Protection from Recruiting Raids — 25
C. New Forms of Compensation — 31

DS

II. NEW JOBS — 35

A. Office Technicians — 40
B. Governmental Relations Experts — 47

III. OBSOLETE JOBS — 52

A. Middle Management Personnel — 58
  1. Quality control experts — 65
  2. Insurance underwriters — 71
B. Two Million to Lose Jobs — 77

	Words
IV. NEW KINDS OF COMPENSATION	84

A. New Stock Option Programs — 90
B. Multiple Fringe Benefits — 96
C. Loss-of-Job Insurance — 101
D. Nonmonetary Alternatives — 107
E. Individualization of Income — 113

V. NEW MANAGEMENT ACTIVITIES — 120

A. Development of Job Standards — 126
B. Research on Salary Plans — 132
C. Emphasis on Needs and Opportunities Rather than Programs — 139, 145
D. Personnel Transfer and Retraining — 153
E. Creation of New Jobs — 158

VI. MECHANIZATION — 163

A. Increased Use of Computers — 169
B. Improved Communication Systems — 176

LESSON 79

79A Preparatory Practice ⑤ *each line three or more times*

Alphabet	Ezra Weber likes the piquancy of orange juice mixed with clover honey.
Figure-symbol	In 1968, storms delayed delivery of 4,370 tons (25% of all shipments).
Third row	Our pitcher, Quentin, threw three powerful pitches and won the series.
Fluency	There are many more trapdoors to the bottom than shortcuts to the top.

| 1 | 2 | 3 | 4 | 5 | 6 | 7 | 8 | 9 | 10 | 11 | 12 | 13 | 14 |

79B Technique Improvement: Stroking ⑳

1. Type each sentence three times.
2. Type a 1' writing on each sentence. Type on the *control* level.

Control Level: When the purpose of your typing is to type with ease and control, drop back in rate and type on the *control level.*

1	Shift keys	Barry and Keith Johnson met in Mexico City in July or early in August.
2	Long reaches	The men received a number of summaries of the stormy political report.
3	Double letters	All his possessions have been transferred to your home in Tallahassee.
4	One hand	As Johnny Carver asserted, Fred was regarded as carefree and careless.
5	Balanced hand	The men may visit the ruins in the ancient city if they get the forms.
6	3d and 4th fingers	As Alex pointed out in his paper, the essay questions were quite easy.
7	Hyphen	They found this to be an up-to-date plan for out-of-town credit sales.
8	Direct reaches	Gregg Bright hunted with Cedric Nunis in the jungle around this river.

| 1 | 2 | 3 | 4 | 5 | 6 | 7 | 8 | 9 | 10 | 11 | 12 | 13 | 14 |

Project 3: Tables with Special Problems

Use full sheets unless directions state otherwise. Prepare original copies only. Erase and correct errors.

Problem 1: Table with Multicolumnar Heading

Double-space the body of the table. Place it in reading position. Decide on spaces between the columns.

Type the one-line headings in the first two columns parallel with the last line of the third column heading.

			Words	
			Prob. 1	Prob. 2
AREA AND POPULATION OF THE WORLD			7	5
Area Given in Kilometers			12	
Continent	Area[1]	Midyear 1967 Estimated Population	14 16 27	7 9 18
Africa	30,312,924	328,134,000	33	27
America, North[2]	24,246,904	304,439,000	40	21
America, South	17,842,516	174,246,000	48	32
Asia[3]	27,530,116	1,907,481,000	55	36
Europe[4]	4,928,906	451,450,000	61	40
Oceania	8,510,947	18,127,000	67	44
USSR	22,402,200	235,543,000	73 78	48 51
World	135,774,513	3,419,420,000	85 89	55 59

Source: The World Almanac, 1969, p. 651. — 98 / 68

[1]Including inland waters, but not some uninhabited polar regions. — 111

[2]Hawaii, Central America, and Caribbean Islands included. — 123 / 80

[3]Excluding USSR, but including all of Turkey. — 132 / 89

[4]Excluding USSR and European part of Turkey. — 141 / 99

Problem 2: Revision of Table

Type the table in Problem 1 again. This time include only the information about the names of the continents and estimated population. Revise the headings and footnotes accordingly. Type the table in exact center.

79C Straight-Copy Checkup ⑮ *two 5′ control-level writings; figure gwam on the better writing*

Full sheet; 70-space line; DS; 5-space ¶ indention

When you type on the control level, drop back in rate and work for ease and precision of stroking.

All letters are used.

	1′	5′	
GWAM			

¶ 1
1.5 SI
5.6 AWL
80% HFW

The serious student who wishes to enter the business world should — 13 | 3 | 56

utilize his school years to develop the traits, skills, and know-how — 27 | 5 | 59

that are generally demanded of all those who want to attain success in — 41 | 8 | 62

it. The student should recognize, for example, the importance of neat, — 56 | 11 | 65

suitable clothing and good grooming. He should learn that if he wishes — 70 | 14 | 68

to get very far in an office job, he must be able to dress well—-even — 84 | 17 | 70

on a limited budget. — 88 | 18 | 71

¶ 2
1.5 SI
5.6 AWL
80% HFW

The student who desires to find a job in the business world will — 13 | 20 | 74

also learn how to express himself in clear, appropriate language. This — 27 | 23 | 77

ability is usually placed at the top of the list of those most needed — 41 | 26 | 80

by the graduate. As a result, he will build his vocabulary with the — 55 | 29 | 82

aid of a dictionary whenever he can. He will learn to spell, and to — 69 | 31 | 85

structure and punctuate his sentences. He will know that writing and — 83 | 34 | 88

speaking skills can be acquired with practice. — 92 | 36 | 90

¶ 3
1.5 SI
5.6 AWL
80% HFW

The able student with an office position as his ultimate goal will — 13 | 39 | 92

learn how to act as well as look the part. While correct clothes and — 27 | 42 | 95

meticulous grooming are important, so are good posture, the right — 41 | 44 | 98

attitude, and a pleasant voice. There are few employers, however, who — 55 | 47 | 101

select an attractive package that has but little of value in it, so the — 69 | 50 | 104

more ability a student has, the better will be his chances of getting — 83 | 53 | 106

the job he really desires. — 88 | 54 | 107

1′ GWAM | 1 | 2 | 3 | 4 | 5 | 6 | 7 | 8 | 9 | 10 | 11 | 12 | 13 | 14 |
5′ GWAM | 1 | 2 | 3 |

79D Skill-Comparison and Transfer Typing ⑩ *two 1′ writings on each sentence; compare gwam*

Words

Goal — Most men can do better work with machines than without them. — 12

Shift keys — Kathy Dow will visit Lisbon, Rome, and Florence this summer. — 12

Rough draft — Far too many of us quit looking for work when we find a job. — 12

Script — A scientist knows that he who fears failure seldom succeeds. — 12

Problem 10: Personal Letter in Modified Block Style with Mixed Punctuation

Letter from: Mrs. Henrietta Taylor, 1985 Balmoral Park, Boston, MA 02127

	Words
¶ 1 On Thursday of last week, one of your	24
vans delivered some furniture that had been in	34
storage for some time in your warehouse in	42
Andover. The dining room table was badly	51
damaged. The top is scratched in a number of	60
places. The base of one of the legs is splin-	69
tered.	70
¶ 2 The upholstery on one of the living room	78
chairs is ripped. Some liquid had been spilled	88
on another chair. At any rate, the fabric is	97
badly stained. Both of the chairs will have to	107
be reupholstered or replaced.	113
¶ 3 Will you please let me know how you	120
wish to handle this matter. I am enclosing a	129
photostatic copy of the shipping order that	138
accompanied the furniture.	143
¶ 4 I shall appreciate receiving a reply from	152
you soon, as we wish to use the table and the	161
two chairs.	164
Supply the appropriate closing lines.	172

Problem 11: Response to Problem 10

Write a courteous response to the letter. Tell Mrs. Taylor that her furniture was fully insured against damage. Enclose an insurance claim form and an envelope, stamped and addressed to you, for the return of the form.

Ask Mrs. Taylor to fill in the form, describing fully the nature of the damage. You will get an insurance adjuster to settle the claim promptly.

Problem 12: Follow-up on Letter Written for Problem 11

Write another letter to Mrs. Taylor, dated a week later than the first one, telling her that you are returning the insurance claim form for her signature. She neglected to sign it. In other respects, the form was filled in satisfactorily.

Problem 13: Letter Requesting Reservations

Letter to: Honolulu Palms Hotel, 7291 Diamond Head Road, Honolulu, HI 96815

Write a letter requesting reservations for six double rooms and a conference room to accommodate ten men. The conference room is to be equipped with a table and chairs for ten.

The reservations are for a four-day period, beginning a month from today. Specify the exact days. Request a confirmation of the reservation.

Problem 14: Modified Block Letter with Mixed Punctuation

Letter from: Honolulu Palms Hotel (see Problem 13)

	Words
¶ 1 Thank you for your request for reserva-	25
tions. It was nice of you to think of the	33
Honolulu Palms Hotel, and we are delighted	42
to be your host. Your reservations are as	50
follows:	52
Arrival: *Give date of arrival.*	58
Departure: *Give date of departure.*	63
Accommodations: 6 double rooms and a	71
conference room.	74
Rate: $22 a day for each double room.	80
$30 a day for the conference room.	88
¶ 2 An advance deposit of $152 is required.	96
Your reservations will be confirmed when	104
we receive this deposit.	109
¶ 3 All of us at Honolulu Palms Hotel are	117
looking forward to your visit with us. You	126
will enjoy our personal hospitality. Everyone	135
will do his utmost to make your conference a	144
happy and productive one.	149
Sincerely yours Richard M. Chow, Manager	158

Letter 15: Response to Problem 14

Write a letter to the Honolulu Palms Hotel to accompany the check for the deposit requested. Indicate that you would like to have in the conference room a portable chalk board and also a bulletin board for the display of charts and posters.

Unless otherwise directed, proceed as follows:
Drill Copy: Full sheet; 70-space line; SS.
Paragraph Copy: Full sheet; 70-space line; DS; 5-space ¶ indention.

Production Copy: Letterhead (or full sheet); current date (unless given); your reference initials; erase and correct your errors. Letter form, carbon copies, and envelopes should be used as indicated.

LESSON 80

80A Preparatory Practice ⑤ *each line at least three times*

Alphabet	The vast exodus of workingmen was probably just one equalizing factor.
Figure-symbol	Lee & Dun's price, $53.40, is 2½ times as high as their 1967–68 price.
First row	Can Mr. Van Bux, the banker, visualize our volume six months from now?
Fluency	A right approach to work that must be done cuts the size of most jobs.

| 1 | 2 | 3 | 4 | 5 | 6 | 7 | 8 | 9 | 10 | 11 | 12 | 13 | 14 |

80B Communication Aid: Spelling ⑤

1. Type these commonly misspelled words twice; study the words as you type them.

2. Close your book; type the words from the dictation of your instructor. Check your work.

chosen confident committee balance calendar buoyant chaperon conquered

temperament statement studying shining similar familiar humorous chord

committing coming copies indictment existence experience guard hurried

| 1 | 2 | 3 | 4 | 5 | 6 | 7 | 8 | 9 | 10 | 11 | 12 | 13 | 14 |

80C Technique Improvement: Response Patterns ㉓

1. Type each sentence three times.
2. Type a 1' writing on each. Use the response pattern indicated.
Stroke: See, think, and type difficult combinations letter by letter.

Word: See, think, and type short, easy words as word wholes.
Combination: Type short, easy words as word wholes; type difficult combinations letter by letter. Blend the two into a smooth typing rhythm.

1	Stroke	Their response to the recent campaign went far beyond my expectations.
2	Stroke	Educational budgets of large companies often exceed those of colleges.
3	Word	When he knows that a thing should be done, he can find a way to do it.
4	Word	We all know that he can do the work the way it can and should be done.
5	Combination	They know that in the long run this project will yield useful results.
6	Combination	No one, however, believes that we need to leave the outcome to chance.
7	Combination	Except for what is marked, they will be glad to accept their shipment.
8	Combination	If he has some time sometime this afternoon, we can discuss his plans.

| 1 | 2 | 3 | 4 | 5 | 6 | 7 | 8 | 9 | 10 | 11 | 12 | 13 | 14 |

Problem 6: AMS Simplified Style

Letter from: Avery Communications Corporation, 24923 Oakcrest Avenue, Baltimore, MD 21234

	Words
INTRODUCING: THE UNCOMPLICATED	21
COPIER	22

Your secretary is a career girl. She is going 32
to use everything she learned at Miss Par- 40
snip's Business School—or die trying. So far, 49
she has reorganized your files, rearranged 58
your schedule, reassured your clients, rebuffed 68
your nuisance callers, repaired your desk 76
lamp, and relaxed your tensions. But she re- 85
fuses to waste her time or yours with that 93
complicated copier you have. 99

We make a copier that makes a career a 107
cinch. It's the Avery 300. It makes the most 117
readable electrostatic copies of anything its 126
size. It has the best lens of its kind, made by 136
the Kineta Camera people. It copies every- 144
thing. 146

The 300 is a workhorse that doesn't quit 154
under pressure. It just plugs in and works, 163
and works, and works. It doesn't need an 171
M.I.T. graduate to make repairs. It probably 180
won't need a repairman at all, because it 189
doesn't have any tricky parts. It runs on 197
metal gears and metal drive chains, instead 206
of nylon gears and rubber belts. In addition, 216
it has a separate drying section. Its only pur- 225
pose is to turn out dry copies. 232

There is nothing more beautiful than a ma- 240
chine that works—unless it is a secretary who 249
does the same thing. The booklet enclosed 258
gives you complete details. Write us for fur- 267
ther information or a free demonstration. 276

LYLE B. THOMPSON - SALES MANAGER 283

Enclosure 285

Problem 7: Response to Problem 6

Write a letter to the Avery Communications Corporation, attention Mr. Thompson. Thank the company for the booklet. Ask for additional information on the copier, such as the kind of original copy that can be reproduced, number of copies it will make in a minute, cost per copy, possibilities of renting the machine, etc. Indicate that you are not ready to buy yet but that, when you are, you will request a demonstration.

Problem 8: Modified Block Letter with Open Punctuation

Letter from: Automatic Dictation Systems, 4499 Neilson Avenue, Youngstown, OH 44502

	Words
Subject: A New Solution to an Old Problem	25

¶ 1 With AUTOMATIC dictation, there is noth- 33
ing to set up or get ready and no machinery 42
to handle. There are no discs, tapes, or cas- 51
settes to fool with; no supplies to buy—ever. 60

¶ 2 The AUTOMATIC handset, which is one 68
third the size of a desk telephone, is all you 77
ever handle. It's as natural as talking on the 86
telephone. You enjoy ease and convenience 95
you never dreamed possible. 101

¶ 3 A sliding switch lets you review one 108
word or your entire dictation, correct your 117
errors, or change your mind. Your secretary 126
will hear perfect, ready-to-type dictation in 135
a clear, natural voice. 140

¶ 4 The transcription unit lights up when 148
there is dictation to be typed. The light goes 157
out when work is caught up. Your secretary 166
will have fewer interruptions, fewer last- 174
minute "rush" jobs. She will love AUTOMATIC 183
dictation! 186

¶ 5 The AUTOMATIC is an "intercom with a 193
memory." You can dictate from any outside 202
telephone or from your home. It will receive 211
salesmen's reports automatically. It keeps 220
your office open 24 hours a day. 227

¶ 6 For more information write for DICTA- 234
TION AIDS, a small book with new ideas on 242
solving an old problem. 249

Yours very truly George P. Ellsworth Assis- 258
tant Sales Manager 262

Problem 9: Response to Problem 8

Send for the booklet and for additional information about the device described in Problem 8. Ask two or three specific questions that you would like to have answered. Include a subject heading in your letter.

80D Building Speed ⑰ *use combination response*

1. Type two 1' writings on each ¶. **2.** Type two 3' writings on all ¶s. **3.** Compute *gwam* for each writing.

All letters are used.

		GWAM	
		1'	3'

¶1
1.5 SI
5.6 AWL
80% HFW

Summarizing is a powerful study tool. To develop it, you must learn to condense into one or two short paragraphs the contents of an entire textbook chapter. This ability will separate the men from the boys on a quiz. A summary should contain in your own words the main ideas in the material you have covered.

13	4	74
27	9	78
40	13	83
54	18	88
62	21	90

¶2
1.5 SI
5.6 AWL
80% HFW

Outlining is another practical aid to learning, as it will help you build the ability to think logically. When you outline, you summarize the text of a chapter and arrange ideas on a scale that shows the importance of one point to another. Just practice outlining the material you read. If you do, you will grow in the ability to think.

14	25	95
28	30	100
42	35	104
56	39	109
68	43	113

¶3
1.5 SI
5.6 AWL
80% HFW

One authority in the learning field recommends the use of a question outline. It is one in which the terse notes normally included in an outline are replaced by questions on the significant points covered in a chapter. If you try this aid, you will learn that it would require almost fiendish ingenuity on the part of an instructor to design a set of questions which you did not anticipate.

13	48	117
27	52	122
41	57	127
55	62	131
69	66	136
79	70	139

1' GWAM | 1 | 2 | 3 | 4 | 5 | 6 | 7 | 8 | 9 | 10 | 11 | 12 | 13 | 14 |
3' GWAM | 1 | 2 | 3 | 4 | 5 |

LESSON 81

81A Preparatory Practice ⑤ *each line at least three times*

Alphabet	They have excused a man who plagiarized quotes from books or journals.
Figure-symbol	Roman & O'Hare's 5% discount ($27.50) reduced our 1968 total to $433.
Hyphen	They cannot re-cover the chair for your son-in-law with that material.
Fluency	The worker who takes pride in his work seldom needs to do a job twice.

| 1 | 2 | 3 | 4 | 5 | 6 | 7 | 8 | 9 | 10 | 11 | 12 | 13 | 14 |

81B Technique Improvement: Response Patterns ⑩ *two 1' writings on each line*

1	Stroke	New concepts and techniques are being tested to deal with the project.
2	Word	The man who knows and knows that he knows is a man who will do things.
3	Combination	Either you or I can go. Neither of us has a session during that hour.
4	Combination	The power of positive thought is, moreover, more than a clever slogan.

| 1 | 2 | 3 | 4 | 5 | 6 | 7 | 8 | 9 | 10 | 11 | 12 | 13 | 14 |

Project 2: Composing Business Letters

Type the following letters in the style directed. Date the letters one week earlier than today. Erase and correct your errors. All letters except the letter in Problem 13 are written to

Longway Corporation
15 Stevens Street
Andover, MA   01810

Gentlemen

You are a correspondent for this company. Type your response to each letter in the modified block style with mixed punctuation. Use today's date. Type your name in the closing lines. Your title is *Correspondent*. Correct your errors.

Type one carbon copy of each response.

Problem 1: Block Style Letter with Open Punctuation

Letter from: Solvtax Data Systems, 1435 Broadway, New York, NY   10018

	Words
¶ 1 There is a cure for tax headaches. It is SOLVTAX, the COBOL software package that calculates all payroll withholding taxes.	25 33 42

¶ 2 No matter what hardware you have, the SOLVTAX module fits right into your main payroll savings in programming, documentation, and systems analysis time. All states approve SOLVTAX.   49 57 66 75 78

¶ 3 Our informative booklet will help you decide how well SOLVTAX can work for you. There's no cost or obligation. Send for your personal copy today.   86 94 104 108

Yours very truly   Benjamin Daniels   Sales Department   116 119

Problem 2: Response to Problem 1

Send for the booklet. Ask if the software package is available in PL/1, as this is the programming language used by your company. Indicate that your company employs about 300 workers with frequent changes in personnel. Find out if SOLVTAX is adaptable to frequent changes.

Problem 3: Modified Block Letter with Mixed Punctuation

Letter from: Graphic Control Systems, 1379 Peachtree Street, N.E., Atlanta, GA   30309

	Words
¶ 1 With the GRAPHICMASTER system you can see how to get things done. You see a graphic picture of your operations, spotlighted in color. You have the facts at eye level. It saves time, cuts costs, and prevents errors.	24 32 42 52 61

¶ 2 The GRAPHICMASTER is the finest "efficiency expert" you can put to work for you. It shows instantly the progress of every operation and alerts you to trouble spots. It is used by successful decision makers everywhere.   68 77 86 95 105

¶ 3 The GRAPHICMASTER is ideal for production, maintenance, scheduling, inventory, sales, traffic, and many other uses. It is a simple, flexible tool. You write or type on cards, and post them on a board. All cards are interchangeable.   112 122 131 141 149 152

¶ 4 The unit, which is made of aluminum, is compact and attractive. Over one million are in use. The complete price is $69.50. Write for a free booklet, or ask for an informative demonstration by our dealer in your city.   160 169 178 188 196

Yours very truly   GRAPHIC CONTROL SYSTEMS   204 205
Herbert Wiley   Vice-President   211

Problem 4: Response to Problem 3

Send for the booklet and request a demonstration. Explain that your company is engaged in the trucking and storage business and that you are interested in a system that will help you to know, day by day, the locations of your various moving vans.

Problem 5: Follow-up on Letter Written in Problem 4

Write another letter to Graphic Control Systems requesting cancellation of the demonstration requested in your earlier letter. You have already purchased a similar device that works on a magnetic principle. You believe it is better suited to your needs. Date the letter a week later than the one in Problem 4.

Information on Typing Letters

Stationery

Business letters are usually typed on 8½- by 11-inch letterhead stationery. For letters of more than one page, plain paper of the same size, color, and quality as the letterhead is usually used for the additional pages. Onionskin or manifold paper is used for carbon copies. Smaller letterheads of 8½ by 5½ or 5½ by 8½ may be used for short letters.

Letter Placement

Some offices use standard side margins for all letters. Others vary the side margins according to letter length. The longer the letter, the narrower the margins. Office typists place letters by judgment. A placement table, such as the one given below, plus practice, will help you develop this intuitive sense. Disregard the table as soon as possible.

How to Use the Placement Table

Column 5 tells you on what line from the top edge of the paper to type the date for business letters of various lengths.

In business letters, the first line of the address is typed on the 4th line space below the date.

Note that each 50-word increase in average-length letters (101-300 words) calls for two fewer line spaces between the top of the paper and the date line.

Letters in which the space between the top edge of the letterhead and the first line of the address approximately equals the space between the last line of the body and the bottom edge appear to be well centered.

Letters that contain such special features as attention and subject lines, long quotations, enumerations, tables, and the like may require adjustment in the date-line placement. Also, when a deep letterhead makes it impossible to type the date on the designated line, type it a double space below the last letterhead line.

Column 3 tells you how wide the side margins should be for letters of different lengths. Note that letters of 101-300 words take 1½-inch margins. Since most letters you type will be of average length, you should get to know the adjustments for these letters quite well in a short time.

Letter Placement Table

	Letter Classification	5-Stroke Words in Letter Body	Side Margins	Margin Description	Date Line Position (From Top Edge of Paper)
①	②	③	④	⑤	
	Short	Up to 100	2″	Wide	Line 20
1	Average	101 – 150	1½″	Standard	18
2		151 – 200	1½″	"	16
3		201 – 250	1½″	"	14
4		251 – 300	1½″	"	12
	Long	301 – 350	1″	Narrow	12
	Two-page	More than 350	1″	Narrow	12

Date Line

The *horizontal* placement of the date line depends on the style of letter being typed, design of the letterhead, office preference, or a combination of these factors.

Block Style. Type date at left margin.

Other Styles. Begin date at center point or type it even with right margin. In this book, the first practice is generally preferred and used.

Business Letters Typed on Plain Paper

If plain paper is used as a letterhead substitute, space down from the top of the paper to type the date as suggested in the foregoing table.

Personal Business Letters Typed on Plain Paper

Deduct 2 lines from the figures given in Column 5 of the Letter Placement Table. Type the return address at this point, followed by the date.

Problem 7: Apostrophe (continued)

Line 1: Double quotation. Line 14: Figures refer to years.

1 i think george said donald said your typewriter is out of order
2 your boss wife mrs lowe is also my daughters english instructor
3 mens suits are lighter easier to clean and more colorful this year
4 womens and girls buying habits are the subject of his timely report
5 nasas space program though very expensive will not be discontinued
6 robert and dales car may be used to transfer the books to the school
7 its an interesting question but its one that cant be answered yet
8 jess new airplane is seldom used since his family moved to illinois
9 tom williams special program was watched by millions of people today
10 he worked for the citizens finance company for more than twelve years
11 this years statement must show a profit or we shall change officers
12 the typist was fired she xd over her errors instead of erasing them
13 he doesnt give many As but he is still considered a superb teacher
14 jerrys sister was in the class of 65 jerry was in the class of 68
15 secy is an abbreviation for secretary not secrecy as i believed

Problem 8: Abbreviations and Parentheses

*Spell out abbreviations as needed. Line 5: Two items in parentheses.
Line 8: Two sentences with parentheses.*

1 several states oh ia and ut have passed this calif law
2 apr june sept and nov are always thirty days in length
3 we have branch offices in ny chgo la and seattle
4 mr k w crenshaw mgr left the office for st paul at 3 30 pm
5 al smith the football hero is now playing in hometown lake league
6 the committees raised one million dollars $1,000,000 for the school
7 his future income will be determined by 1 education and 2 ability
8 i shall see ann her niece im not sure why but i shall see her
9 the new book contains the information you need for this job page 21
10 the meeting was set for 7 00 pm by the mgr mr a j brookings

Problem 9: Numbers and Symbols

Spell out the numbers as needed.

1 The office should have 9 typewriters and 4 duplicating machines.
2 79% of our single female clerks quit within 1 year.
3 There were 13 absences on Tuesday, 15 on Wednesday, and 2 on Thursday.
4 60 tourists 20 drivers and 12 guides were detained at the border.
5 I bought 2 10' lengths of pipe; she bought 15 4' lengths.
6 Look for this quotation in Volume XXV, #8, of the college paper.
7 He carried the 3-pound pack over the 20-mile hike with the Boy Scouts.
8 My new address is 1 15th Street; my old address was 42 5th Street.

PD PERRY & DERRICK, INC.

111 Lincoln Park / Newark, New Jersey 07102 / Telephone 201-227-0453

	Words in Parts	5' GWAM

Begin date at center on Line 12

	February 15, 19--	4	1
	DS		

Mailing notation   AIRMAIL   5   1
DS

Address

Miss Evelyn Terry, Office Manager   12   2
Standard Steel Equipment Company   19   3
270 - 53d Street   22   4
Brooklyn, NY 11232   26   5
DS

Salutation   Dear Miss Terry   29   6
DS

The booklet you requested about letter format is en-   40   8
closed. The format features described are those adopted   51   10
by this company. This letter follows them.   60   12

The first line of each paragraph is indented five   10   14
spaces. The date, complimentary close, company name,   21   16
Body   and the dictator's name are started at the center point   32   18
of the paper. We use open punctuation. In this style,   43   21
punctuation marks are omitted after the date, address,   54   23
salutation, and closing lines unless an abbreviation is   65   25
used, in which case the period is typed as part of the   76   27
abbreviation.   79   28

Although we do not usually show the company name   89   30
in the closing lines, we have done so here to illustrate   100   32
for you the correct handling of it. Since the dictator's   112   34
name is typed in the closing lines, only the typist's   123   36
initials are used in the reference notation.   131   38

Special mailing notations are typed in all capital   142   40
letters at the left margin, a double space below the date.   153   43

After you have had an opportunity to examine your   10   45
copy of Styling Business Letters, I shall appreciate   25   48
your sending us your impressions of it.   33   49

Complimentary close   Sincerely yours   36   50
DS

Company name   PERRY & DERRICK, INC.   41   51

Richard S. Perry   *3 blank lines*

Typed name and official title   Richard S. Perry, Manager *(4th line space)*   46   52
DS

Reference initials   mev   47   52
DS

Enclosure notation   Enclosure   49   52

STYLE LETTER 3: *Modified Block with Indented Paragraphs and Open Punctuation (Typed in Pica Type)*

Problem 4: Colon, Hyphen, and Dash

Line 7: A quotation.

1 the following parts have been shipped to you a space bar and platen
2 the question is this how many clerks are needed to complete the job
3 the class meets from 10 30 am to 1 15 pm on thursdays and fridays
4 a wide variety of 30 60 and 90 day training classes are available
5 this man became a well liked public official during his two year term
6 one out of four married women 28 percent to be exact now have jobs
7 people will seldom fail if they exert their maximum efforts   miles
8 these items were sent postpaid one 5 inch file and one 2 hole punch
9 i need the answer to this question how many feet are in a kilometer
10 the building committee will meet at 9 30 am and 2 30 pm on monday
11 i travelled about ninety five miles today to attend this amateur play
12 he may charge this item for a 30 or a 60 day period with no interest

Problem 5: Quotation Marks

Line 3: One sentence. Line 6: End with exclamation point.

1 life liberty and the pursuit of happiness is in your constitution
2 you will regret the decision he said because you are incorrect
3 john said the car in the accident was red others said it was blue
4 did ronald say the first electronic computer was completed in 1946
5 perhaps he said was the first electronic computer invented in 1946
6 i couldnt have said electronic computers have been used since 24
7 his article computers in the business office was in business week
8 the education bottleneck is a chapter from the education revolution
9 she said you can never be but he still said i am a fast typist
10 tuesdays wall street journal quoted the article called office jobs

Problem 6: Apostrophe

Line 6: One sentence. Lines 7 and 8: Add ' or 's, as needed. Line 13: Figures refer to years.

1 dr walters sons secretary miss love is very competent in her job
2 womens mens and childrens shoes are on sale at johns shoe store
3 our large stock of boys and girls sweaters will be on sale in march
4 the ymcas classes under joe doe jrs leadership are very popular
5 joes father is a fireman while tom and petes father is a policeman
6 thats your book his has a scratch on its cover so its not as nice
7 james typing of tables is much better than bess typing of letters
8 al childress store is just a short distance from harold stern shop
9 mendels department store is across the street from the citizens bank
10 three years work was done when he got the letter in yesterdays mail
11 the manager okd the report but the owner xd out the first sentence
12 the teacher is very proud of giving over half the class fs in speech
13 the class of 70 beat the class of 72 in the track meet on wednesday
14 bob howe his secretary always signs his letters robt howe secy

81C Production Orientation and Skill Building ⃝35

Problem 1

1. Type the letter on page 144 in the style shown. The body contains 217 five-stroke words. Consult the table for placement directions, taking into account the additional lines required for the company name in the closing and for the enclosure notation.

2. Type on the *exploration level*; do not correct errors.

3. With a pencil, mark the corrections that need to be made.

Problem 2

1. On plain paper type a 5′ writing on the letter from your corrected copy. Do not correct your typing errors. Compute *g-pram*.

$$\text{G-PRAM} = \frac{\text{Gross (total) words typed}}{\text{Length (in minutes) of writing}}$$

2. Type the letter again on the *control level*. Erase and correct your errors as you type.

LESSON 82

82A Preparatory Practice ⃝5 *each line at least three times*

Alphabet   The exact propinquity of the moving red object was quickly recognized.

Figure-symbol Memo #38 says, "Bel & Bel's May 27 order ($1,694.50) is a cash order."

Double letters Miss Poole, from Tallahassee, will see Tennessee and Mississippi soon.

Fluency   Training is learning the rules; experience is learning the exceptions.

| 1 | 2 | 3 | 4 | 5 | 6 | 7 | 8 | 9 | 10 | 11 | 12 | 13 | 14 |

82B Production Skill Building ⃝15

Using the letter on page 144, type the writings described at the right on the *control level*. Do not erase and correct your errors. Compute *g-pram* for each writing.

1. Type three 1′ writings on the date, mailing notation, address, salutation, and the first paragraph.

2. Type three 1′ writings on the last paragraph, complimentary close, company name, dictator's name and title, reference initials, and enclosure notation.

3. Type a 5′ writing on the entire letter.

82C Production Typing: Letters in Modified Block Style ⃝30

Problem 1

Letter placement table on p. 143; 134 words; indented ¶s; open punctuation

	Words
Mr. James T. Bolder ǀ Placement Director ǀ	11
Underwood Community College ǀ Dyke, VA	18
22935 ǀ Dear Mr. Bolder ǀ (¶ 1) Our office	25
staff begins summer vacations June 1, and we	34
usually rotate our vacations so that only	42
a few people are away from the office during	51
any one week. Even so, we are often short-	60

	Words
handed during our busiest season. (¶ 2) To	67
rectify this situation, we want to hire two or	77
three temporary employees for the months of	86
June, July, and August. Such replacements will	95
need above-average office skills and should,	104
since they will be moved from job to job,	113
be adaptable to change. Naturally, we will	121
provide any necessary job instruction. (¶ 3) If	130
you can recommend several students who are	139
looking for summer work, we shall be happy	147
to make arrangements with them for inter-	155
views. ǀ Very truly yours ǀ W. P. Stone,	163
Office Manager	167

Project 1: Communication Aids

Type each problem on a separate sheet of paper, with double spacing and a 3-inch top margin. Capitalize and punctuate as needed.

Problem 1: Capitalization

Sentence 1: Name of book.

1 i can use the directions that appear in business computers as a guide
2 his article appears in the january issue of administrative management
3 the title of their article is furnishings help set learning climate
4 she spent a week at lake tahoe before going to yosemite national park
5 we bought a beautiful oriental rug from a chinese merchant in bangkok
6 your president is looking for examples of roman art in northern italy
7 the sertoma club meets in the arctic room of the royal canadian hotel
8 the directions say that she should use india ink in signing the forms
9 remember this rule capitalize titles that come before a proper name
10 we talked to president johns about the plans of mr good our cashier
11 she referred to paragraph 3 on page 23 of reorganization plan no 230
12 he needs a course in accounting and plans to enroll for accounting 12

Problem 2: Comma

1 on january 18 1969 they opened a new branch office in salem oregon
2 we heard that in 1968 250 companies used this plan in cashing checks
3 i can type take dictation operate a mimeograph and compose letters
4 we may try this rapid easy way to check letters reports and tables
5 mr bye our manager occupies the office which is on the first floor
6 when you read this authentic detailed report you will agree with me
7 this course which is recommended by many leaders is now open to you
8 several men have applied for the position and one of them may get it
9 to qualify for the position candidates must have training in writing
10 consider these facts mr holmes before you decide to leave this job
11 if this computer can do the job we should consider it very carefully
12 after all all the members who were there had done their work quietly

Problem 3: Terminal Punctuation; Semicolon

Sentence 6: One sentence.

1 is learning how to use this machine worth the cost emphatically yes
2 she asked how we investigated employee conduct objectively and fairly
3 will you please send us seven copies of the pamphlet when it is ready
4 before considering discipline did the employer investigate the facts
5 how do you put an end to complaints about the temperature you cant
6 some schools use elaborate training centers others use a simple room
7 he had the experience needed consequently he got the job in seattle
8 send the books paper and files by air and ship the maps by express
9 we handle this publication however it is being revised at this time
10 this is a compact inexpensive model but it can handle complex tasks

Problem 2

88 words; mixed punctuation; indented ¶s

	Words
Miss Betty N. Toland	135 Madison Avenue		11
Portsmouth, VA 23704	Dear Miss Toland		19
(¶ 1) Our office has received a request from a	27
firm in Alexandria asking for the names of	36
persons who might be interested in working	45
for them during the summer. (¶ 2) If you	52
are still looking for summer employment, will	61
you please complete the enclosed card and	69
return it promptly to our office. Be sure to	79
list both your local and Alexandria addresses.	88
(¶ 3) When the company has received your	95
records, someone will contact you to arrange	104
for an interview. Sincerely yours	James T.	113
Bolder	Placement Director	Enclosure	121

Problem 3

73 words; mixed punctuation; indented ¶s

	Words
Mr. W. P. Stone, Office Manager	Atlantic	11
Fruit Company, Inc.	1323 Spring Valley	19
Drive	Alexandria, VA 22312	Dear Mr.	26
Stone	(¶ 1) Thank you for writing to us	34
inquiring about students who are seeking sum-	42
mer employment. (¶ 2) I am enclosing per-	49
sonnel record cards for three of our students	59
who are planning to spend this summer in	67
Alexandria. They should be well qualified for	76
the type of employment you mentioned. Our	85
faculty recommends them. (¶ 3) If we can	92
help you further, please write to us again.	101
Very truly yours	James T. Bolder	Place-	109
ment Director	Enclosures	114

66

LESSON 83

83A Preparatory Practice ⑤ *each line at least three times*

Alphabet	David Cox, the lazy, obsequious janitor, is working for small payment.
Figure-symbol	Our contract, #785–03, dated March 12, 1968, allows us a 4½% discount.
Inside keys	Phillip Dexter requested them to apply for the quiz questions quickly.
Fluency	We do not have time to do a job right—but we find time to do it over.

| 1 | 2 | 3 | 4 | 5 | 6 | 7 | 8 | 9 | 10 | 11 | 12 | 13 | 14 |

83B Paragraph Guided Writings ⑩

1. Type four 1′ writings on the *exploration level.* Record *gwam* for the best writing.

2. Type three 1′ writings on the *control level.* Record *gwam* for the most accurate writing.

1.5 SI
5.6 AWL
80% HFW

	Words
A man's ability to reason and his capacity to solve problems are	13
closely related to the number of words he knows. Most experts agree,	27
however, that memorizing new words will do very little to add to your	41
mental stature. If word knowledge is retained, a large vocabulary will	55
make it possible for you to understand and assimilate more. Keep in	69
mind, though, that a man is not smart because he has a good vocabulary.	84
It is the other way around.	89

3

GWAM
1' 5'

¶ 1
1.5 SI
5.6 AWL
80% HFW

Every typewriter has a scale that is remarkably useful in centering and setting margin and tabulator stops at specified points. It is often referred to as the cylinder scale. It begins with zero at the left, and the numbers extend to the right the entire length of the carriage. A point on this scale corresponds to the center of your paper. You must remember this particular point, as you will use it very frequently. When an individual heading or when material of some particular line length is to be centered with even left and right margins, half the copy should be placed on the left and half on the right of the central point. The carriage is then moved to the correct point, or the margin stops are set at correct positions before you begin to type.

1'	5'	
14	3	54
28	6	57
43	9	60
57	11	63
71	14	66
85	17	68
99	20	71
113	23	74
128	26	77
142	28	80
152	30	82

¶ 2
1.5 SI
5.6 AWL
80% HFW

Most machines have still another scale on the paper bail on which the figures synchronize with those on the cylinder scale. The scale on the paper bail will help you determine the position of margins and table columns in the top part of your paper. This particular scale can also be used, however, to determine the margins and tabulator positions of material that is to be copied. Just place the material under the bail with the left edge of the paper at zero; then notice the margin and table points on the scale.

13	33	84
28	36	87
42	39	90
57	42	93
71	45	96
85	48	99
99	50	102
104	51	103

1' GWAM | 1 | 2 | 3 | 4 | 5 | 6 | 7 | 8 | 9 | 10 | 11 | 12 | 13 | 14 |
5' GWAM | 1   2   3 |

4

GWAM
1' 5'

¶ 1
1.5 SI
5.6 AWL
80% HFW

In addition to the several scales that appear on modern typewriters, you will find a number of gadgets and devices that are designed to make you ever ready with the right approach to the most puzzling typing problem. A line indicator or gauge tells you automatically how many lines or inches remain to the bottom edge of the paper on which you are typing.

14	3	52
28	6	55
42	8	58
57	11	61
71	14	64

¶ 2
1.5 SI
5.6 AWL
80% HFW

Every machine comes equipped with a bell that rings––on clear days––when you approach the end of a line. This feature permits you to keep your eyes constantly on the copy from which you are working. The majority of typists invariably look anyway. Why? The reasons are not immediately clear, but a plausible explanation is that we may be more adept at seeing than we are at hearing.

12	17	67
26	20	69
40	22	72
54	25	75
68	28	78
77	30	79

¶ 3
1.5 SI
5.6 AWL
80% HFW

Some typewriters are equipped with one or more keys on which the heads may be removed and new ones attached in a few seconds. There is no limit to the special symbols you can obtain for your typewriter. On some machines, you can also get a half or full space between letters merely by depressing a special key. On others, you can regulate the vertical spacing mechanism for four or five lines to the inch, instead of the usual six. What innovations will manufacturers of typewriters think of next!

13	32	82
28	35	85
43	38	88
57	41	91
72	44	94
86	47	97
100	50	99

1' GWAM | 1 | 2 | 3 | 4 | 5 | 6 | 7 | 8 | 9 | 10 | 11 | 12 | 13 | 14 |
5' GWAM | 1   2   3 |

Information on Addressing Envelopes

To hasten the sorting and distribution of first-class mail, the U.S. Post Office Department now uses Optical Character Readers to read electronically the ZIP Code and the name of the city and to sort the letters into appropriate bins. This agency asks that the following directions be observed.

Placement. The city and state line is optically scanned. The address lines must be higher than ½ inch from the bottom of the envelope, but no higher than 3 inches from the bottom. This 2½-inch "read zone" is 8 inches long, and it must not be closer than 1 inch to either the right or left edges of the envelope.

Extraneous information, regardless of its nature, will not interfere with reading if it is placed above the address block. The space below the address block should be kept completely clear to the bottom of the envelope.

Spacing. The address lines should be arranged in block form. Typing in single-space style is recommended by the Post Office Department.

The city and state names and the ZIP Code should appear in that sequence on the bottom line. Four-line addresses may be used so long as the city line complies with the foregoing placement directions.

State Abbreviations. The Post Office Department recommends the use of two-letter abbreviations for state names. Approved forms appear on page viii. These abbreviations should be typed in all caps, without an ending period.

In the typing of names of states in letter addresses, the recommended practice is to type the two-letter state abbreviations and ZIP Codes. If the ZIP Code is not known or available, the state name is spelled in full or typed according to the standard abbreviation.

Notations. Postal directions (such as AIRMAIL, SPECIAL DELIVERY, etc.) are typed in capitals below the stamp and at least 3 line spaces above the address. Addressee instructions (*Hold for Arrival, Please Forward, Personal*, etc.) should be typed a triple space below the return address and 3 spaces from the left edge of the envelope. Addressee instructions may be either underlined or typed in all capitals.

If it is not convenient to locate account numbers, dates, attention lines, and other similar items outside the read zone, they may be entered on any line of the address block above the street name or box number.

Personal Titles. Always use an appropriate personal title on a letter, envelope, or card addressed to an individual. When a woman's marital status is not known, use *Miss* as the personal title. (The abbreviation *Ms.* may also be used.)

Small Envelope. Use a small envelope (6½ by 3⅝ inches) for a one-page letter without enclosures.

Large Envelope. Use a large envelope (9½ by 4⅛ inches) for a letter of more than one page and for those with enclosures.

Observe the addresses on the small and large envelopes illustrated below. The notations indicate recommended placement for good appearance. At the same time the addresses appear in the read zones.

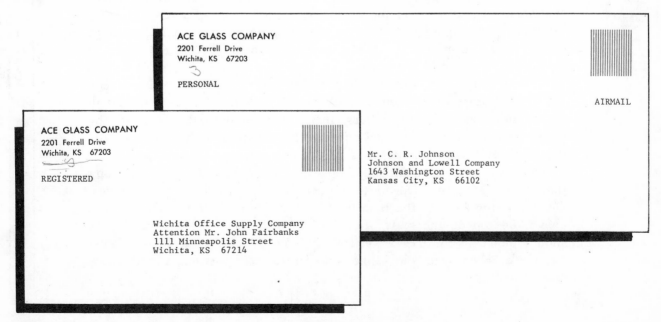

SUPPLEMENTARY PROJECTS

Supplementary Growth Index Writings

1

	GWAM
	1'	5'

¶ 1
1.5 SI
5.6 AWL
80% HFW

Since the typewriter was invented more than one hundred years ago, it has undergone many alterations. The early machines typed only in capital letters, and the typist could not see what he typed. The type hit the paper on the underside of the cylinder. To examine his copy, the typist was required to turn the carriage back until he could see the print. When he was satisfied that everything was in order, he snapped the carriage back into place and went ahead with his work. Errors were generally ignored because they were not seen—at least not by the typist.

1'	5'
13	3	51
27	5	54
41	8	57
56	11	60
70	14	63
84	17	65
99	20	68
114	23	71

¶ 2
1.5 SI
5.6 AWL
80% HFW

Time marches on, and with its passing have come many improvements in the typewriter. A personalized control device will allow you to regulate the touch to equal the power in your fingers. If you turn a dial or move a lever in one direction, you reduce the tension on the type bars. A move in the other direction increases the tension. You can set the mechanism to suit yourself. When your hands are cold or tired, for instance, you can set the machine for a light touch. When a firm touch is desirable, however, you can increase the tension. In this manner, you can adjust the machine as needed to get even rhythm and satisfactory speed.

1'	5'
13	25	74
28	28	77
42	31	80
56	34	82
70	37	85
84	40	88
98	42	91
112	45	94
125	48	96
129	49	97

1' GWAM | 1 | 2 | 3 | 4 | 5 | 6 | 7 | 8 | 9 | 10 | 11 | 12 | 13 | 14 |
5' GWAM | 1 | 2 | 3 |

2

	GWAM
	1'	5'

¶ 1
1.5 SI
5.6 AWL
80% HFW

All typewriters come equipped with several scales. The claim is that they measure everything except the calories in your lunch. Those examined here appear on most typewriters. A paper-guide scale facilitates the centering of stationery in the machine or over some particular point. One can move the guide easily left or right on the scale to position cards or odd-size paper. On several machines, the scale begins with zero at the left, and the numbers extend to the right. On others, the zero appears in the center of the scale, and the numbers extend in either direction. On still others, marks appear on either end of the scale. When paper is inserted so that the marks at either edge of the paper are in balance, the paper is said to be centered.

1'	5'
13	3	51
27	5	53
41	8	56
56	11	59
69	14	62
84	17	65
98	20	68
113	23	70
127	25	73
141	28	76
152	30	78

¶ 2
1.5 SI
5.6 AWL
80% HFW

All machines have an aligning scale that helps you line up copy that has been reinserted in the typewriter for corrections or fill-ins. Generally, the base of the figures and letters in the copy should be just above the top of the scale. In addition, one of the letters or figures should be centered over a vertical line on the scale. If these simple steps are taken, you should be able to reinsert stationery and make exact corrections.

1'	5'
13	33	81
27	36	84
42	39	87
57	42	90
71	45	92
84	47	95
88	48	96

1' GWAM | 1 | 2 | 3 | 4 | 5 | 6 | 7 | 8 | 9 | 10 | 11 | 12 | 13 | 14 |
5' GWAM | 1 | 2 | 3 |

83C Production Typing: Modified Block Style Letters (35)

Beginning with this lesson, vertical lines are no longer used to indicate opening and closing line endings. Arrange these lines correctly. In addition, add punctuation marks where needed.

An official title may follow the name of the addressee; it may be on a line with the company name; or it may be on a line by itself. (See page 149.)

Problem 1: Medium-Length Letter

236 words; open punctuation; indented ¶s; small envelope

	Words
Mr. James T. Bolder Placement Director	11
Underwood Community College Dyke, VA	18
22935 Dear Mr. Bolder (¶ 1) Some time ago	25
I wrote to you asking for the names of stu-	34
dents who wanted summer work, and you sent	42
the names of three people to me. We have	51
tested these students; perhaps you would be	60
interested in our conclusions. (¶ 2) Miss	67
Toland did well on the tests. She needed	75
more time than the others to transcribe her	84
shorthand notes; but her letter was neat,	93
properly placed, and correct in style. She	101
began the filing tests slowly, but her speed	110
increased as she became acquainted with the	119
procedures. (¶ 3) Mr. Martin took his short-	127
hand notes rapidly, and he transcribed them	136
quickly and accurately. His letter was free of	145
errors. He did well with the machines test,	154
but he was much slower than the others at	163
filing. (¶ 4) Miss Basset is one of the fastest	171
shorthand writers we have ever tested; but	180
her transcript contained misspellings and	188
other inaccuracies. The letter was not attrac-	198
tively placed on the page, and her typing was	207
not so neat as that of the others. She was	216
fast (but not accurate) on the filing and the	225
machines tests. (¶ 5) Although we had	231
planned to hire only one student, we hired	240
two—Miss Toland and Mr. Martin. Thank	248
you for providing us with the type of employ-	257
ees we need. Very truly yours W. P. Stone,	266
Office Manager	269/285

Problem 2: Medium-Length Letter

177 words; mixed punctuation; indented ¶s; small envelope

	Words
Mr. L. W. West Farmer, West & Lincoln	11
133 Byer Street Edwardsville, VA 22456	19
Dear Mr. West (¶ 1) Miss Lorna Basset,	26
about whom you inquired in your recent let-	34
ter, is a student at our school. Her record	43
indicates she should be graduated in January.	52
(¶ 2) Always a friendly and cooperative	59
person, Miss Basset accepts responsibility	68
willingly; she has been both secretary and	76
president of the Arts Club on our campus.	85
She dresses neatly and tastefully. Her grades	94
are average; she attends her classes regularly.	104
(¶ 3) According to her teachers, Miss Basset	112
is a very rapid, enthusiastic worker. She	121
writes shorthand and types at very high rates	130
of speed, but her letters are not always neat	139
and accurate. (¶ 4) It would appear to us that	147
Miss Basset has an excellent potential for a	156
job that provides additional training and help-	166
ful supervision. We therefore recommend her	175
to you for summer work, with the thought	183
that she might return to you as a full-time	192
employee when she finishes school. Sincerely	201
yours James T. Bolder Placement Director	210/225

Problem 3: Short Letter

84 words; open punctuation; indented ¶s; large envelope

	Words
June 27, 19—— Professor Fred R. Saxton 461	9
Washington Avenue Iowa City, IA 52240	16
Dear Professor Saxton (¶ 1) A promotion	23
plan for the book PRODUCTION PROCEDURES	31
is enclosed for your approval. You will recall	41
that our contract provides for your approval	50
of promotion plans. (¶ 2) When all final	57
proofreading is finished late in October, PRO-	66
DUCTION PROCEDURES will probably be ready	75
to go to press; but plans to promote the book	83
should be settled before August 1. May we	92
therefore have your prompt approval for each	101
plan we suggest. Very truly yours Edward	110
Caster Senior Editor Enclosure	117/130

Problem 3: Outline

2" top margin; see p. 185

	Words
STOCKS	1
I. COMMON STOCK	5
A. No Fixed Dividends	9
B. Voting Privilege Usually	15
II. PREFERRED STOCK	20
A. Dividends Usually Paid First	27
1. Cumulative (unpaid dividends accumulate)	36
2. Noncumulative (dividends in arrears not paid)	46
3. Participating (sharing residual dividends with common	58
stockholders)	61
4. Nonparticipating (receiving only agreed percent	72
of dividends)	75
B. Voting Privilege Usually Absent	82
III. STOCK VALUES	87
A. Par Value Stock	91
B. No Par Value Stock	96
C. Market Value of Stock	101
D. Book Value of Stock	106
IV. STOCKHOLDERS MEETING	112
A. Usually Held Annually	117
B. Elections Conducted	122
1. Board elected by stockholders	129
a. Personal vote	133
b. Proxy	136
2. Officers elected later by Board	143

Problem 4: Purchase Order

See p. 225

	Words
Ordered From Meade Sports Goods Company 417 Hooper Street Norfolk, VA 25313	13
Order No. 1879 **Date** *(current)* **Terms** 1/10, n/30 F.O.B. Richmond **Ship Via** Gold	23
Star Trucking Lines	27

Quantity	Cat. No.	Description	Price	Total	
12	SR129	Marsh's Jet Spin Reels	9.72	116.64	36
10	SR135	Marsh's Buddy Lightweight Spin Reels	7.12	71.20	48
8	SR136	Bing's Spinlite Special Spin Reels	17.82	142.56	59
18	SR140	Aladdin's Freespeed Spin Reels	9.17	165.06	70
16	SR142	Zig's Spin Wondereels	10.73	171.68	79
6	TB607	Aladdin Aluminum Tackle Boxes	6.40	38.40	89
					90
				705.54	91

84A Preparatory Practice ⑤ *each line at least three times*

Alphabet   Jeff York amazed us by stating his quixotic view of the labor problem.

Figure-symbol On May 27, 1964, George paid Sedge–Brown $513.02, just $4.98 too much.

Inside keys   Five navy tugs tried to enter the harbor before fog ruined visibility.

Fluency   The man who keeps his eyes fixed on his goal can walk a straight path.
               | 1 | 2 | 3 | 4 | 5 | 6 | 7 | 8 | 9 | 10 | 11 | 12 | 13 | 14 |

84B Building Speed and Control ⑩

1. Type three 1' writings on the *exploration level*.
2. Type three 1' writings on the *control level*.

3. Compute *gwam*. Record the rate of your most accurate and your fastest writings.

1.5 SI
5.6 AWL
80% HFW

Carbon paper, with the glossy side down, is placed on a sheet of
plain paper. Second sheets of thin paper are generally used for carbon
copies. The letterhead paper is then laid on the carbon paper, and the
several sheets are inserted into the typewriter so that the face of the
letterhead is toward the writer. The dull side of the carbon paper will
be toward you when the sheets are inserted in proper position for typing.
               | 1 | 2 | 3 | 4 | 5 | 6 | 7 | 8 | 9 | 10 | 11 | 12 | 13 | 14 |

Problem Typing Information

MAILING NOTATION IN A LETTER

If a special mailing notation is used in a letter, type it at the left margin midway between the date and the first line of the inside address. If the notation is to be typed on the carbon copy only (blind carbon notation), insert a piece of heavy paper between the ribbon and the original (first) sheet. The paper should be thick enough to prevent the imprint of the type from showing on the original sheet.

TITLES IN THE ADDRESS

Use a personal title (*Mr., Mrs., Miss.*, etc.) in the address when the letter is to an individual. An official title (indicating the position held) may be typed (1) on the line with the name, (2) on the line with the company name, or (3) on a separate line. Capitalize the title. Use the style that will give the best balanced lines.

May 31, 19--

Mailing notation	REGISTERED MAIL
Title on line with name	Mr. E. P. Johnson, Manager Smith Real Estate Company 1001 Kansas Avenue Omaha, NE 68110
Title on line with company name	Mr. Lawrence P. Robertson Manager, Ohio Tractors, Inc. 2200 Greensburg Road Canton, OH 44720
Title on separate line	Miss Anne K. Taylor Dean of Women North Idaho Junior College Coeur d'Alene, ID 83814

Type for 25 minutes. Erase and correct errors. You will need an interoffice memorandum form, a purchase order, and full sheets of blank paper. When time is called, compute your *n-pram.*

Problem 1: Interoffice Memorandum with Table

SS body;
see p. 179

			Words
TO: David E. Moore	**DATE:** *(Current)*		6
FROM: Robert Daniels			9
SUBJECT: Bonding Agents	**FILE:** IM-A-768		14

As a result of our recent article in <u>Ceramics</u>, we have had many inquiries from people associated with the building industry about the relative qualities of the three leading brands of adhesives now on the market. — 28 / 43 / 58

In response to these inquiries, we have conducted tests on these brands—Belmont, Luxor, and Dye's—with results as shown below. — 71 / 84

COMPARATIVE QUALITIES OF THREE BONDING AGENTS				Words
	Belmont	Luxor	Dye's	94 / 101
Waterproof	Excellent	Average	Poor	108
Water Resistance	Excellent	Excellent	Excellent	118
Flexibility	Average	Poor	Poor	124
Bonding Strength	Excellent	Average	Average	132
Workability	Excellent	Poor	Excellent	140

The excellence of the Belmont product is evident, but it should be kept in mind that its price is about three times that of the other two. — 153 / 168

You may use this information in whatever ways will serve you best. Complete information about the tests is available from our office. — 181 / 196

Problem 2: Table with Horizontal Rules

Full sheet; SS; decide spaces between columns; add horizontal rules; see p. 204

REGISTRATION OF COPYRIGHTS BY SELECTED MEDIA				Words
1950 to 1965				9 / 12 / 40
Subject Matter of Copyright	1950	1960	1965	48 / 62
Total	210,564	243,926	293,617	69
Books	50,456	60,034	76,098	74
Periodicals	55,436	64,204	78,307	81
Lectures, Sermons, Addresses	1,007	835	848	91
Musical Compositions	52,309	65,558	80,881	99
Works of Art	4,013	5,271	5,735	106
Drawings or Plastic Works of Scientific or Technical Character	1,316	768	1,239	112 / 123
Photographs	1,143	842	860	129
Motion Picture Photoplays	782	2,755	2,536	139 / 153

Source: U.S. Bureau of the Census, <u>Statistical Abstract of the United States: 1966</u> (87th ed.; Washington: U.S. Government Printing Office, 1966), p. 526. — 174 / 189 / 194

84C Production Typing: Modified Block Letter with Variations ㉟

Problem 1: Enclosure for Problem 2

Margins: 2" top; 1" side; 5-space ¶ indention; DS; SS and indent numbered ¶s from side margins

	Words
ERASING ON CARBON COPIES	5

TS

(¶ 1) Erase and correct all typing errors. Use 13
a hard eraser in correcting errors on the origi- 23
nal copy. A soft eraser works best on carbon 32
copies. In correcting errors when carbon cop- 41
ies have been made, proceed as follows: 50

1. Move the carriage to the extreme 57
   right or left so that the eraser 64
   crumbs will not fall into the 70
   machine. 72

DS

2. Place a small card directly behind 80
   the original. Erase the error on 87
   the original copy. 91

3. Transfer the card behind the first 100
   carbon copy, and erase that copy. 107

4. Continue erasing all carbon copies 115
   in this manner, moving from front 122
   to back. 124

5. Strike the correct key or keys 132
   lightly. Repeat the stroking until 139
   the desired shading is achieved. 145

Problem 2

166 words; open punctuation; indented ¶s; 1 carbon copy; large envelope

	Words

Miss Lori Bellmont, Secretary Webster Allen 12
Corporation 1700 Broadway Denver, CO 19
80202 Dear Miss Bellmont (¶ 1) I am en- 26
closing the report you requested on erasing 34
on carbon copies. It is one we distribute to 44
all office personnel who use typewriters in our 53
company. I hope you will find it helpful. 62
(¶ 2) Some of our typists use correction 69
cover-ups that are principally of two types: 78
chalk-coated paper or liquid correction fluid. 88
Both applications are quite satisfactory. (¶ 3) 96
When using the chalk-coated paper, place the 105

	Words

coated side down over the error. Retype the 114
error in order to transfer the chalk dust to 123
the incorrectly typed characters. Remove the 132
paper and type in your correction. (¶ 4) 139
Liquid correction fluid looks much like white 149
or colored nail polish and is available in 157
shades to match various colors of paper. 166
Choose a tint to blend with the paper you are 175
using. Paint over the error, let the fluid dry, 185
then type the copy desired. Sincerely yours 194
Alphonso Lopez Office Manager Enclosure 202/220

Problem 3: Company Name in Closing Lines

92 words; open punctuation; block ¶s; 1 carbon copy; large envelope

If the company name appears in the closing lines, type it in all capitals, a double space below the complimentary close as shown in the illustration. The name of the writer is then typed on the 4th line space below the company name.

```
                    Yours very truly

                    CONTINENTAL PROTECTION CO.


                    William E. Hathaway, Jr.
                    District Manager

xx

Enclosure
```

	Words

Mr. Ernest L. Hawthorne 1365 Peachtree 11
Street Atlanta, GA 30309 Dear Mr. Haw- 19
thorne (¶ 1) A man buys life insurance so 26
that he is provided with protection, but he 35
may discover one day that he has not needed 43
this kind of protection. Of what possible use 53
is his policy to him? (¶ 2) This question (and 61
others like it) is answered in our novel book- 70
let Insurance in Action, which is enclosed. 83
Our agent, Mr. Vince Bradley, will be glad 92
to answer any additional questions confront- 100
ing you. Call him; his number is in your tele- 109
phone book. Yours very truly CONTINEN- 117
TAL PROTECTION CO. William E. Hathaway, 125
Jr. District Manager Enclosure 132/144

LESSON 150

150A Preparatory Practice ⑤ *each line three or more times*

Alphabet   Elizabeth Jacks should mix five quarts of gray paint for Hugh Budwell.

Figure-symbol   The blue sedan (Model 950--315 hp) has a Blue Book value of $2,786.40.

One hand   Drews was requested to decrease the minimum number of pollution tests.

Fluency   The first and last rule of writing clear copy is knowing your subject.

| 1 | 2 | 3 | 4 | 5 | 6 | 7 | 8 | 9 | 10 | 11 | 12 | 13 | 14 |

150B Growth Index ⑩ *one 5' writing; compute* nwam

All letters are used.

GWAM
1' | 5'

¶ 1
1.5 SI
5.6 AWL
80% HFW

Credit is a vital sales tool. Without it, many companies could   13 | 3 | 57
not stay in business. Often the more credit firms grant, the larger   27 | 5 | 59
will be their total annual sales. This principle is based on the   40 | 8 | 62
fact that a credit sale is easier to make than a cash sale. Statistics   54 | 11 | 65
show that a credit buyer gets more and in larger amounts. A credit   68 | 14 | 68
customer is usually a steady one. All sales must be profitable, however,   83 | 17 | 70
and this calls for good business credit.   91 | 18 | 72

¶ 2
1.5 SI
5.6 AWL
80% HFW

What is credit? It is the ability a buyer has to acquire goods   13 | 21 | 75
or services from a seller in exchange for his word to pay a specific   27 | 23 | 77
amount at a specific future time. Thus, firms do not grant credit; they   41 | 26 | 80
accept it. Companies offer their goods or services. The buyer, on the   56 | 29 | 83
other hand, either offers cash or his credit. If he offers credit,   69 | 32 | 86
you either accept or reject his credit and business. Either decision is   84 | 35 | 89
basically yours to render.   89 | 36 | 90

¶ 3
1.5 SI
5.6 AWL
80% HFW

Firms, in appraising a buyer as a credit risk, examine him from   13 | 38 | 92
four angles. The first of these is his character. His former dealings   27 | 41 | 95
are analyzed and judged. One writer said, "It is more important to   41 | 44 | 98
know a customer's philosophy than his income. If he is a scoundrel,   55 | 47 | 101
there is no need to continue." Those who have the desire to pay their   69 | 50 | 104
bills generally have the ability. Finally, the debtor's memory should be   84 | 53 | 107
as good as that of the creditor.   90 | 54 | 109

1' GWAM | 1 | 2 | 3 | 4 | 5 | 6 | 7 | 8 | 9 | 10 | 11 | 12 | 13 | 14 |
5' GWAM | 1 | 2 | 3 |

85A   Preparatory Practice ⑤ *each line at least three times*

Alphabet	We hope Mr. Frazier will quickly adjourn the executive board meetings.
Figure-symbol	Memo #7091 said: Buy 25½ dozen @ 46¢ and 38½ dozen @ 27¢ immediately.
Long words	Management development must challenge the manager to question success.
Fluency	Hard work can often help a person overcome many handicaps he may have.

| 1 | 2 | 3 | 4 | 5 | 6 | 7 | 8 | 9 | 10 | 11 | 12 | 13 | 14 |

85B   Production Skill Builder ⑮ *type two 5' writings on the letter on page 144; compute g-pram.*

85C   Production Typing: Modified Block Style with Variations ㉚

Letters of Two or More Pages

Use plain paper for the second and subsequent pages of letters. Begin the heading about an inch from the top edge of the sheet. Type the heading at the left margin in *block form* or in the *horizontal form* (one-line arrangement).

Leave 3 blank lines between the heading and the first line of the resumed letter; use the same side margins as for preceding page.

Note. Do not resume the body of a letter with the last part of a divided word. Include at least two lines of a paragraph at the bottom of a page and at least two lines at the top of the succeeding page.

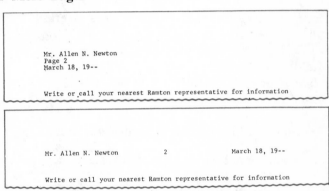

```
Mr. Allen N. Newton
Page 2
March 18, 19--


Write or call your nearest Ramton representative for information
```

```
Mr. Allen N. Newton          2          March 18, 19--


Write or call your nearest Ramton representative for information
```

Headings for Letters of Two or More Pages—Block Form and Horizontal Form

Problem 1: Two-Page Letter

422 words; open punctuation; block ¶s; 1 carbon copy; large envelope

	Words
March 18, 19-- Mr. Allen N. Newton,	7
Vice-President Bedford–Lowe, Ltd. 450	15
Massachusetts Avenue Niagara Falls, NY	23
14305 Dear Mr. Newton (¶ 1) The Harlowe	30
National Bank, a multimillion dollar institu-	38
tion serving New York City and Long Island	47
City, is one of the first banks to establish	56
separate budgets for its 24 branches and 40	65
departments. This step requires the prepara-	74
tion of a complex monthly budget report,	82
which resulted in a three-day headache for the	91
Accounting Department each month. This	99
was the case, at any rate, until a Ramton 200	109
electric printing calculator turned the entire	118
operation into a routine one-hour job. (¶ 2)	126
With the Ramton 200, a monthly budget sum-	134

	Words
mation for each branch can be programmed	142
by mathematical functions once. The Ramton	151
200 then continues to perform the operations	160
automatically while variables such as deposits,	170
rates, and loans are fed into it. The results	179
are printed on paper tape for verification and	189
filing. As a consequence, the budgets go out	198
three days to a week earlier. (¶ 3) The Ram-	205
ton's ability to do difficult calculations in	215
milliseconds makes it invaluable to Harlowe	223
National in other ways. It can be programmed	233
to compound interest on a continual daily	241
basis. Moreover, it can prepare a last-minute	250
analysis of future profits for each branch and	260
department. With conventional methods, this	269
operation would have taken all night. The	277
Ramton 200 has the job done in an hour.	286
(¶ 4) All arithmetic functions are performed	293
by touching figures on the simple control keys.	303

directors' meetings are held once a month. 106
The fees for meetings attended are $450 for 115
nonemployee directors. Employee directors 123
do not receive any fees. (¶ 4) The 12 nomi- 131
nees for directors were elected. 138

Proposal to Limit Charitable Contributions 155

(¶ 5) In commenting on this proposal, one 162
stockholder stated that contributions before 171
taxes were equal to approximately 6½ cents a 180
share and to only 3¼ cents after taxes. He 189
stated that he was very happy to give in this 198
manner. The proposal was defeated by a vote 207
of 1,510 votes for and 17,161 votes against. 216
(¶ 6) At the meeting of the Board of Direc- 223
tors, which followed the stockholders meeting, 233
all officers were reelected to their positions. 243

Ralph C. Morris   Eugene Bailey 249
Chairman of the Board   President 255

Problem 2: Last Page of Leftbound Manuscript

This is page 6 (last page) of report; see p. 185

Words

(¶ 1) While tremendous advances have been 7
made in science and technology, our knowl- 15
edge of how to develop and employ men lags 24
far behind. Frank H. Cassell, Director of the 33
United States Employment Service, summed 41
up the present state of affairs in this way: 51
"We can create miracles from molecules, but 59
we are only beginning to get some grasp of 68
what people can do if given the right oppor- 77
tunity and incentive to develop their talents."[5] 87
The need to develop our manpower is today's 95
new frontier. (¶ 2) We often judge a nation's 104
greatness by its art, scientific achievements, 113
and raw materials. While there is nothing 122
wrong with this method of assessing a nation's 131
leadership, there is a new measure that sur- 140
passes all others. That measure is the state 149
of a nation's manpower. (¶ 3) We have only 156
recently begun to recognize the real value of 165
investing in people. As a result, education is 171
being thought of as our greatest industry. Its 185
products are the human resources of this 193
nation.[6] 195

[5] Frank H. Cassell, "Manpower—Today's Frontier," California Management Review (Spring, 1968), p. 3. (*29 words*)
[6] Ronald Gross and Judith Murphy, The Revolution in the Schools (New York: Harcourt, Brace & World, Inc., 1964), p. 8. (*28 words*)

Problem 3: Letter on Executive-Size Stationery (7¼″ by 10½″)

Modified block; open punctuation

Words

(*Current date*) mr ira m hammond jr 3712 9
elfindale street springfield mo 65804 dear mr 19
hammond (¶ 1) Thank you for selecting the 26
Manor Hotel as your home away from home. 34
It was a pleasure to have you with us. (¶ 2) 42
You will help us greatly if you give us your 51
frank opinion of our facilities and service. We 61
recognize how important it is for all our em- 70
ployees to give friendly, efficient service and 80
for all equipment to be in faultless condition. 89
(¶ 3) Compliments will be passed on to em- 96
ployees; constructive criticism will be given 106
our immediate attention. cordially julius 114
weaver chairman of the board 120/134

Problem 4: Agenda for Meeting

DS between items; arrange attractively on full sheet

Words

ARCADE SOCIETY 3

Agenda for Meeting, April 9, 19— 10

1. Call to Order 13
2. Minutes of March Meeting 19
3. President's Report on Plans to Revise Membership Regulations 28 / 32
4. Treasurer's Report 37
5. Report of Committee on Scholarships on Contributions Received for Aid of Foreign Students in American Schools 45 / 53 / 60
6. Report of Progress on Plans for the Annual Dinner Meeting in June by the Program Committee 68 / 75 / 79
7. Adjournment 82

Multiplication and division are both fully automatic. You simply index the figures, touch the control keys, and there's your answer—printed on tape. For all its simplicity, the Ramton 200 is a full-fledged calculator. It has an automatic constant multiplier, automatic divisor alignment, and automatic retention of quotient. (¶ 5) Ramton makes and sells more different kinds of calculators than any other company in the world. You are thus assured of finding the right calculator for your particular operation without having to pay for more computing sophistication than you actually need. (¶ 6) Write or call your nearest Ramton representative for information on the full line of full-value Ramton calculators. You can bank on them. Yours very truly RAMTON MACHINES, INC. Joseph Keane, Sales Manager

Words: 313, 321, 330, 339, 349, 358, 367, 375, 384, 393, 402, 410, 419, 427, 436, 446, 454, 462, 463/484

Problem 2: Writer's Name Omitted in Closing Lines

94 words; date of letter, January 12; open punctuation; indented ¶s; 1 carbon copy; large envelope

When the writer's name is not included in the closing lines, type his initials before yours at the end of the letter, thus: WSB:*your initials.*

Mr. J. Harmon Roberts Station Manager Radio Station WRNC Euclid, OH 44123 Dear Mr. Roberts (¶ 1) With this letter we are enclosing five copies of a two-minute commercial message we should like to have presented on the air from your studio at 10:58 a.m. for 14 consecutive days, commencing with the first Monday of next month. If possible, we should like to have the announcement read by Stan Givens of your announcing staff. (¶ 2) It is our understanding that the time for this spot announcement is part of that we contracted for in our agreement of January 2 with you. Very truly yours Advertising Manager WSB:*your initials* Enclosures 5

Words: 18, 26, 35, 43, 52, 60, 69, 77, 86, 94, 103, 112, 120, 126, 127/142

LESSON 86

86A Preparatory Practice ⑤ *each line at least three times*

Alphabet — Major Forbes quickly recognized the power of an auxiliary naval force.

Figure-symbol — By buying the stock at 124¼ and selling it at 86½, Lance lost $395.70.

Capitals — The President of the United States visited Chicago, Omaha, and Tucson.

Fluency — If you can succeed the first time, it is time to try something harder.

| 1 | 2 | 3 | 4 | 5 | 6 | 7 | 8 | 9 | 10 | 11 | 12 | 13 | 14 |

86B Building Speed and Control ⑩ *type 84B, page 149, as directed there*

86C Production Skill Building: Letters in Modified Block Style ㉟

Type these problems as a 25' writing. Correct your errors. Type a carbon copy and an appropriate envelope for each letter. Compute your *n-pram.*

Page 148, 83C, Problem 2
Page 150, 84C, Problem 2
Page 150, 84C, Problem 3
Page 152, 85C, Problem 2, above

N-PRAM (NET PRODUCTION RATE A MINUTE)

N-pram refers to the rate on production copy on which errors are erased and corrected.

PENALTIES FOR ERRORS:

Deduct 10 words.......for each error not erased on an original copy

Deduct 5 words........for each error not erased on a carbon copy

$$\text{N-PRAM} = \frac{\text{Gross (total) words} - \text{Penalties}}{\text{Length (in minutes) of writing}}$$

Problem 3: Block Style Letter

Open punctuation; 1 carbon copy

	Words
walter l davis esq. washburn, hosler & locke	13
936 commerce building springfield mo 65821	22
dear mr davis (¶ 1) This letter confirms our	29
telephone conversation of this morning in	38
which you and your firm were appointed our	47
legal representatives in the case of Ramsey v.	56
Worthington. (¶ 2) I am having a complete	63
list of our transactions with both litigants	72
documented, and a copy of it will be sent to	81
you. Mr. McLeeds has withdrawn completely	90
from the case; he will give you his files. If	99
you need still further information, let me	108
know personally. sincerely yours irvin h dia-	117
mond president cc mr raymond mcleeds	125/144

Problem 4: Modified Block Letter with Table

Indented ¶s; open punctuation

	Words
bond—moore sports equipment company 1475	11
kilvington avenue nashville tn 37211 atten-	24
tion sales department gentlemen (¶ 1) Will	32
you please send us a quotation for the follow-	41
ing merchandise as soon as possible. All	49
prices should be quoted f.o.b. our store.	58

		Words
14 doz.	Lead Bass Casting Sinkers	64
50 pkgs.	Nylon Snelled Fang Hooks	71
8 doz.	Standard June Bug Spinners	78
12 doz.	Standard Trolling Spinners	85

	Words
(¶ 2) Please state all terms clearly, noting	93
quantity and cash discounts. yours very truly	102
durston & wallace burton e stanley director	111
of purchases	114/130

LESSON 149

149A Preparatory Practice ⑤ *each line three or more times*

Alphabet Jack and Beth Powell may take a quiz next week if the board gives one.

Figure-symbol O'Dell paid $729.38 (less 10%) for Model #4560 at Birdwell & Smothers.

Vowels Despite his diet, he ate various pieces of chocolate candy and sweets.

Fluency We know that success comes to the men who are too busy to look for it.

| 1 | 2 | 3 | 4 | 5 | 6 | 7 | 8 | 9 | 10 | 11 | 12 | 13 | 14 |

149B Production Skill Building ⑩ *type 142B, page 246, as directed*

149C Production Measurement: Reports ㉟ *errors corrected; figure n-pram*

Type for 25 minutes. Correct errors. To type the problems in this lesson, you will need three full sheets of blank paper. When time is called, compute your *n-pram*.

Problem 1: Partial Report of Stockholders Meeting

Unbound manuscript form; SS; see p. 241

	Words
REPORT OF MORRIS MOTORS	5
STOCKHOLDERS MEETING	9
(¶ 1) The 25th Annual Meeting of Morris	16
Motors stockholders was called to order by	24
Ralph C. Morris, Chairman of the Board of	33
Directors, who presided. Mr. Morris wel-	41
comed the stockholders present at the meet-	49
ing as well as several officers.	56
Election of Directors	65
(¶ 2) The 12 nominees named in the proxy	72
statement were nominated. (¶ 3) A stock-	78
holder inquired as to the number of directors'	88
meetings and fees paid. Mr. Morris said that	97

LESSON 87

87A Preparatory Practice (5) *each line at least three times*

Alphabet
Walter expects to have two dozen tickets for the July banquet meeting.

Figure-symbol
To work this problem: Add (+) 186,549 to 327,060; subtract (−) 3,672.

Third row
They went to her party, for they were quite sure Betty would be there.

Fluency
Believe about half of what you hear—and be sure it is the right half.

| 1 | 2 | 3 | 4 | 5 | 6 | 7 | 8 | 9 | 10 | 11 | 12 | 13 | 14 |

87B Growth Index (15) *two 5' control-level writings; figure gwam on better writing*

All letters are used.

		GWAM	
		1'	5'

¶1
1.5 SI
5.6 AWL
80% HFW

Communication experts agree that the average letter costs about
two and a half dollars to produce. Included in the cost are the time
of the dictator and typist, paper, postage, and fixed charges, such
as wear and tear on the equipment used in the process. With costs going sky high, every avenue must be explored to keep them in check. Pro-
ficiency of the staff can be upgraded, and all possible steps must be
taken to reduce the cost of "getting out the mail."

1'	5'	
13	3	58
26	5	61
40	8	63
54	11	66
69	14	69
83	17	72
93	19	74

¶2
1.5 SI
5.6 AWL
80% HFW

When executives study some of the communications going through
the mails, they may wonder if letters are worth what they cost. Very
likely, many are not. The ability to write can be acquired. The
principles of clear writing can be mastered by almost anybody. One
must first be able to gather and organize the data he needs; then he
must know how to put his data into words that convey exactly what he
wants to say. Those who write letters should become skillful in the art.

13	21	77
27	24	79
40	27	82
53	29	85
67	32	87
81	35	90
96	38	93

¶3
1.5 SI
5.6 AWL
80% HFW

Finally, every effort must be made by the staff to cut costs.
The experts say that a majority of letters are about thirty percent
longer than necessary, and long letters are usually very fuzzy. Clarity
and brevity go hand in hand. Analyze the letters you write. With a
pencil, strike out the words and phrases that are not needed. Rewrite
the letter. Does not its meaning shine through more lively and clearly?
It is a way to cut costs.

13	40	96
26	43	98
41	46	101
55	49	104
69	51	107
84	54	110
89	55	111

| 1' GWAM | 1 | 2 | 3 | 4 | 5 | 6 | 7 | 8 | 9 | 10 | 11 | 12 | 13 | 14 |
| 5' GWAM | | 1 | | | 2 | | | 3 | | | | | | |

87C Production Measurement: Business Letters (30) *20' timing; errors corrected; compute* n-pram

Type the four letters on page 154. Make a carbon copy of each
letter. Address an envelope of appropriate size for each letter.

SECTION 24 ▶ MEASUREMENT: Basic and Production Skills

LESSONS 148–150

Unless otherwise directed, follow these procedures:
Drill Copy: Full sheet; 70-space line; SS.
Production Copy: When complete directions are not given, use your own judgment. Make your work neat and attractive. Correct your errors.
Page References: When appropriate, reference is given for a quick review of problem procedures. No extra time is allowed for reference, however.

LESSON 148

148A   Preparatory Practice ⑤ *each line three or more times*

Alphabet	Pizarro's powerful army unjustly vanquished the boxed-in Inca kingdom.
Figure-symbol	Our Check #75921 for $340.68, covering your Invoice #537, is enclosed.
Long reaches	Only the hungry baby's babbling disturbed the dignity of the ceremony.
Fluency	Until we meet the problem, we do not need to worry about its solution.

| 1 | 2 | 3 | 4 | 5 | 6 | 7 | 8 | 9 | 10 | 11 | 12 | 13 | 14 |

148B   Paragraph Guided Writings for Speed ⑩ *type 128D, page 221, as directed*

148C   Production Measurement: Communication Forms ㉟

Materials: To complete the problems in this lesson, you will need letterheads, carbon paper, onionskin, and envelopes.

Type for 25 minutes. Use the current date and your initials. Correct your errors. Make a carbon copy and address an envelope for each letter. When time is called, compute the *n-pram*.

Problem 1: Modified Block Letter

Mixed punctuation; centered subject line

	Words
mr john s scranton vice-president cantwell	12
and cramm's 878 amber street houston tx	21
77022 dear mr scranton subject: el rancho	29
patio furniture (¶ 1) Thank you for meeting	37
with me yesterday to discuss our new line of	46
furniture, El Rancho Patio. (¶ 2) When I re-	53
turned to my office this morning, I told our	62
sales manager, Mr. John Bartel, that your	71
store was considering an adoption of the El	79
Rancho line. He was, of course, pleased and	88
authorized me to offer you a 5 percent dis-	97
count on your initial order. (¶ 3) I shall be	105
in Houston next month and shall telephone	113
you then to learn if I can give you any fur-	122

	Words
ther information about the El Rancho Patio	130
line. sincerely yours miles a brookhart sales	140
representative A copy of our Manufacturer's	150
Warranty is enclosed.	154/172

Problem 2: AMS Simplified Letter

Open punctuation; see p. 176

	Words
mr frank c green 898 evergreen drive augusta	13
ga 30904 policy no 743891 (¶ 1) Our records	21
reveal the very gratifying fact that the final	30
premium payment for your policy has been	38
received. You now have a contract that is	47
paid in full. May we congratulate you upon	56
the attainment of this objective, which you	65
planned so many years ago. (¶ 2) If at any	72
time you should desire information concern-	81
ing this policy or assistance in connection with	90
your insurance estate, please call on us. Our	100
services are always at your disposal. (¶ 3) So	108
that our records may always be up to date,	117
Mr. Green, we shall appreciate your notifying	126
us promptly of any change in your address.	135
victor m young – vice-president cc mr george	145
thom agent	147/158

Problem 1

138 words; mixed punctuation; modified block; indented ¶s

	Words
Mr. Franklin R. Stern 158 South Maple	11
Road Odin, IL 62870 Dear Mr. Stern	18

(¶ 1) Thank you for permitting us to open one of our charge accounts in your name. We appreciate your patronage. (¶ 2) Our credit manager tells me that you have selected the Budget Account type of credit service. Your choice is a wise one; the Budget Account allows a generous 90 days for payment, with only one third of the account to be payable the tenth of each month following a purchase. Terms such as these are one of the privileges we provide for our customers; and there is, of course, no charge of any kind for them. (¶ 3) We sincerely hope this will be the beginning of a long and pleasant friendship. If at any time you have a suggestion for improving our service, please let us hear from you. Cordially yours   DIAMOND & COULTER   L. S. Roost, Manager

169/180

Problem 2

104 words; open punctuation; modified block; indented ¶s; reference initials not needed

	Words
Miss Betty N. Toland 135 Madison Avenue	11
Portsmouth, VA 23704 Dear Miss Toland	19

(¶ 1) Will you please complete as soon as possible the enclosed personnel record card and return it to this office. We must have the card before we can include your name on our payroll. (¶ 2) Print all information clearly, and be certain to include your full name and address and your social security number. In addition, let us know how you wish to handle your salary check. You may either get it at the payroll office or have it sent to your bank for deposit. (¶ 3) We are pleased to know you will be working with us this summer. Sincerely yours   (Miss) Fern Ann Royal   Payroll Clerk   Enclosure

135/147

Problem 3

129 words; open punctuation; modified block; block ¶s; writer's initials: HVL

	Words
Miss Charlene Marie Lampel 1204 Spring	11
Garden Drive Aurora, IL 60538 Dear Miss	19

Lampel (¶ 1) Our records indicate that checks drawn to your order in payment of dividends on stock of this Corporation, as described on the enclosed application, have not been paid by the bank on which the checks were drawn. (¶ 2) If the dividend checks are in your possession, we request that they be cashed or deposited promptly. If they have been lost or destroyed, please complete and execute the enclosed application and return it to us. Upon receipt of the application, we shall arrange for the issuance of replacement checks, provided your application is found to be in good order. (¶ 3) For your convenience, a return envelope requiring no postage is enclosed. Very truly yours   Assistant Secretary   Enclosures 2

161/174

Problem 4

117 words; open punctuation; modified block; block ¶s

	Words
Mr. William Senn Bell Advertising Manager	12
McMillan & Smith, Inc. 901 Euclid Avenue	20
Cleveland, OH 44115 Dear Mr. Bell (¶ 1)	27

Thank you for sending us your spot commercial to broadcast for 14 consecutive days, commencing with the first Monday of next month. Stan Givens will record your message, and it will be played at 10:58 in the morning on each of the requested days. (¶ 2) We are pleased to announce that Mr. Paul Jacks will join our staff next week as our advertising consultant. He has handled radio advertising accounts for more than ten years and is highly adept in finding out if advertising campaigns are worth what they cost. He will be glad to help you with any advertising problems you may have. Cordially yours   J. Harmon Roberts   Station Manager

154/175

LESSON 147

147A Preparatory Practice ⑤ *each line three or more times*

Alphabet   This unique, exciting bazaar was planned by Jack, Velma, and Florence.

Figure-symbol   For $274.31 (plus tax), Mr. Stone can take UAL Flight 580 at 6:19 a.m.

Outside reaches   Zeno mopped his brow, then powered the axe halfway through the quartz.

Fluency   Assuming you retire at 60, you are now preparing for 40 years of work.

| 1 | 2 | 3 | 4 | 5 | 6 | 7 | 8 | 9 | 10 | 11 | 12 | 13 | 14 |

147B Growth Index ⑮ *Use 141B, page 244, for two 5' writings; compute nwam on better one*

147C Sentence Guided Writings ⑩

Type two or more 1' writings on each sentence with the guide called each 15, 12, or 10 seconds.   Try completing a sentence and returning your carriage as the guides are called.

		GWAM		
		15"	12"	10"
1	I was pleased to hear from you about the position open in your office.	56	70	84
2	Thank you for giving me the opportunity to talk to you about this job.	56	70	84
3	I shall try to live up to the high standards of your firm in this job.	56	70	84
4	Thank you for the offer of a position on the sales staff of your firm.	56	70	84

| 1 | 2 | 3 | 4 | 5 | 6 | 7 | 8 | 9 | 10 | 11 | 12 | 13 | 14 |

147D Communication Aid: Composing ⑳

1. Type the paragraph below.
2. In a second paragraph, accept the offer. Restate the offer and the beginning date of employment. Indicate your pleasure at having been selected.

3. Proofread Paragraph 1, marking it for correction.
4. Edit and correct your paragraph; then retype both paragraphs.

I am pleased to offer you a position in our Accounting Department at a beginning monthly salary of $500. If you accept this offer, your employment is to start on Monday, June 5, at 8:15 a.m. Your duties will be in the general area of bookkeeping and accounting. As I told you during your interview, we expect this position to develop into one of head of our Credit Department. Our firm is a rapidly growing one, so the opportunities for advancement are very good for the right man. Please let me know if you will accept my offer.

SECTION 15 ▶ BUSINESS LETTERS WITH SPECIAL FEATURES
LESSONS 88–94

Unless otherwise directed, proceed as follows:
Drill Copy: Full sheet; 70-space line; SS.
Paragraph Copy: Full sheet; 70-space line; DS;
5-space ¶ indention.

Production Copy: Letterhead (or full sheet), current date (unless given), and your reference initials should be used. Erase and correct errors. Prepare carbon copies and envelopes of appropriate size.

LESSON 88

88A Preparatory Practice ⑤ *each line at least three times*

Alphabet — Czar Alexei quickly delivered his bellicose judgment on foreign power.

Figure-symbol — Didn't Invoice #87456–90 allow us a 3 1/5% discount––or was it 3 2/5%?

Double letters — The committee added bookkeeping and speech to the school's curriculum.

Fluency — Habits are like muscles––the more we use them, the stronger they grow.

| 1 | 2 | 3 | 4 | 5 | 6 | 7 | 8 | 9 | 10 | 11 | 12 | 13 | 14 |

88B Skill-Comparison Typing ⑮ *three 1' writings on each ¶; compare gwam and number of errors on the writings*

All letters are used.

	GWAM	
	1'	5'

¶ 1
1.3 SI
5.2 AWL
90% HFW

Mark Twain once wrote that nothing so needs to be changed as the habits of others. What he referred to, no doubt, was the wasteful, unfriendly habits all men get into from time to time. Generally, most people have many excellent habits, also; and these can prove to be of use. If a good habit is set, it is as hard to change as a bad one. In your daily typing practice, it will pay you to give all your attention to building the right kind of habits.

1'	5'
13	3	56
27	5	59
41	8	62
55	11	64
69	14	67
83	17	70
91	18	72

¶ 2
1.5 SI
5.6 AWL
80% HFW

Is your vocabulary all you want it to be? If you are like the majority of us, it will call for improvement. You can begin at once to utilize words that are unfamiliar and to integrate them into your normal speech. Try reading aloud from well-written books or articles; such reading will make you pronounce the words you may skip. Look for unique words that have appeal. Learn any meanings that they convey; then practice using them very diligently.

13	21	74
26	23	77
40	26	80
54	29	82
68	32	85
81	34	88
91	36	90

¶ 3
1.7 SI
6.0 AWL
70% HFW

The soybean is a life capsule for a greatly overpopulated world. It is used in animal feeds that help multiply the production of such items as filet mignons, drumsticks, and pork chops. As a food ingredient, a field that has scarcely been scratched, it increases the production of many of our top supermarket delicacies. This ubiquitous legume is one of the best food multipliers for any community popping with people.

13	39	92
27	42	95
41	45	98
57	48	101
71	50	104
86	53	107

1' GWAM | 1 | 2 | 3 | 4 | 5 | 6 | 7 | 8 | 9 | 10 | 11 | 12 | 13 | 14 |
5' GWAM | 1 | 2 | 3 |

Application for Employment

NELSON & SONS COMPANY

1185 LOUISE STREET   WICHITA, KANSAS 67203   316-123-7117

■ ■

PLEASE TYPE

Date __June 15, 19--__

Name _____ David _____ Charles _____ Edward _____
　　　　 Last 　　　　　First 　　　　　　 Middle

Address _254 Slaton Hall, Bentley Coll., Wichita, KS 67207_ Telephone Number _852-3000_
　　　　 Street and Number 　　　　　　 City 　　 State 　 ZIP Code 　　　　　　　　 Ext. 148

Position Desired _Clerk_ 　　　　　　　　　　 Social Security No. _799-23-1864_

　　　　　　　　　　　　　　　　 (During 　　　　　　　　　　　　　　　　 (Summer)
How Long Have You Lived at the Above Address? _2 years_ school term) Do You Live with Your Parents? _Yes_
　　 Yes/No

Date and Place of Birth _June_ _4_ _1948_ _Topeka_ _Kansas_ 　 Citizen of United States? _Yes_
　　　　　　　 Month 　 Day 　 Year 　　 City 　　　 State 　　　　　　　　　　 Yes/No

Weight _185_ 　 Height _5_ _11_ 　 Right or Left Handed _Left_
　　　 Pounds 　　　　　 Feet 　 Inches

　　　　　　　　　　　　　　　　　　　　　　　　 No. of Dependents
Single (X) Married ( ) Widowed ( ) Separated ( ) Divorced ( ) Other than Self _____

EDUCATION

	School Name	Address	Major	From Year	To Year	Grad. Degree
Grammar	Fullbright Element.	Topeka, Kansas		1954	1962	Diploma
High School	Holcomb High School	Topeka, Kansas	Gen'l Course	1962	1966	Diploma
Business						
Evening						
University or College	Bentley College	Wichita, Kansas	Office Mgt.	1966		
Other						

PREVIOUS EMPLOYMENT

From Mo. Yr.	To Mo. Yr.	Name and Address of Employer	Position	Salary	Reason for Leaving
June 1964	Sept. 1966	Okewa Youth Camp Coffeyville, Kansas	Assistant to Director	$25 week	Returned to school
Sept. 1966	Sept. 1967	Williamson's Bookstore Wichita, Kansas	Salesclerk	$1.50 hour	New position
Sept. 1967		Bentley College Wichita, Kansas	Student Assistant to Professor	$1.75 hour	

PERSONAL REFERENCES *

Name	Address	Occupation
Mr. Bruce Tobey	Holcomb High School Topeka, Kansas	Principal
Dr. Frank I. Ellis	College of Bus. Admin. Bentley Coll., Wichita, KS	Chairman
Mr. B. V. Dalton	Okewa Youth Camp Coffeyville, Kansas	Director

* If you have never been employed, give names of two responsible persons (not relatives) to whom we can refer.

Signature *Charles E. David*

Model Copy of an Application Blank

88C Manipulative Drill: Correcting Copy by "Squeezing" or "Spreading" Letters ⑮

"SQUEEZING" AN OMITTED LETTER WITHIN A WORD

First, erase the word.

Typewriters Without Half-Space Mechanism: "Squeeze" letters into available space by using backspace key and typing as explained at the left.

Typewriters with Half-Space Mechanism: Position carriage in the space preceding erased word; then:

1. Depress and hold down space bar; strike first letter of erased word.
2. Release space bar, press it down again and hold it; strike second letter of erased word. Continue in this manner until the correction is made.

Electric Typewriters, but Not the Selectric: Use same process as for squeezing at the beginning or end of a word.

"SQUEEZING" AN OMITTED LETTER AT THE BEGINNING OR AT THE END OF A WORD

Typewriters Without Half-Space Mechanism: Move carriage to the space or letter following omission. Depress backspace key halfway and hold it in position as you type omitted letter.

Typewriters with Half-Space Mechanism: Move carriage to last space before omission. Depress and hold down space bar; type omitted letter.

Electric Typewriters: Move carriage to proper position for inserting omitted letter. Hold carriage in position as you type the letter.

"SQUEEZING" AND "SPREADING" OF LETTERS ON THE SELECTRIC TYPE-WRITER

A detailed explanation of these two operations is given on page xii of the Reference Guide.

"SPREADING" TO CORRECT A WORD WITH AN ADDED LETTER

First, erase the word.

Typewriters Without Half-Space Mechanism: Space twice after word preceding error; then:

1. Depress backspace key halfway; strike first letter of erased word; release backspace key, and hit space bar once.
2. Depress backspace key halfway; strike second letter of erased word. Continue in this manner until correction is made.

Typewriters with Half-Space Mechanism: Position carriage for first letter of erased word; then:

1. Depress and hold down space bar; strike the first letter.
2. Release space bar; press and hold it down; strike the second letter. Continue in this manner until the correction is made.

Electric Typewriters: Spreading is not feasible on electric machines.

PROCEDURE Study the explanatory material carefully. Then, type the problem sentences exactly as they are shown at the right and make the corrections by "squeezing" or "spreading." Compare your corrected sentences with those illustrated below. Repeat if time permits.

```
Friday was a very busy day for the staff.
The edition was well worth his effort.
Several of them worked until six o'clock.
The boys checked every page of the issue.
```

SENTENCE 4 Add *s* to *boy.*

1 Friday was a very usy day for he staff.

2 Thhe edition was welll worth his effort.

3 Several of thm worked untl six o'clock.

4 The boy checked every pag of the issue.

88D Skill-Comparison and Transfer Typing ⑮ *three 1' writings on each sentence; compare gwam*

		Words
Goal	Nothing is so rare as the use of a word in its true meaning.	12
One hand	John Plum traced the baggage to my street address in Waseca.	12
Rough draft	We are glad to write to you about this new, unique book.	12
Script	His success depends on his ability to work well with others.	12

LESSON 146

146A Preparatory Practice (5) *each line three or more times*

Alphabet   Parker says this exciting jazz was arranged from lovely baroque music.

Figure-symbol   The report for 1968 showed a profit of $327,450, or a net gain of 17%.

One hand   In my opinion, the mill weavers should request oil for the extra loom.

Fluency   In letters the thought is central, and it should be clearly expressed.

| 1 | 2 | 3 | 4 | 5 | 6 | 7 | 8 | 9 | 10 | 11 | 12 | 13 | 14 |

146B Communication Aid: Spelling (5)

1. Type these commonly misspelled words twice; study the words as you type them.

2. Close your book; type the words from your instructor's dictation. Check your work.

chosen confident committee balance calendar buoyant chaperon conquered

committing coming copies indictment existence experience guard hurried

abrupt absorbent accelerate accessory accommodate acknowledgment fiery

146C Technique Improvement: Combination Response (10) *each line 5 times; flowing rhythm*

1   The past is of use to us only as it can make the life of today fuller.

2   Being a leader is largely a matter of knowing how to work with people.

3   It makes a difference whether they go into a thing to win or to drift.

4   The will to win is a big aid to all the men who want to do big things.

5   The final games are to be played by two of the best teams in the city.

| 1 | 2 | 3 | 4 | 5 | 6 | 7 | 8 | 9 | 10 | 11 | 12 | 13 | 14 |

146D Production Typing: Completing an Application Blank (30)

Problem 1: Letter Returning Form

Type this letter as a personal business letter. Decide on the letter style and form of punctuation.

Words

Room 254, Slaton Hall Bentley College   8
Wichita, KS 67207 June 15, 19-- Mr. Lyle   16
C. Nelson, President Nelson & Sons Company   25
1185 Louise Street Wichita, KS 67203 Dear   33
Mr. Nelson (¶ 1) Thank you for asking me   41
to visit with you in your office last Thursday. 50
I enjoyed discussing employment possibilities   60
with you. Touring your plant was an un-   67
expected pleasure. (¶ 2) The application form   76
you asked me to complete is enclosed. It   84
appears to be complete; but if there is any   93
further information you would like to have,   102

Words

please let me know. (¶ 3) If you decide you   109
want me to take the tests you mentioned, I   118
can make arrangements to do so when it is   126
convenient for you. Sincerely yours Charles   135
E. David Enclosure   139/172

Problem 2: Typing an Application Form

Type a copy of the application form shown on page 252. Arrange your copy carefully; keep your typing just above the printed lines. Try to have your typing as free of errors as possible.

Problem 3: Personal Application Form

Complete another application form. This time, assume *you* are the applicant. Use the information you would give an employer.

89A Preparatory Practice ⑤ *each line three or more times*

Alphabet	Al Gray became exhilarated as we kept justifying his five quiz scores.
Figure-symbol	A & D Mine sold 8,764 tons of #130 coal (259 more tons than in March).
Inside keys	The navy frigates fought the battle for fifteen hours before retiring.
Fluency	One of our most wonderful experiences is to find that work can be fun.

| 1 | 2 | 3 | 4 | 5 | 6 | 7 | 8 | 9 | 10 | 11 | 12 | 13 | 14 |

89B Communication Pretest: Capitalization and Punctuation ⑮

Full sheet; DS; 3″ top margin

Type each sentence once as you capitalize and punctuate it. Do not number the sentences.

Later lessons of this division contain rules and other aids to help you build communication skill. Correcting the following sentences will give you an opportunity to assess your present knowledge of capitalization and punctuation.

Sentence 8: Type the title of the play in all capital letters. Titles of plays may also be underlined or enclosed in quotation marks (with principal words capitalized).

1 from july 10 1967 to july 20 1968 we built and sold 49 new houses

2 a short simple explanation of the process we use appears in the book

3 the man we hire for this position must be alert reliable and honest

4 this book which has just been published is very helpful to teachers

5 when we finish the job we plan to take a short vacation trip to iowa

6 we have the funds but we are reluctant to buy your wire recorder now

7 in 1967 32 books were added to our price list in 1968 18 pamphlets

8 miss lees my secretary picked up our tickets for the play king lear

9 after closing the exhibit mr hamilton will send the books to peoria

10 it is true however that these cuts do not affect our office workers

Production Typing Information

ATTENTION LINE IN A LETTER

While the attention line is still used, there is a growing preference for addressing a letter to an individual or department rather than to the company. When the attention line is used, type it a double space below the inside address and a double space above the salutation. Since it is part of the address, the recommended placement is at the left margin. The attention line may also be centered.

```
                              January 14, 19--


Elliott Plastics, Inc.
1025 West Hazel
New Haven, CT  06511

Attention Research Director

Gentlemen
```

Problem 2: Personal Data Sheet

2" top margin; 60-space line;
uniform vertical spacing

Words

DATA SHEET   2

Charles E. David   5

Address   8

    254 Slaton Hall   11
    Bentley College   14
    Wichita, Kansas 67207   19
    Telephone: 852–3000, Extension 148   26

Personal Information   34

    Age, 20. Single. Weight, 185 pounds. Height, 5 feet 11 inches.   47

Education   51

    Graduate, General Course, Holcomb High School, Topeka, Kansas.   64
    Sophomore, Office Management, Bentley College, Wichita, Kansas. 77

Experience   80

    Assistant to Director, Okewa Youth Camp, for two summers.   92
    Salesclerk, Williamson's Bookstore, on Saturdays for one year. 105
    Student Assistant to Doctor Erwin M. Keithley, Professor of Com-   118
    munications, Bentley College, for one year.   127

References   131

    Mr. Bruce Tobey, Principal, Holcomb High School, Topeka, Kansas.   144
    Dr. Frank I. Ellis, Chairman, College of Business Administration,   157
    Bentley College, Wichita, Kansas.   164
    Mr. B. V. Dalton, Director, Okewa Youth Camp, Coffeyville, Kansas.   178
    Mr. Larry Bond, Manager, Williamson's Bookstore, Wichita, Kansas.   191

mattie m. Austin

LESSON 145

145A Preparatory Practice (5) *each line three or more times*

Alphabet   Jack Foxe quizzed the two players about the length of an average game.

Figure-symbol   He wrote, "Sell 875 @ $63\frac{1}{4}$¢ ea., 130 @ $29\frac{1}{4}$¢, and the remainder @ $49\frac{1}{2}$¢."

Double letters   The committee expressed a desire to have your bookkeeper's assistance.

Fluency   It takes a great deal more than just an age of 21 to make a man of us.

| 1 | 2 | 3 | 4 | 5 | 6 | 7 | 8 | 9 | 10 | 11 | 12 | 13 | 14 |

145B Building Control (15) *type 103B, page 183, as directed*

145C Production Typing: Composing Letter of Application and Data Sheet (30)

Problem 1

Compose and type a letter of application for a job you would like to have for the summer. Assume a friend has told you of the opening. The firm to which you are applying is George Johnson & Son Company (provide a local address).

Problem 2

Construct and type a data sheet to accompany your letter. Use your own name, address, and qualifications in the data sheet. Arrange the data neatly on a full sheet of paper.

89C Production Typing: Attention Lines; Mailing and Enclosure Notations ㉚

Problem 1: Letter with Attention Line

132 words; open punctuation; modified block;* attention line at left margin

A letter addressed to a firm but containing an attention line should use the salutation *Gentlemen*.

	Words
January 14, 19-- Elliott Plastics, Inc. 1025	9
West Hazel New Haven, CT 06511 Atten-	17
tion Research Director Gentlemen (¶ 1) We	24
are currently engaged in research for the Gov-	33
ernment space program, and the project we are	42
working on involves the construction of cer-	51
tain new space vehicles. We are hoping you	60
can help us with a problem we now face.	68
(¶ 2) We urgently need a highly viscous sub-	75
stance that retains its adhesive quality under	85
extreme conditions and that has a marked	93
degree of flexibility. No glue now on the	102
market can meet our specifications. (¶ 3) We	110
shall be grateful if you will immediately notify	119
us if your firm is doing any research that could	128
result in the type of cementing material we	137
need. One of our men can fly to New Haven for	147
further discussions with you at any time. Sin-	156
cerely yours M. E. Borman Chief Technician	165/177

*Unless indented paragraphs are specified, modified block form requires block paragraphs.

Problem 2: Letter with Attention Line and Mailing and Enclosure Notations

120 words; mixed punctuation; modified block; centered attention line; mailing notation (see p. 144); carbon copy

	Words
January 17, 19-- AIRMAIL Brant Aircraft, Inc.	9
56 Chevoit Drive Chattanooga, TN 37411	17
Attention Mr. M. E. Borman, Chief Techni-	25
cian Gentlemen (¶ 1) Your letter about re-	33
search in adhesives has been referred to me	42
for reply. (¶ 2) Until the first of June, our	50
laboratory had been at work on adhesives re-	59
search; but since we gained most of the goals	68
we set out to reach, the project was ended	77

	Words
and another begun. The problem confronting	85
you was not seriously studied at any time by	94
our group. (¶ 3) The products we perfected	102
are all patented, and they are on the market.	111
They were surely among those you tested;	120
their names are typed on the enclosed card.	129
(¶ 4) We regret we cannot help you with your	136
problem. We can, however, offer you access	145
to any of our files. Very truly yours Oscar E.	155
Battle Director of Research Enclosure	163/175

Problem 3: Letter with Attention Line and Multiple Enclosure Notation

172 words; open punctuation; modified block; indented ¶s; attention line at left margin; carbon copy

	Words
January 20, 19-- Brant Aircraft, Inc. 56	8
Chevoit Drive Chattanooga, TN 37411	16
Attention Chief Technician Gentlemen (¶ 1)	23
I have discovered through discussions with	32
my customers that your firm is trying to	40
locate a gripping substance or device that has	49
exceptional flexibility under extreme condi-	58
tions. (¶ 2) I have represented fastening	65
manufacturers for 28 years; and, to the best	74
of my knowledge, there is no glue that will	83
do that kind of job. To find such a glue has	92
been the object of many researches, all of	101
which show that any "flexible fixative" lacks	110
strength and holding power. (¶ 3) Have you	118
thought of using rivets or pins instead of	126
glue? Our company markets many fine fas-	134
teners that can expand and contract with little	144
danger of breaking. They are available; they	153
are inexpensive; and they may well be the	162
solution to your problem. (¶ 4) I am enclos-	169
ing copies of our price lists and will stop at	179
your offices next week to explain the prin-	187
ciples involved and answer questions. Very	196
truly yours J. Donald Carr Eastern Repre-	204
sentative Enclosures: 4 price lists	212/224

LESSON 144

144A Preparatory Practice ⑤ *each line three or more times*

Alphabet We quickly brought the extra juice the five puzzled athletes demanded.

Figure-symbol The policy is #8763–412590–N*. (The "N" shows two types of coverage.)

Drill on **ea** These ears of corn are easier to eat than were the ears I ate earlier.

Fluency Often it is the person who knows everything who has the most to learn.

| 1 | 2 | 3 | 4 | 5 | 6 | 7 | 8 | 9 | 10 | 11 | 12 | 13 | 14 |

144B Sentence Guided Writings ⑩

Type two or more 1′ writings on each sentence with the guide called each 15, 12, or 10 seconds. Try completing a sentence and returning your carriage as the guides are called.

		GWAM 15″ 12″ 10″
1	I know that I can do the work with a little more ease each day I type.	56 70 84
2	Many a man has done well at the last hour because he would not let go.	56 70 84
3	I should hold my eyes on the copy at all times if I am to build skill.	56 70 84
4	You must keep your arms and wrists quiet; let the fingers do the work.	56 70 84

| 1 | 2 | 3 | 4 | 5 | 6 | 7 | 8 | 9 | 10 | 11 | 12 | 13 | 14 |

144C Paragraph Guided Writings ⑩ *type 83B, page 146, as directed*

144D Production Typing: Letter of Application and Data Sheet ㉕

Problem 1: Letter of Application

Type this letter as a personal business letter. Decide on the letter style and form of punctuation.

Words

Room 254, Slaton Hall Bentley College 8
Wichita, KS 67207 June 10, 19–– Mr. Lyle 16
C. Nelson, President Nelson & Sons Company 25
1185 Louise Street Wichita, KS 67203 Dear 33
Mr. Nelson (¶ 1) Mr. Harry Carlton has told 41
me that you usually hire several college stu- 50
dents to work for your company during the 58
summer. He suggested that I write to you 67
and ask to be considered for a job this sum- 75
mer. (¶ 2) I am 20 years old and a sophomore 83
at Bentley College, where my studies are con- 92
centrated in the area of office management. 101
Both my high school and college grades have 110
been average or better. My extracurricular 119
activities include membership on the college 128
football, track, and debating teams. In high 137

Words

school, I was coeditor of the school news- 145
paper; I work as a reporter on the college 154
paper. (¶ 3) Mr. Carlton informed me that 161
you expect your employees to be punctual, 170
reliable, and industrious. He explained also 179
that the work can be strenuous. I am not 187
afraid of hard work, Mr. Nelson; my health 196
is excellent; and I have always engaged in 204
physical activity. (¶ 4) I am eager to explain 213
to you personally why I want a job this sum- 221
mer and why I would particularly like to work 231
for your company. My telephone number is 239
852–3000, Extension 148. A personal data 247
sheet is enclosed. Sincerely yours Charles E. 257
David Enclosure 261/282

90A Preparatory Practice ⑤ *each line three or more times*

Alphabet   The truculent Javanese quickly exhibited zeal for more fighting power.

Figure-symbol   The * on page 358 of <u>The Story of 1760</u> refers you to pages 74 and 209.

Quiet hands   The populace celebrated the queen's birthday--she was 66 in September.

Fluency   Believe in luck; but the harder you work, the more luck you will have.
                | 1 | 2 | 3 | 4 | 5 | 6 | 7 | 8 | 9 | 10 | 11 | 12 | 13 | 14 |

90B Communication Aid: Comma ⑳

Full sheet; 1½" top margin; 70-space line; SS with DS between items

1. For the heading, type COMMA.
2. Type the rules and examples given below (with numbers); underline the side headings.
3. Compose and type six sentences, each sentence illustrating one rule. Number these sentences to correspond with the rules.

	Words
Rules	3
• Space once after the parenthesis	
(1) In citing a date within a sentence, set off the year with commas.	17
(2) When two or more adjectives modify a noun, separate them by commas	32
if they bear equal relationship to the noun.	41
(3) Words in a series are separated by commas.	50
(4) Use a comma after a dependent clause that precedes its principal	64
clause.	66
(5) Use commas to set off a nonrestrictive appositive, but do not set	80
off a restrictive appositive.	86
(6) When two unrelated groups of figures come together, separate them	100
with a comma.	103
Examples	106
(1) On May 24, 1969, we transferred our account to a bank in Phoenix.	120
(2) This firm is known to all of us for giving honest, alert service.	134
(3) They like to receive letters that are short, clear, and friendly.	148
(4) When you learn the facts, you will change your mind about my car.	162
(5) Mr. Poe, our manager, is ill. He has read the book COST SYSTEMS.	176
(6) In 1967, 135 firms used this plan. During 1968, 32 discarded it.	190
<u>Other Examples</u> *(Compose six sentences, each sentence illustrating one rule.)*	196

DS — DS — TS — DS — TS — DS markers appear beside the items.

Production Typing Information

SUBJECT LINE

A *subject line*, when used, is typed a double space below the salutation. In the block style or the AMS Simplified letter style (page 176), the subject line is typed even with the left margin. In other styles it may be typed (1) even with the left margin, (2) at paragraph point, or (3) centered.

The word *Subject*, when used in the subject line, is followed by a colon and is typed in all capitals or with only the first letter capitalized. It may also be omitted (as in the AMS Simplified letter style).

```
                                      March 9, 19--

AIRMAIL - SPECIAL DELIVERY

Dr. Henry L. Allen
Town House Hotel
271 Continental Drive
Minneapolis, MN  55430

Dear Henry

        SUBJECT:  Bold Journey Project

     Last week I wrote to General Hunt telling him of
our lack of progress in solving the adhesives problem.
```

Centered Subject Line in a Letter

143C Production Typing ㉕

Problem 1: Memorandum to Graduates

Full sheet; 1″ side margins

Words

TO: Business School Graduates **FROM:** Arthur 7
L. Carlson, Dean **DATE:** (*Current*) **SUBJECT:** 13
Application Letters (¶ 1) In writing applica- 21
tion letters, use plain white paper of good 30
grade. Type your letters. Do not use hotel, 39
club, or fraternity stationery. Never use the 48
letterhead of the business in which you may 57
now be employed. Your letters should be 65
neatly typed, as they will reflect your profes- 74
sional standards. (¶ 2) In a direct, opening 82
statement, apply for the position. If you have 92
learned of the opening from an acquaintance 101
of the employer, use his name. A personal 109
touch is always helpful. (¶ 3) State your 116
understanding of the requirements of the posi- 125
tion. A short, direct statement or two will 134
suffice. (¶ 4) Show how your education and 142
experience match the requirements of the job. 151
From your qualifications, choose the facts that 161
will convince the employer you can handle the 170
position. Hold back details that are not rele- 179
vant. (¶ 5) Show some of your personality. 187
Tell the employer why you are interested in 196
his type of business. Give only such personal 205
details as you think may be of interest to him. 215
(¶ 6) Give at least three references. Indicate 224
that you have been given permission to use 232
their names. Generally, give both business 241
and personal references. (¶ 7) Finally, request 250
an interview. Tell the employer how and 258
when he may reach you. 263

Problem 2: Letter Inquiring about Opening

Using the current date, your address, and your
name, write this letter as a personal business letter.
Decide on the letter style and form of punctuation.

Words

mr irving l stone attorney-at-law broadway 21
building spokane wa 99203 dear mr stone 29
(¶ 1) Do you anticipate an opening in your 37
office for a secretarial assistant? If you do, 46
I should like to make formal application for 55
the position. (¶ 2) I shall be graduated from 63
Spokane College this June with a major in 72
business. I can 75

    type 76

    take dictation 79

    arrange appointments 84

    handle routine office duties 89

(¶ 3) I have held a number of typing, steno- 97
graphic, and secretarial positions in campus 106
and Spokane offices during the summer 113
months. This experience has been most benefi- 122
cial, especially in helping me to decide on a 132
legal secretarial career. (¶ 4) A reply will be 140
most appreciated. If you expect to have an 149
opening in your office, I can arrange to see 158
you at your convenience. very truly yours 167
(*your name*) 171/196

Problem 3: Request for Letter of Reference

Same procedure as in Problem 2

Words

mr leonard m pierce president pierson-brick 21
company 8315 marquette street spokane wa 29
99204 dear mr pierce (¶ 1) Will you please 37
write a letter of reference for me to Mr. Irving 47
L. Stone, Attorney-at-Law, Broadway Build- 55
ing, Spokane, Washington 99203. I am ap- 63
plying for a secretarial position in Mr. Stone's 73
office and believe that my experience as a 81
stenographer in your office last summer will 90
carry a great deal of weight. (¶ 2) I believe 99
that Mr. Stone would be most interested in 107
knowing when I worked for you, in what 115
capacity, and how well I handled my duties. 124
I shall appreciate your writing this letter for 134
me. very truly yours (*your name*) 142/173

90C Production Typing: Letters with Subject and Attention Lines ㉕

When a long company name appears in the closing lines of a letter, as in Problem 2, begin the closing lines 5 or more spaces to the left of the center point.

Problem 1

129 words; open punctuation; modified block; indented ¶s; centered subject line; carbon copy

Words

March 9, 19–– AIRMAIL - SPECIAL DELIVERY   8
Dr. Henry L. Allen Town House Hotel 271   16
Continental Drive Minneapolis, MN 55430   24
Dear Henry SUBJECT: Bold Journey Project   33
(¶ 1) Last week I wrote to General Hunt   40
telling him of our lack of progress in solving   49
the adhesives problem. I asked him for one   58
more month to extend our research. (¶ 2)   65
This morning I received a reply from him in   74
which he bluntly states that we may have no   83
extension of time, and he says that we will be   92
held to our contract as it now stands. (¶ 3)   100
Will you therefore finish the work you are   109
now doing and return at once. You must be   117
here before Monday; for if we stop the Mengl   126
study, you must help us decide what areas we   135
should begin to explore next. (¶ 4) I am   142
sending you a Xerox copy of General Hunt's   151
letter so that you will appreciate fully   159
our position. Sincerely yours M. E. Bor-   167
man Chief Technician Enclosure   174/190

Problem 2

114 words; open punctuation; modified block; attention and subject lines at left margin; carbon copy

Words

March 9, 19–– Brant Aircraft, Inc. 56 Chevoit   9
Drive Chattanooga, TN 37411 Attention De-   17
partment of Research Gentlemen Subject: 26
Bold Journey Project (¶ 1) The Federal   32
Space Administration has proposed that we   40
replace your company on the contract for the   49
Bold Journey Project. They have stressed   58
that time is of the utmost importance. (¶ 2)   66
If we agree to undertake this project, are you   75
willing to let us have as soon as possible all   85
the data you have collected? This action will   94
avoid any duplication of effort. It will also be   104
helpful if you will allow our Director of Re-   113
search, Dr. Conrad Miller, to work with your   122
staff for a few days to become familiar with   131
the problems involved. He would, of course,   140
work at our expense. (¶ 3) We shall appre-   147
ciate a prompt reply. Sincerely yours MIDLAND-   157
CONTINENTAL AIRFLIGHT CO. Guy S. Wear,   165
President   167/179

LESSON 91

91A Preparatory Practice ⑤ *each line three or more times*

Alphabet	Six books on safe driving, due July 2, will emphasize crash equipment.
Figure-symbol	The note ("27¢ for stamps") was among receipts of $3,680.94 on May 15.
Long words	Punctuation, pronunciation, and enunciation show communication skills.
Fluency	Each of us has 24 hours in his day; what we do with them is important.

| 1 | 2 | 3 | 4 | 5 | 6 | 7 | 8 | 9 | 10 | 11 | 12 | 13 | 14 |

91B Building Speed ⑩ *1' writing on each ¶, 88B, page 155; then a 3' writing on all ¶s; compute gwam*

142C Skill-Comparison Typing ⑳ *two 1' writings on each sentence; compare gwam*

Goal | The top men in a firm work with people as well as they work with jobs.

Figures | Express dimensions in figures: 15 feet by 13 feet 7 inches by 2 feet.

Long reaches | We filed an application for the funds before reading the announcement.

Shift keys | Larry Rohy and Walter Zahl will go to Quincy, Patterson, and Santa Fe.

Long words | He is likely to influence the next generation of intellectual leaders.

Double letters | Gregg will succeed in getting the committee's letters to their office.

Hyphen | Our vice-president is on a far-reaching trip to get all-round players.

One hand | In my opinion, minimum wage rates were agreed upon in Edwards in July.

| 1 | 2 | 3 | 4 | 5 | 6 | 7 | 8 | 9 | 10 | 11 | 12 | 13 | 14 |

142D Communication Aid: Composing ⑮

1. Type the paragraph below.
2. In a second paragraph, grant the appointment on the date specified. Set a time for the appointment and indicate that it can be changed if not convenient.

3. Proofread Paragraph 1, marking it for correction.
4. Edit and correct your paragraph; then retype both paragraphs.

I shall be in Cleveland on Friday, May 5, and should like to see you for a few minutes if your appointment calendar permits. The reason for this request is that I should like to look into employment opportunities in your company. I am graduating from the School of Business, Ohio State University, with a major in advertising, and am desirous of bringing my qualifications to your attention.

LESSON 143

143A Preparatory Practice ⑤ *each line three or more times*

Alphabet | Willard Young packed a dozen quarts of plum jam in the box for Violet.

Figures | The 29 vessels--marked "Circa 1780 B. C."--were 245 to 360 years older.

Adjacent keys | Freddy needed his cooperation in order to start the logs rolling away.

Fluency | It does not take long for the man with push to pass the man with pull.

| 1 | 2 | 3 | 4 | 5 | 6 | 7 | 8 | 9 | 10 | 11 | 12 | 13 | 14 |

143B Skill-Comparison Typing ⑳ *type 142C, above, as directed*

REPLY REFERENCE NOTATION

Some writers ask that a reply to a letter mention a file or case number. If the letterhead indicates a printed position for this information (usually at the top of the letterhead), supply it. If not, type the reply reference notation as you would type a subject line (page 159). The word *Reference* or *Re:* may be typed before the notation.

CARBON COPY NOTATION

Carbon copies of letters are occasionally sent to interested persons. The carbon copy notation informs the addressee to whom copies were sent and is typed a double space below the last typed line at the left margin. A *blind carbon copy notation* (one which does not appear on the original) is typed as directed on page 149.

91C Production Typing: Special Notations ㉟

Problem 1: Letter with Mailing and Reply Reference and Enclosure Notations

96 words; mixed punctuation; modified block; reply reference notation at left margin; carbon copy

	Words
SPECIAL DELIVERY Mr. Leo J. Richards, Man-	12
ager Gunther Plumbing Company 7412 Ore-	20
gon Trail Youngstown, OH 44512 Dear Mr.	28
Richards Re: File #202-B (¶ 1) Enclosed are	36
three copies of the contract we revised some	45
days ago when we met in the office of Stephen-	54
son and Volk. Please fill in the missing infor-	64
mation required on pages 2 and 3, and return	73
the original and one copy of the contract to	82
us. (¶ 2) As soon as possible, please obtain	90
a bond and send it to us in triplicate. (¶ 3)	98
Enclosed with this letter is an insurance form	107
in triplicate. Please have your insurance car-	117
rier complete these forms and mail them	125
directly to us. Very truly yours JAMES INDUS-	134
TRIES, INC. David E. Cork General Manager	143
Enclosures 6	146/168

Problem 2: Letter with Reply Reference and Carbon Copy Notations

135 words; open punctuation; modified block; indented ¶s; centered reply reference notation; 3 carbon copies

	Words
March 11, 19-- Mr. Jerry E. Wagner, Presi-	8
dent Apex Electronics Corporation 8100 La-	16

Dear Sir

Reference: Your File #31-082

The Federal Space Administration has granted us a 10-day extension on our contract for the Bold Journey Project. We now believe we shall be able to satisfy the contract, and assignment to you will not be necessary.

Very truly yours

M. E. Borman
Chief Technician

xx

cc Mr. Guy S. Wear
Mr. James J. Hess

	Words
verne Avenue Oklahoma City, OK 73135	24
Dear Sir Reference: Your File #31–082 (¶ 1)	32
The Federal Space Administration has granted	41
us a 10-day extension on our contract for the	50
Bold Journey Project. We now believe we	58
shall be able to satisfy the contract, and	67
assignment to you will not be necessary.	75
(¶ 2) We received a letter similar to yours	83
from the Northeast National Airflight Com-	91
pany, of Saginaw, Michigan. The Space Ad-	99
ministration had apparently planned to assign	108
our contract for the Bold Journey Project to	117
two companies, yours and Northeast National	126
Airflight. (¶ 3) If we should not be able to	134
meet our new deadline, as we now believe we	143
can, we shall be quite willing to give your	152
company and the Northeast National Airflight	161
Company all the help we can. Very truly	169
yours M. E. Borman Chief Technician cc Mr.	178
Guy S. Wear Mr. James J. Hess	184/205

Problem 3: Composing a Letter

Write a letter for Mr. Richard's signature (Problem 1). Use file reference notation and punctuation style you desire. Indicate that original and one copy of contract are enclosed with information inserted as requested. Indicate, also, that bond will be obtained shortly and that insurance forms have already been sent to carrier.

Address letter to Mr. David E. Cork General Manager James Industries, Inc. 81912 Valentine Drive Dayton, OH 45431

SECTION 23 ▶ PREPARING FOR EMPLOYMENT APPLICATION

LESSONS 142–147

Unless otherwise directed, follow these procedures in Section 23:

Drill Copy: Full sheet; 70-space line; SS.
Production Copy: When complete directions are not given, use your own judgment. Make your work as neat and attractive as possible. When you are asked to type letters, use the style and punctuation you prefer. Address envelopes as needed. Correct your errors. You need not make carbon copies.

LESSON 142

142A   Preparatory Practice ⑤   *each line three or more times*

Alphabet Daniel Joyer's macabre mask, "Banquo's Ghost," won five or six prizes.

Figure-symbol At the meeting, 289,356 stockholders (70%) voted "no" on Proposal #14.

Second row Jason thanked the Highland laddies and lassies for dancing the flings.

Fluency The nation's future lies in the plans and actions of its young people.
| 1 | 2 | 3 | 4 | 5 | 6 | 7 | 8 | 9 | 10 | 11 | 12 | 13 | 14 |

142B   Production Skill Building ⑩   *two 3' writings; compute gwam on each*

Unbound manuscript form

Words

We are shifting in this county from a product-oriented culture to one of an idea-oriented one. More and more, Education is being thought of of as our greatest industry. Little Do you wonder, for more people are engaged in this industry then in any other: 51 million students and 2 million instructors teachers on a full-time bases, and the number is growing. Our The country's outlay expenditure for education is $50 billion a year and so is exceeded only by our expenditure for defense.

Economies Economists have only recently begun to recognize the real value of investing in people. A trained man or woman has a capital value in the economy that should be considered along with plant, equipment, and inventories.

Many economists are now stressing emphasizing education as the key to our economic and social advance progress. They trace all the greatness of America, not along to only vast, natural resources, but to foresighted investment in human capital. as well. More than anyone other people in history, we in the United States have hitched our star to Education.

Words
12
27
39
53
65
78
90
103
116
129
135
144
157
169
180
196
198

LESSON 92

92A   Preparatory Practice ⑤ *each line at least three times*

Alphabet   Ezra quickly fixed the broken vase with just mucilage and brown paper.

Figure-symbol   Ken's stock, bought at 135½, sold for 248¼ in the 1966–67 bull market.

Adjacent keys   There were three points on Kili's eastern slope free of rough weather.

Fluency   All of us need a lot of pushing and guiding if we are to do good work.
                | 1 | 2 | 3 | 4 | 5 | 6 | 7 | 8 | 9 | 10 | 11 | 12 | 13 | 14 |

92B   Communication Aid: Comma ⑳

Full sheet; 1½″ top margin; 70-space line; SS with DS between items

1. For the heading, type COMMA.
2. Type the rules and examples given below (with numbers); underline the side headings.
3. Compose and type six sentences, each sentence illustrating one rule. Number these sentences to correspond with the rules.

	Words
Rules	3
(1) Use commas to set off a nonrestrictive clause.	14
(2) Use a comma to separate coordinate clauses joined by one of the pure conjunctions (and, but, for, or, neither, nor).	27 / 38
(3) Use a comma to point off an introductory phrase containing a verb.	52
(4) Use commas to set off parenthetic words, phrases, and clauses that may be omitted without harming the structure of the sentence.	66 / 79
(5) Use commas to set off words of direct address.	89
(6) Use a comma to separate city and state names.	99
Examples	103
(1) This trip, which is recommended in all guide books, costs little.	117
(2) A position is open, but I cannot interview anyone to fill it yet.	131
(3) To qualify for a job, he must know how to write forceful letters.	145
(4) This is one job, for example, on which she can use expert advice.	159
(5) Thank you, Mr. Cole, for sending the portraits to me so promptly.	173
(6) Our annual meeting will be held in Cleveland, Ohio, on August 21.	187
Other Examples *(Compose six sentences, each sentence illustrating one rule.)*	192

DS appears to the left of Rules; TS, DS, TS, DS markers appear in margin.

Production Typing Information

POSTSCRIPT

Type the postscript a double space below the reference initials line or the last typed line. The postscript need not be preceded by the letters "P.S."; it is indented or blocked to agree with the style used in other paragraphs of the letter.

```
                          H. R. Wilkins, President
xx

Enclosure

So that your employees will be taking no chances, we shall
accept the return of any boats not satisfactory and make
a full refund.  We guarantee your complete satisfaction.
```

141C Production Measurement (30) *20' writing; erase and correct all errors*

Problem 1: Letter on Executive-Size Paper

(Sheet 7¼" by 10½")

	Words
(Current date) mr hunter a langley area man-	9
ager mott supply company 802 touchstone	17
avenue dayton oh 45427 dear hunter (¶ 1)	25
For months we have watched our costs rise	34
and have waited patiently for them to return	43
to normal. Apparently we have waited too	51
long, for our current monthly report shows	60
a net loss. Therefore, we must increase some	69
of our prices, effective the first of next month.	79
(¶ 2) Please look over the proposed price in-	87
creases and the short advertisement we plan	96
to send with the new price list. Both are	104
enclosed. We want your frank comments.	112
(¶ 3) You may notify your customers that our	120
prices will be advanced soon; we can accept	129
orders at our present rates, however, for the	138
remainder of this month only. sincerely yours	148
b f savage vice-president enclosures 2	156/175

Problem 2: Program of Meeting

Half sheet (5½" by 8½")

	Words
MANAGEMENT SOCIETY ANNUAL MEETING	7
Longfellow Hotel, Niagara Falls	13
October 10, 19--	17
10:00 a.m. Cascade Room	21
Opening Statements	25
Richard Adams, President, Manage-	32
ment Society	34
Address: "Consumer Innovators"	41
Herbert Simon, Professor of Com-	47
puter Sciences, Purdue University,	54
Lafayette, Indiana	58
Open Forum	61
Leader: Oscar B. Osborne, Market-	67
ing Consultant, Rochester, New York	75
12:30 p.m. Viewpoint Dining Room	82
Luncheon and Introduction of Visitors	90
Address: "Technological Obsolescence"	98
Benjamin L. Gerber, Management	104
Consultant, Buffalo, New York	110
Business Meeting	114
3:15 p.m. Adjournment	119

Problem 3: Partial Notice of Meeting of Stockholders

	Words
CREST MOTORS CORPORATION	5
Notice of Annual Meeting of Stockholders	13
To Be Held April 16, 19--	18

(¶ 1) PLEASE TAKE NOTICE that the annual | 25
meeting of the stockholders of Crest Motors | 34
Corporation will be held on Friday, the 16th | 43
day of April, 19--, at two o'clock in the after- | 53
noon, at 123 Washington Boulevard, Detroit, | 61
Michigan. (¶ 2) The annual meeting will be | 69
held for the purpose of electing seven direc- | 80
tors and for the purpose of considering and | 87
acting upon the proposals set forth in the | 95
attached Proxy Statement. (¶ 3) The record | 103
of stockholders entitled to vote at said meet- | 112
ing will be taken at the close of business, | 121
April 5, 19--. | 124

By Order of the Board of Directors | 131
Edward E. Fardo, Secretary | 136

Problem 4: Partial Report of Stockholders Meeting

REPORT OF STOCKHOLDERS MEETING | 6

(¶ 1) The regular annual meeting of stock- | 13
holders was held in Detroit, Michigan, on | 22
April 16, 19--. The number of votes cast by | 31
proxy or in person was equal to 89.4% of the | 40
outstanding common stock. The following | 48
action was taken at the meeting: | 55

(1) Election of the following directors: | 63
John F. Baldwin   Clyde McGraw | 69
Alfred Glasser, Jr.   David Roche | 75
F. E. Henricks   A. B. Schmidt | 81
Norman Snyder | 84

(2) Approval of proposals to increase the | 94
number of shares of common stock | 100
from 10,000,000 shares to 15,000,000 | 108
shares. | 109

(¶ 2) At the meeting of the Board of Direc- | 117
tors which followed the stockholders meeting, | 126
Mr. Fred Hillary, Assistant Vice-President, | 134
was elected Vice-President. All other officers | 144
were reelected to their positions. | 151

Harvey Doyle	Thomas Sorrell	157
Chairman of the Board	President	163

92C Production Typing: Capitalizing and Punctuating Letter Parts ㉕

Problem 1

128 words; mixed punctuation; modified block; centered attention line; capitalize and punctuate as you type

	Words
burton & nelson industries inc 319 jefferson	12
drive durham nc 27705 attention purchas-	21
ing agent gentlemen (¶1) Here is your	28
opportunity to make it possible for your em-	37
ployees to buy for their children at wholesale	46
price a toy sailboat of rare design. Place the	56
enclosed folder on your bulletin board or show	65
it to your employees, accumulate the individ-	72
ual orders, and send them to us. (¶2) We	81
shall bill the boats at $36 per dozen, 2%	90
10 days, f.o.b. Lansing, Michigan. The price	99
of each boat is thus $3, which is just half of	108
what they would cost in retail stores. More	117
than a hundred thousand of these boats have	126
been sold in retail stores at prices ranging	135
from $6 to $8.75. (¶3) We look forward to	143
receiving your order soon. We can fill it im-	152
mediately. very truly yours maddox specialty	161
company h r wilkins, president enclosure	171
(*Postscript*) So that your employees will be	177
taking no chances, we shall accept the return	186
of any boats not satisfactory and make a	194
full refund. We guarantee your complete	202
satisfaction.	205/219

Problem 2

116 words; open punctuation; modified block; attention and reply reference notations at left margin

	Words
springfield seed & bulb company 8271 dart-	11
mouth road springfield ma 01106 attention	20
mr will jackson gentlemen re order no 281	29
(¶1) Please cancel Order No. 281. We shall	37
replace it with another order, which you will	46
receive from us in a day or two. (¶2) Our	54
first order is out of line with the current de-	63

	Words
mand for seeds and bulbs. Our sales have	72
been far below our expectations, and we do	80
not want to overstock. (¶3) Our supply of	88
your brochure PLANTING HINTS TO GROWERS	97
is very nearly exhausted. Our customers tell	105
us that it is very helpful. They like the	114
clear, practical explanations and vivid il-	122
lustrations. Will you please send us another	132
box of 500 copies. I can assure that we	140
shall put them to good use. very truly yours	150
garden supplies inc robert thompson, manager	159/174

Problem 3

82 words; open punctuation; modified block; attention and reply reference notations at left margin

	Words
airmail berkshire contracting company 931	11
clayton avenue evansville in 47715 attention	21
mr d b anderson gentlemen reference file no	30
3155 (¶1) Two copies of a contract with the	38
Evansville Mortgage Company, 17511 Elm-	46
hurst Drive, Evansville, are enclosed for the	55
installation of plumbing equipment. Please	64
sign the owner's copy of the contract and	72
return it to us as soon as possible. (¶2) The	81
specifications for the installation are attached	90
to the contractor's copy of the contract. We	100
can send you an additional set of the specifica-	109
tions if you need them. very truly yours	118
moore engineering company fred morris,	125
architect enclosures 2	130/144

Problem 4: Composing a Letter

Write a letter for Mr. Anderson's signature (Problem 3). Use file reference notation and punctuation style you desire. Indicate that the signed copy of the contract is enclosed. Ask Mr. Morris to send an additional set of specifications.

Address letter to: Mr. Fred Morris Architect Moore Engineering Company 3147 Colonial Avenue Evansville, IN 47710

140C   Production Skill Building ㉚

Make pencil notations of the problems at the right to be typed for 20 minutes. When time is called, compute your *n-pram*.

Page 237, 136C, Problem 1
Page 239, 137D, Problem 1
Page 240, 138D, Problem 1
Page 241, 138D, Problem 2

LESSON 141

141A   Preparatory Practice ⑤ *each line three or more times*

Alphabet	His proclivity to work explains his fine grade on a major botany quiz.
Figure-symbol	Ray Cook sent 530 bills in 1968, reducing his bad debts losses $8,427.
First row	Has Maxine Mazon or Bob Vanz, members of this club, climbed Mt. Blanc?
Fluency	This is a good week to do all the things you promised to do last week.

| 1 | 2 | 3 | 4 | 5 | 6 | 7 | 8 | 9 | 10 | 11 | 12 | 13 | 14 |

141B   Growth Index ⑮ *two 5' writings; compute* nwam *on the better one*

All letters are used.

	GWAM 1'	5'

¶ 1
1.5 SI
5.6 AWL
80% HFW

Why is learning to ride bicycles such a difficult task? Actually, there is nothing new to learn. We learned body balance, pedaling, and steering at a very early age; therefore, we have all the required skills necessary to stay on a bicycle from the very first day. Most of us must practice riding the tricky bicycle several times before we are really successful. Why? If we have the ability needed, why can't we do the job on our first attempt?

13	3	57
28	6	59
42	8	62
57	11	65
71	14	68
85	17	71
90	18	72

¶ 2
1.5 SI
5.6 AWL
80% HFW

We can fail at a task when we have no confidence in our ability. Those who expect to succeed, will ride a bicycle; those who can but are not certain they can, will tumble off. Surely, the difference between those who succeed and those who fail is the quality of confidence. Confidence will propel us forward, unafraid. Naturally, overconfidence is foolish; but many times it is wiser to bite off more than we can chew than to die of malnutrition.

13	21	75
28	23	77
42	26	80
55	29	83
70	32	86
83	35	87
90	36	90

¶ 3
1.5 SI
5.6 AWL
80% HFW

Confidence is a tilt of the chin; his friend, Determination, a gleam in the eye. Learn to recognize both of these qualities. Together, they are a formidable team. They can help you reach the goals that many another person can only philosophize about. The slogans, "I can because I know that I can" and "I will," should be memorized and recited frequently. Using the aid of the two slogans, you can attempt a really great job; and you will win.

13	38	92
26	41	95
39	44	98
53	47	100
66	49	103
79	52	106
90	54	108

1' GWAM | 1 | 2 | 3 | 4 | 5 | 6 | 7 | 8 | 9 | 10 | 11 | 12 | 13 | 14 |
5' GWAM | 1 | 2 | 3 |

93A Preparatory Practice ⑤ *each line at least three times*

Alphabet	All of his money exhausted, lazy Jacques is now verging on bankruptcy.
Figure-symbol	The fractions 1/9, 5/45, and 7/63 are proper fractions. What is 80/2?
Quiet hands	The very first jet plane flight was made in 1942 in an XP-59 Aircomet.
Fluency	A smile will cut your load in half; a frown only heaps up your burden.

| 1 | 2 | 3 | 4 | 5 | 6 | 7 | 8 | 9 | 10 | 11 | 12 | 13 | 14 |

93B Manipulative Drill: Tabulation ⑩

2 half sheets; DS; 10 spaces between columns; type in exact center

1. Review the steps for horizontal placement of columns given at the right.
2. Tabulate the words; study spellings as you type.
3. Close your book; type the words from dictation.

Columns			Words

advice	beacon	chagrin	4
commitments	judgment	losing	10
missile	misspelling	muscles	16
permitting	personal	personnel	22
privileges	promptly	recognize	28
recommend	separate	similar	33
subtle	traveled	vertical	38

Intercolumns

HORIZONTAL PLACEMENT OF COLUMNS

1. Move margin stops to ends of scale; clear tabulator rack.
2. From center of page backspace 1 space for each 2 letters and spaces in longest line of each column and for each 2 spaces left between columns. Set *left margin stop* at this point.

   Note. Carry forward to the intercolumn the extra space that may occur at the end of the longest line of a column; to the next column the extra space that may occur in an intercolumn. If an extra space occurs at the end of the longest line of the final column, drop it.

3. From left margin stop, space forward *once* for each letter and space in longest line of first column and for each space to be left between first and second columns. Set a *tab stop* at this point for the second column. Follow a similar procedure for additional columns.

93C Skill-Comparison and Transfer Typing ⑤ *one 1' writing on each sentence; compare* gwam

		Words
Goal	She knows that every time she speaks, her mind is on parade.	12
Figures	Our plant can produce 5,973 gallons of paint every 24 hours.	12
Rough draft	We ~~were~~ are pleased to welcome your a to our family of stockowners.	12
Script	Please write or call if we can be of any further assistance.	12

93D Production Skill Building: Business Letters with Special Features ㉚ *20' timing; errors corrected; figure* n-pram

Make a pencil notation of the problems listed at the right. Type each letter with a carbon copy, and address an envelope for each letter. Arrange your material conveniently; work continuously.

Page 158, 89C, Problem 2
Page 160, 90C, Problem 2
Page 161, 91C, Problem 2
Page 163, 92C, Problem 3

Unbound report form; SS descriptive copy; DS and TS between parts as indicated

Words

PROPOSED AMENDMENTS AND REVISIONS TO   7
THE CONSTITUTION AND BYLAWS   13

DS

Stockton Chapter, Management Society   20

TS

Amendment 1   25

DS

All references within the Constitution   33
and Bylaws to the word "National" shall be   41
changed to read "International."   48

TS

Amendment 2   53

DS

ARTICLE I – OFFICERS AND DIRECTORS   60

DS

Section 1. Shall be amended as follows: 68

DS

Officers – The officers of this chapter shall   79
be President, a First Vice-President, a Sec-   87
ond Vice-President, Secretary, and Treasurer,   97
all of whom shall be members exofficio of the   106
Board of Directors.   110

DS

Section 3. Shall be amended as follows: 118

DS

Nominations – The Advisory, Long-   127
Range Planning, and Nominating Committee   135
shall submit, to the Chapter at the next regu-   142
lar meeting prior to the April annual meeting,   154
a report placing in nomination one candidate   163
for each office to be filled by election.   171

DS

Words

Section 8. Shall be amended as follows: 180

Duties of Vice-Presidents – In the ab-   192
sence of the President, the First Vice-President   202
shall perform all the duties of the office of   211
President. He shall also have such other   220
powers and duties as the Board of Directors   228
may delegate to him.   233

TS

Amendment 3   237

ARTICLE II – COMMITTEES   242

Section 1. Shall be amended as follows: 250

Standing Committees: The President   261
shall appoint the following committees from   270
the members of the Chapter: 276

a. A Program Committee shall make all   284
arrangements for regular meetings of the   292
Chapter as well as coordinate special pro-   300
grams through a Program Services Commit-   308
tee.   309

b. A Membership Committee shall solicit   317
and investigate applications for membership   326
and recommend to the Board whether they   334
be accepted or declined in accordance with   342
provisions of Article IV of the Bylaws.   350

LESSON 140

140A Preparatory Practice ⑤ *each line three or more times*

Alphabet   Jeffrey Belkman awarded five prizes to the aquatic experts in Georgia.

Figure-symbol   * Billed as "285 sets @ 76¢ a set," the listing caused a $149.03 error.

Inside keys   Mighty heights jut from the five beautiful, but formidable, mountains.

Fluency   Do the little things well, and the big things take care of themselves.

| 1 | 2 | 3 | 4 | 5 | 6 | 7 | 8 | 9 | 10 | 11 | 12 | 13 | 14 |

140B Guided Paragraph Writings for Speed and Control ⑮ *135E, page 235, as directed*

LESSON 94

94A   Preparatory Practice ⑤ *each line three or more times*

Alphabet   The vicious mix-up was quickly organized by those foreign journalists.

Figure-symbol   By waiting until May 30, he paid 5½% instead of 2¼%, losing $1,479.86.

Double letters   The embarrassed bookkeeper will be accessible and can accommodate you.

Fluency   We may have a second chance, but it is never so good as the first one.

| 1 | 2 | 3 | 4 | 5 | 6 | 7 | 8 | 9 | 10 | 11 | 12 | 13 | 14 |

94B   Growth Index ⑮ *two 5' control level writings; figure gwam on better writing*

All letters are used.

		GWAM		
		1'	5'	

¶ 1
1.5 SI
5.6 AWL
80% HFW

All letters convey two messages. One is expressed in words; the other, by the impression it makes on the reader. The second is the hidden quality you put into an envelope each time you mail a letter. The written message is important; let there be no doubt on this point. A letter must say what it should, and it should say it clearly and succinctly. Nobody likes to receive fuzzy letters in which ideas defy interpretation. A clear letter is usually a welcome caller.

13 | 3 | 60
27 | 6 | 62
41 | 8 | 65
55 | 11 | 68
69 | 14 | 71
83 | 17 | 74
95 | 19 | 76

¶ 2
1.5 SI
5.6 AWL
80% HFW

Almost everyone disapproves of men or women who overdress or who do not dress appropriately for their calling. As a writer remarked, "I hate to see men overdressed; a man ought to look like he is put together by accident, not added up on purpose." How you dress is very important; so are the letters you send out to represent you. They should reflect a company at its very best. Letters gain admittance more easily than callers, but this privilege should not be abused.

13 | 22 | 79
27 | 24 | 81
41 | 27 | 84
55 | 30 | 87
68 | 33 | 90
82 | 35 | 92
95 | 38 | 95

¶ 3
1.5 SI
5.6 AWL
80% HFW

In an office setting, you must be observant of the many hidden qualities that are part of any good letter. A firm will often be judged on the typing and on the care you take in spelling, punctuating, and proofreading your work. Somehow, a letter that is faulty in these basic points does not impress a reader with the purpose of its message. The letters you type must express the dignity and sincerity with which a company conducts business affairs.

13 | 41 | 98
26 | 43 | 100
40 | 46 | 103
54 | 49 | 106
69 | 52 | 109
83 | 55 | 112
94 | 57 | 114

1' GWAM | 1 | 2 | 3 | 4 | 5 | 6 | 7 | 8 | 9 | 10 | 11 | 12 | 13 | 14 |
5' GWAM | 1 | 2 | 3 |

94C   Production Measurement: Business Letters with Special Features ㉚ *20' timing; errors corrected; compute n-pram*

Type the four letters on page 166. Make a carbon copy of each letter. Address an envelope of appropriate size for each letter.

139B Production Skill Building ⑮ *two 5' writings; compute* gwam

Words

As a spokesmen for Budlong's management, I am happy to welcome   11

you as a stockholder in Budlong Financial Cooperation. We   22

appreciate your expressions of confidense in this company and   35

assure we intent to continue our roll as the nationa's leading   49

institutions.   54

No doubt as you know, our subsidaries make an im-   64

portant contrivution to to the financial structure of the   78

American and Canadian economies. In putting money to word   90

usfully, our subsidiaries avance well over six million dol-   102

lars a year too consumers and business organizations for the   114

fulfillment of their neess. We financed majoy retail pur-   125

chases to familye and lent them money directly. We also   137

provide a broad ranch of finanacing, factoring, and leasion   149

services to industry. We provide installment financing for   161

parants, covering school and college expenses, and construct   173

and lease college dormitories and dinning halls.   182

We also ensure cars against colision and and other damage   195

and write life, health, and acident insurence.   204

The Annual meetings of stockholders are on the forth Tuesday   218

in April. We sincerely hope you will be to attend the meetings   230

in the furture. For those who cannot attent, a reprt on the   242

procedings will be send to all stockholders after meetings.   255

Your questions or comments about activities will allways be   267

welcome.   270

139C Production Typing ㉚

Problem 1: Letter on Executive-Size Stationery (7¼″ by 10½″)

Type 139B as the body of a letter to Mr. Stephen Corcoran, 5778 Nantuckett Avenue, Durham, NC 27703. The sender is M. D. Sundeen, President. Use the current date, an appropriate salutation, and a complimentary close. Center the letter on executive-size stationery. Leave 1″ side margins. *(298/310 words)*

Problem 1

134 words; open punctuation; modified block; centered subject line

Words

Dr. William E. Kerr 52 Tally Ho Lane Alexandria, VA 22307 Dear Dr. Kerr SUBJECT: Challenge to Trophy Fishermen (¶ 1) Early last month, I had the opportunity of presenting our story on Arctic fishing at Great Pine Lodge, Great Bear Lake, Northwest Territories, to your Lions Club. I hope that I properly conveyed the story of what it's like to fish in the fourth largest freshwater lake in all of North America. (¶ 2) Dr. Kerr, I am enclosing a copy of our new 20-page color brochure. Possibly this folder can provide additional information to you and your friends when discussing Arctic fishing in the Northwest Territory. (¶ 3) If there is any additional information you desire, please call or write. Thank you again for allowing me to tell you about fishing on Great Bear Lake. Sincerely yours GREAT PINE LODGE Jim Castle General Manager Enclosure

11
20
27
36
45
54
62
71
81
89
97
106
115
124
132
141
150
158
167
173/185

Problem 2

119 words; mixed punctuation; modified block; attention line and reply reference notation at left margin

Words

Property Management Company 7294 El Miradero Avenue Glendale, CA 91201 Attention Mr. Leonard Carpenter Gentlemen Re: File #842-N (¶ 1) Yesterday we examined the Formica tops on the backbars in the Royal Hotel Drugstore and found that four pieces, amounting to 19 linear feet, should be replaced. (¶ 2) We suggest that the Formica be eliminated underneath the coffee urns and that two urn pans be used between the Formica sections instead. This new arrangement will eliminate any future trouble with the Formica top. (¶ 3) We offer to build, deliver, and install the Formica tops and the two Monel Metal urn pans for the sum of $170. We can do this work almost immediately. Please let us know soon if you want us to make these repairs. Very truly yours Harley Davidson Chief Engineer cc Mr. Richard Perry

10
19
28
34
44
52
61
68
77
86
95
103
112
120
128
136
145
154
163/184

Problem 3

119 words; open punctuation; modified block with indented ¶s; centered subject line; capitalize and punctuate

Words

airmail mr michael wunsch, office manager langston–forbes chemical company 15 roosevelt avenue e | tacoma wa 98404 dear mr wunsch subject membership roster (¶ 1) As in 1968, the firm of Epson–Alexandre has been authorized to photograph our members for the new membership roster for 1969–1970. (¶ 2) A representative of Epson–Alexandre will contact you to arrange a mutually convenient appointment to take your photograph for this purpose. (¶ 3) Your consent to be photographed will not obligate you in any way. You may obtain personal portraits from the several proofs which will be shown you, but only if you so desire. (¶ 4) The value of our roster depends on the amount of membership participation in this project. Our goal is to obtain a photograph of every member. sincerely yours arthur mcintosh director

12
20
29
36
45
54
62
69
78
87
94
103
112
120
129
137
147
155
164/186

Problem 4

95 words; mixed punctuation; modified block; capitalize and punctuate; writer's initials: JDD

Words

mr and mrs dwayne schramm 39 mound view court topeka ks 66614 dear mr and mrs schramm (¶ 1) Are you interested in knowing the present market value of your lovely home? (¶ 2) We have never before experienced a greater demand for fine homes in your prestige area; and, needless to say, obtainable prices are startling. (¶ 3) If you will be kind enough to return the enclosed card, we shall be glad to make an appointment at your convenience. Please be assured that our professional opinion will be given entirely in confidence and without obligation. sincerely yours greater topeka investment company vice-president enclosure

11
20
27
36
43
52
62
70
79
88
97
106
119
127
132/145

Problem 2: Board Minutes

1 original; 1 carbon copy; SS; leftbound manuscript form

MINUTES OF THE MEETING OF THE BOARD OF DIRECTORS

August 18, 19––

TS

Words

A special meeting of the Board of Directors was held on Friday, August 18, 19––. Members present were Messrs. Bradley, Dawson, Glidden, Holstein, May, McClintock, Roberts, and Wahl. Members absent were Messrs. Lipscomb and Puckett.

The Chairman stated that the purpose of the meeting was to consider the offer of merger with the Dodge Bank and Trust Company. Statements of Condition of the Merchants State Bank and Dodge Bank and Trust Company as of August 1, 19––, were placed in the hands of each member present. Copies of these statements are attached and are made a part of these Minutes.

According to the terms of the proposed merger, holders of shares of Dodge Bank and Trust Company will receive shares of the combined bank on a share-for-share basis, and holders of shares of the Merchants State Bank will retain their present shares. Holders of common stock of the Dodge Bank and Trust Company may, at their option, receive in cash $62 for each share of common stock held.

After a careful study and discussion of the terms of the proposed merger, the members of the Board present unanimously voted to direct the President to notify the stockholders of the terms of the proposed merger and of the Board recommendation that this merger be approved.

There being no further business, the meeting was adjourned at 4:15 p.m.

Respectfully submitted,

Secretary

	Words
	10
	13
	26
	39
	53
	60
	73
	86
	99
	113
	127
	133
	146
	160
	174
	189
	202
	211
	224
	238
	252
	266
	279
	281
	286
	287

LESSON 139

139A Preparatory Practice ⑤ *each line at least three times*

Alphabet	We must analyze and prove the exact question before the judge asks it.
Figure-symbol	Your Invoice #246–80 says, "Pay this total: $57.91." We paid $57.39.
Long reaches	My boy, "Sunny," is excited about the 60 rabbits he raised as a hobby.
Fluency	On the other hand, everyone who is on the level has his ups and downs.

| 1 | 2 | 3 | 4 | 5 | 6 | 7 | 8 | 9 | 10 | 11 | 12 | 13 | 14 |

SECTION 16 ▶ SPECIAL COMMUNICATION FORMS

LESSONS 95–102

Unless otherwise directed, proceed as follows:
Drill Copy: Full sheet; 70-space line; SS.
Paragraph Copy: Full sheet; 70-space line; DS; 5-space ¶ indention.

Production Typing: Follow specific directions given with each problem; correct errors.
Materials Needed: Letterheads (or full sheets); carbon sheets; file copy sheets; Desk-Fax and interoffice communication forms; envelopes of appropriate size.

LESSON 95

95A Preparatory Practice ⑤ *each line three or more times*

Alphabet	Mazie was probably enjoying her quiet visit to Cape Cod for six weeks.
Figure-symbol	Exactly 25.167% of the solids (384 pounds) must be added at 10:29 a.m.
Home row	Daylight was fading; Hal adjusted the waning little spark of gaslight.
Fluency	Although the turtle took just one step at a time, he gained the prize.

| 1 | 2 | 3 | 4 | 5 | 6 | 7 | 8 | 9 | 10 | 11 | 12 | 13 | 14 |

95B Building Speed and Control ⑳

1. Type a 1′ writing on each paragraph on the *exploration level*.
2. Type a 1′ writing on each paragraph on the *control level*.

3. Type two 5′ writings on all paragraphs on the *control level*. Figure *gwam*.

All letters are used.

		GWAM	
		1′	5′

¶1
1.5 SI
5.6 AWL
80% HFW

There are only a half dozen operating parts of a typewriter that are used frequently. You can add several words to your rate by using expertly any one of the six. Getting high typing rates is more often a case of eliminating useless motions than working more rapidly. Just analyze what you do when you use the shift and tabular keys, the space bar, the carriage return, the margin release, or backspace key. Note the movements you make. Cut out any that are not necessary.

13	3	59
27	5	62
41	8	64
55	11	67
69	14	70
83	17	73
95	19	75

¶2
1.5 SI
5.6 AWL
80% HFW

Manipulating the shift is part of typing. You should employ the correct method in shifting for a capital. If you are using a standard machine, hold your left elbow in regular position, stretch the little finger to the shift key, depress and hold down until the capital has been struck and released. If you do an inadequate job or have a capital suspended in midair or only partly visible, there is a better way to type. Practice until you improve.

13	22	78
27	24	81
41	27	83
56	30	86
70	33	89
85	36	92
90	37	93

¶3
1.5 SI
5.6 AWL
80% HFW

Do you begin without a pause after a carriage return is made on a manual typewriter? If not, practice to improve. When you return the carriage, use a short throw with the elbow held close to the body. When a return is completed, drop the hand to normal position, and begin typing on the next line without pausing. The entire operation takes only split seconds; and it will, if you practice the techniques correctly.

13	40	96
26	42	99
41	45	101
54	48	104
68	51	107
82	53	110
96	56	112

1′ GWAM | 1 | 2 | 3 | 4 | 5 | 6 | 7 | 8 | 9 | 10 | 11 | 12 | 13 | 14 |
5′ GWAM | 1 | 2 | 3 |

LESSON 138

138A Preparatory Practice ⑤ *each line three or more times*

Alphabet   Always loquacious, Hazel gave Pam her subject for the next day's talk.

Figure-symbol   For a 30½% discount, call Mr. Hanna at this number: 271–6598, Ext. 4.

Quiet hands   The piquant taste of the lemonade temporarily slakes our heavy thirst.

Fluency   Please keep in mind that your stroking must be sharp, clean, and even.

| 1 | 2 | 3 | 4 | 5 | 6 | 7 | 8 | 9 | 10 | 11 | 12 | 13 | 14 |

138B Communication Aid: Composing ⑮

1. Type the paragraph below.
2. In a second paragraph, accept the invitation. Indicate the title of your presentation.
3. Proofread Paragraph 1, marking it for correction.
4. Edit and correct your paragraph; then retype both paragraphs.

Will you please speak to the members of Delta Pi Epsilon at a dinner meeting on Wednesday, October 14, 19--. The meeting is set for the Victory Room of Robaires, 4296 Melrose Avenue. We plan to have dinner at 6:30, and your talk will follow immediately. Delta Pi Epsilon is an honorary fraternity devoted to the improvement of business and economic education. You may select your own topic. I shall appreciate hearing from you soon.

138C Building Speed and Control ⑤ *137C, page 238, as directed*

138D Production Typing ㉕

Problem 1: Letter on Executive-Size Stationery (7¼″ by 10½″)

Type the following letter on executive-size stationery. When stationery is narrower than the regular 8½″ width, regulate line length by setting appropriate margins. Such letter margins are usually 1″ wide.

	Words
august 18 19-- mr vernon e caster president	10
dodge bank and trust company dodge wi 54625	19
dear mr caster (¶ 1) At a special meeting of	26
our Board of Directors held today, the terms	36
of the offer of a merger between the Mer-	44
chants State Bank and Dodge Bank and Trust	53
Company were thoroughly explored. (¶ 2) It	60
is the unanimous recommendation of our	68
Board of Directors that the terms of the pro-	77
posed merger be approved, and I have been	85
directed to notify the holders of shares of	94
common stock in the Merchants State Bank	102
of a special meeting to be held on September	111
30 for the purpose of voting on the proposed	120
merger. (¶ 3) In carrying out the directions	128
of the Board of Directors, I do so with confi-	137
dence that this proposed merger will be to the	147
mutual advantage of all holders of stock in	156
both banks. I look forward with much inter-	164
est to working with you as one of the officers	174
of the resulting institution. cordially yours	183
j d may president	

138/203

		Words in Guide	Line
Goal sentence	The talent of success is nothing more than doing what you can do well.	56	14
Hyphens	The well-known speaker talked about up-to-date methods in office work.	56	14
Double letters	Ann can now notify all her classes that the 22 books will arrive soon.	56	14
Figures	We can now ship 147 of the 593 wall fixtures you ordered on August 27.	56	14

95D Technique Improvement: Response Patterns ⑩ *each line three times on the response level indicated*

1	Stroke	Several residents mailed Form X, thereby establishing legal residence.
2	Stroke	These discrepancies were immediately corrected by improved scheduling.
3	Stroke	Mae inquired at local stationery stores for stationary light fixtures.
4	Word	She will take an ad in your paper if you will add one more line to it.
5	Word	No problem is so big that it lacks an answer. Learn to think clearly.
6	Word	This is the kind of work I like to do and the work I can do very well.
7	Combination	I know their themes were not submitted; there are no more papers here.
8	Combination	Some people will try anything once; others will try it once too often.
9	Combination	To make your work look neat, keep the right margin as even as you can.

| 1 | 2 | 3 | 4 | 5 | 6 | 7 | 8 | 9 | 10 | 11 | 12 | 13 | 14 |

95E Manipulative Drill: Tabulation ⑩

2 half sheets; DS; 8 spaces between columns; type in exact center

1. If necessary, review the steps for horizontal placement of columns, 93B, p. 164.
2. Tabulate the words; study spellings as you type.
3. Close your book; type the words from dictation.

			Words
access	adjourn	analyzed	5
allotment	commitments	convey	11
dictionary	dilemma	disappointed	17
exceptions	exhibited	extension	23
familiarize	grateful	receive	29
referred	schedule	stymied	34
vehicles	vicious	visibility	40

LESSON 96

96A Preparatory Practice ⑤ *each line three or more times*

Alphabet	The jarring impact of the earthquake paralyzed six old Bavarian towns.
Figure-symbol	Change Ray's total (19½) to 20; add it to Ann's totals (357 and 684½).
Second row	Ask Gladys if she has a half tank of gas; she has less than she knows.
Fluency	He would rather do one thing really well than do many things half way.

| 1 | 2 | 3 | 4 | 5 | 6 | 7 | 8 | 9 | 10 | 11 | 12 | 13 | 14 |

137D Production Typing ㉕

Problem 1: Program of Meeting

Type a copy of the following program. Plan your work so that the program will be attractively placed on a single page. Correct your errors.

	Words
MADISON ACCOUNTANTS ASSOCIATION	6
Continental Hotel, Madison DS	12
November 10, 19-- DS	15
TS	
3:00 p.m. Copenhagen Room	20
Address: "Tax Laws and the Accountant"	28
Ernest B. Towner, Comptroller, National	36
Tractor Co., Milwaukee	41
Panel Discussion	45
Harold Fields, Senior Partner, Fields,	53
Gunther & Jackson, Madison; George	60
Gentry, Lawyer, Green Bay; Ralph M.	68
Kinney, Chief Accountant, Hooker &	75
Sons, Madison	78
5:15 p.m. Rio de Janerio Room	84
Social Hour	87

	Words
6:00 p.m. Quebec Room	91
Buffet Dinner	94
7:30 p.m. Copenhagen Room	98
Address: "Court Decisions on Taxes"	106
Alex M. Pfeiffer, Partner, Price & Pfeiffer, Madison	114
	117
Panel Discussion	121
William Gibbs, President, Gibbs Manufacturing Co., Madison; Wilmert Perkins,	128
	137
Comptroller, Hunter–Miller Company,	144
Milwaukee; Sydney B. Phillips, Vice-President, Webb Aerospace Corporation,	152
	160
Madison; Thomas Justiz, Tax Consultant, Chicago	168
	170
Open Forum Discussion	175

Problem 2: Speech (First Part)

This is the first part of a speech that Mr. Bernard Gladstone, President of Marvel Motors, will deliver at a meeting of the stockholders. Type in unbound manuscript form. Use triple spacing and 10-space paragraph indentions for easy reading. Correct your errors. Prepare a title for the speech. Leave 3 blank spaces after the title.

	Words
To the Members of the Marvel Family:	8

(¶ 1) Since I came to work for Marvel Motors in 1930, vast changes have taken place in our Company, the environment in which it operates, and the standards of success that we have set for ourselves. (¶ 2) We had our fair share of problems in the ensuing years. In 1930, Marvel Motors, with 19 percent of the market, was just starting to gain momentum as a successful competitor. The economy was booming, but there were prophets of gloom in those days, too. (¶ 3) I recall a statement made by a nationally known economist in the middle 1920's who said, "One car per family is the measure of ultimate use of the automobile for the same reason that one bathtub and one telephone serve the needs of the family unit." This type of pessimistic vision led to his prediction in 1927 that the number of vehicles on the road at that time--22 million cars and trucks--represented the saturation point for motor vehicles in this country. (¶ 4) Today--some 40 years after the saturation point for motor vehicles in this country had been estimated at 22 million--we have over 88 million vehicles on the roads and a growing demand that continues to push the figures higher. (¶ 5) The results of our performance during the past year have been made available to you through our Annual Report. Because demand for automotive products fluctuates from year to year, we can obtain a better indication of both short- and long-term performance by analyzing a longer time span. With this in mind, let us review the past year in relation to our performance over the past 10 years. This is a representative period during which substantial growth was realized by Marvel Motors and the automotive industry.

96B Skill-Comparison and Transfer Typing ⑩ *two 1' writings on each sentence, 95C, page 168, without the call of the guide; compare rates*

96C Communication Pretest: Punctuation Marks ⑩

Full sheet; 2" top margin; DS; 70-space line

The following sentences will pretest your knowledge of the punctuation marks to be studied in this section. As you type, make necessary corrections and insert the punctuation marks emphasized at the left of the sentences.

1	Terminal punctuation	may i hear from you soon about this matter so that i may file a claim
2	Terminal punctuation	does mr jackson know how long this young man has worked in my office
3	Exclamation point	get on the bandwagon hurry remember the contest ends this tuesday
4	Semicolon	i ordered those pens a month ago i have not received any of them yet
5	Semicolon	i saw the notice on the board last month therefore i was forewarned
6	Semicolon	if he goes he will drive but since he is busy he may not go at all
7	Hyphen	twenty five of the men will report for work before the end of the day
8	Hyphen	i know that the machine is available for a 10 20 or 30 day period
9	Hyphen	lewis has a free and easy manner on his weekly coast to coast program
10	Dashes	sympathy the kind we all treasure is two hearts tugging at one load

| 1 | 2 | 3 | 4 | 5 | 6 | 7 | 8 | 9 | 10 | 11 | 12 | 13 | 14 |

96D Production Typing: Manuscript and Telegram ㉕

Problem 1: Unbound Manuscript

Type in unbound manuscript form with a 2" top margin; number the pages. If necessary, refer to directions on page 185.

PREPARING TELEGRAMS

TS

(¶ 1) Almost all telegrams are transmitted to Western Union offices by telephone, teleprinter, or Desk-Fax. When they are transmitted by telephone or teleprinter, one or more copies of the message are typed on plain paper for the files. The file copy should show the class of service specified, account to be charged if other than that of the sender, date and time the message was filed, name and address of the recipient, message, sender's name and possibly his title, and reference initials of the typist. The form in which these data are typed on the paper is flexible. (¶ 2) Desk-Fax (or Telefax) machines are installed in companies that send and receive a large number of messages. When this service is used, telegrams are typed on special forms that are later placed on the cylinder of the transmitter. An electronic eye then scans the message and flashes it to a similar machine located at the nearest telegraph center, which in turn flashes it to its destination. The Desk-Fax also receives telegrams by the same process. (¶ 3) The senders of domestic messages (those communicated within the continental United States) have two classes of service available:

SS and indent numbered items 5 spaces from both margins

1. Full-Rate Telegram. This is the speediest service available. The minimum

Rules

(1) Use parentheses to set off parenthetical or explanatory matter.

(2) Use parentheses when an amount expressed in words is followed by the same amount in figures.

(3) Parentheses may be used to enclose item enumerations.

(4) A punctuation mark follows the second parenthesis if it punctuates the sentence as a whole.

(5) A punctuation mark is placed inside the parentheses if it applies to the parenthetical material.

(6) A reference in parentheses at the end of a sentence is placed before the period unless it is a complete sentence in itself.

Examples

(1) Ralph (my cousin) lives in the capital city of Arizona (Phoenix).

(2) I can sell my home to them for thirty thousand dollars ($30,000).

(3) John set three goals: (1) speed, (2) control, and (3) good form.

(4) I will call him (the lawyer, I mean), but I shall call you first.

(5) Bring the late report with you. (We have a copy of the old one.)

(6) You will find the pictures you desire in the new book (page 137).

Other Examples

137C Building Speed and Control ⑤

1. Type two 1' writings on the *exploration level.* Compute *gwam* on the better one. All letters are used.

2. Type two 1' writings on the *control level.* Compute *nwam* on the better one. Compare the *gwam* and *nwam* rates.

All letters are used.

Some persons do not believe that time is important. They appear to
have an excess of it; and, as a consequence, they become quite bored and
lazy. They forget to realize that every minute contains a potential
meant just for them. Minutes inexorably change into days; days rapidly
turn into months and years; and Time copies the history of our lives.
We write another page every day. What kind of story is it? What kind of
story will it be? Only Time and you will determine.

1.4 SI
5.6 AWL
85% HFW

2. **Overnight Telegram.** Overnight telegrams may be sent any time up to midnight for delivery the next morning. The minimum charge is based on 100 words. For longer messages, a charge is made for each additional word.

(¶ 4) There are a few important points to keep in mind in preparing a telegram. The class of service desired, the point of origin, and the date should be indicated. One complete address is free. The address on a telegram should thus include all the information that will be helpful in locating the addressee quickly. Even a telephone number or the business title of the addressee may be used without charge. The ZIP Code need not be included. (¶ 5) Only one signature may be included without extra charge. A title, name of department, or name of firm may be added. The name of the city from which a message is sent is shown without charge in the date line of the delivered message.

heading TELEGRAM at the top, as shown.

TELEGRAM Telegram May 2, 19--, 9 a.m. William B. Biggs, President Pacific Industries, Inc. 41892 Van Ness Boulevard San Francisco, California (¶) Arriving San Francisco Wednesday. Can you meet me to discuss supplying materials for the Wilmott contract? Quick delivery vital. Telegraph reply. Charles Holman, Manager Monarch Builders, Inc. (*your initials as typist*)

TELEGRAM

Telegram

May 2, 19--, 9 a.m.

William B. Biggs, President
Pacific Industries, Inc.
41892 Van Ness Boulevard
San Francisco, California

Arriving San Francisco Wednesday. Can you meet me to discuss

supplying materials for the Wilmott contract? Quick delivery

vital. Telegraph reply.

Charles Holman, Manager
Monarch Builders, Inc.

xx

File Copy of Telegram on Plain Paper

LESSON 97

97A Preparatory Practice ⑤ *each line three or more times*

Alphabet

Our quiz grades quickly improved, but we failed the June examinations.

Figure-symbol

I wrote, "P & L Co., 936 Oak St., 1,840 prs. @ 72¢ per pr. (less 5%)."

Capitals

D. H. Achs, P. G. Hasko, and R. I. Quinn live in Salt Lake City, Utah.

Fluency

We must prepare ourselves for work that must be done in the year 2000.

| 1 | 2 | 3 | 4 | 5 | 6 | 7 | 8 | 9 | 10 | 11 | 12 | 13 | 14 |

97B Communication Aid: Terminal Punctuation ⑮

Full sheet; 1½" top margin; SS with DS between items; 70-space line

1. For the heading, use TERMINAL PUNCTUATION.
2. Type the rules and examples (with numbers) on page 171.
3. Compose and type an additional sentence to illustrate further each rule. Number these sentences to correspond with the rules.

136C Production Typing: Typing on Half-Size Stationery; Chain-Feeding Envelopes ㉚

Letter on Half-Size Stationery

Problem 1: Letter Typed on 5½- by 8½-inch Stationery

¾" side margins; date on Line 10

	Words
july 15, 19–– mr carmen marinella 5840 pawtucket street hartford	13
ct 06114 dear mr marinella (¶1) On Tuesday, August 10, Mr.	25
Charles M. Daily, owner of the Morse Building, will be in Hartford.	39
He informs me that he is willing to meet with our Board of Directors	53
that afternoon at 2:30 to discuss the sale of his building to us. (¶2)	66
As you know, our company has tried unsuccessfully for a number of	79
years to buy the Morse Building. The price asked has always been	92
much too high. (¶3) I do not yet know what proposals Mr. Daily	104
is ready to make, but I should like as many as possible of the Board	118
members to be present. We may need to make a quick decision.	131
sincerely yours kenneth banks chairman	
	139/151

Problem 2: Letter Typed on Half-Size Stationery

Type the letter in Problem 1 again. Address it to the first name on the list in Problem 3. (*150 words*)

Problem 3: Chain-Feeding Envelopes

Chain-feed fourteen small envelopes, typing two for each of the following addresses. Feed seven of the envelopes by Method 1 (back feeding) and seven by Method 2 (front feeding). (See page 236.) Add a personal title to each name.

richard s anderson 84090 pelham road hartford ct   06107

george l burke 9321 beardsley street bridgeport ct   06607

l v campbell 548 alcazar street new brunswick nj   08904

carmen marinella 5840 pawtucket street hartford ct   06114

martin c morales 3196 mediterraneo san juan pr   00924

randolph x scott 3458½ passaic street newark nj   07104

john scott williams 2992 colfax avenue e | elizabeth nj   07204

LESSON 137

137A Preparatory Practice ⑤ *each line three or more times*

Alphabet   In waves, jagged ice chunks quickly excised big lumps of frozen earth.

Figure-symbol   The note said, "The problem is 37 x 96 — 458; time: 1′ 20″ /s/ John."

Capitals   I moved from Elm Street, Orange, Texas, to Pine Avenue, Red Oak, Iowa.

Fluency   A man needs work to do, and there is work in the world for each of us.

| 1 | 2 | 3 | 4 | 5 | 6 | 7 | 8 | 9 | 10 | 11 | 12 | 13 | 14 |

after the——
parenthesis

      (2) A request in the form of a question is usually punctuated with a   DS   33
period.   35

      (3) Use a question mark after a direct question——not after an indirect   49
question.   51

      (4) Use an exclamation point after a word, a phrase, or a sentence to   65
indicate strong emotion or to carry sharp emphasis.   76
             TS

<u>Examples</u>   79
   DS

      (1) The mastery of an art requires technical proficiency and insight.   93

      (2) Will you please have Mr. Johns sign the six copies of the report.   107

      (3) When did you hire her? He asked how long she has worked for you.   121

      (4) Your sales met your quota! Congratulations! You earned a bonus!   135
             TS

<u>Other Examples</u> (*Compose four sentences, each sentence illustrating one rule.*)   141

97C   Production Typing: Telegrams (30)

Problem 1: File Copy of Telegram

Full sheet; 2" top margin; 60-space line; DS message; style shown on p. 170; add heading TELEGRAM

Telegram May 2, 19—, 1 p.m. Gerald M. Marshfield Crystal Supply Company 700 Post Road St. Louis, Missouri (¶) Meeting with Holman Wednesday to consider supplying materials for Wilmott contract. Assemble Monarch Builders order we discussed for prompt shipment. Will advise. William B. Biggs, President Pacific Industries, Inc. (*your initials as typist*)

Problem 2: File Copy of Overnight Telegram

Directions given for Problem 1

Overnight telegram May 2, 19—, 3:30 p.m. William B. Biggs, President Pacific Industries, Inc. 41892 Van Ness Boulevard San Francisco, California (¶) Inventory of Smo-lite needed for Wilmott contract depleted. Remainder of order can be on cars and ready to leave within 24 hours. Advise. Charles Holman, Manager Monarch Builders, Inc. (*your initials as typist*)

Problem 3: Telefax Message

Type the Telefax message illustrated below. Make one carbon copy.

Call Letters. These identify Desk-Fax station.

Class of Service. Indicate by letters NL or NL (Col) if the overnight message is sent collect. If FR or no letters appear, messages are sent full rate.

Type only within outlined border.

Typist's reference initials may be typed at the left margin.

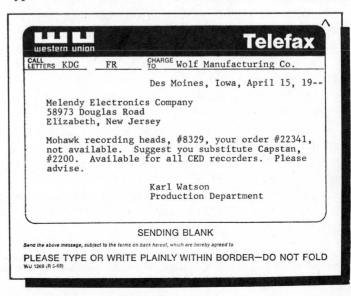

LESSON 136

136A Preparatory Practice ⑤ *each line three or more times*

Alphabet   The misty jungle quivered as herds of zebra panicked in excited waves.

Figure-symbol   "My rate of return," he says, "can be $32\frac{1}{2}\%$ ($1,385 ÷ $4,260) by 1979."

Long words   The secured obligation includes extension of my original indebtedness.

Fluency   Lucky is the man who has a clear idea of what he wants his life to be.
    | 1 | 2 | 3 | 4 | 5 | 6 | 7 | 8 | 9 | 10 | 11 | 12 | 13 | 14 |

136B Communication Aid: Composing ⑮

1. Type the paragraph below.
2. In a second paragraph, acknowledge the request. Indicate that the booklet is being sent. No charge.
3. Proofread Paragraph 1, marking it for correction.
4. Edit and correct your paragraph; then retype both paragraphs.

I understand that you publish a booklet with the interesting title

<u>Joint Tenancy: Can It Work for You?</u> I am a student in the Law School

of the University of Washington and should very much appreciate receiv-

ing a copy of this booklet from you. If there is a charge for it, let

me know. I shall send a check to you.

Chain-Feeding Envelopes

METHOD 1—BACK FEEDING

Stack the envelopes *face up* on the left side of the typewriter.

Insert the first envelope to typing position; place a second envelope behind the cylinder in the "feed" position.

Address the first envelope. As you twirl the first envelope out of the machine with the right hand, feed another envelope in the "feed" position with the left hand.

As the first envelope is removed, the second envelope will be moved into typewriting position. Continue the "chain" by placing a new envelope in the "feed" position each time the addressed envelope is removed.*

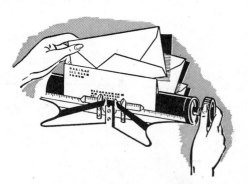

Back-Feeding Envelopes

METHOD 2—FRONT FEEDING

Stack the envelopes face down, flap toward you, on the left side of the typewriter.

Address the first envelope; then roll it back (toward you) until a half inch shows above the alignment scale.

Insert the next envelope from the front, placing it between the first envelope and the cylinder.

Turn the cylinder back to remove the first envelope and to position the second one. Continue the "chain" by feeding all envelopes from the front of the cylinder.

*Some typewriters require three envelopes simultaneously around the platen for backfeeding. When this is necessary, insert an envelope between the bottom of the preceding envelope and the platen.

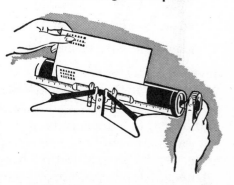

Front-Feeding Envelopes

Moines, Iowa, April 17, 19-- Virgil Carter Company 2002 Speedway Moline, Illinois (¶) Submit best price on 12 #2200 magnetic core matrices with 256 bit capacity. Ben Byrom General Manager

18, 19-- General Precision, Inc. 732 Washington Avenue Pleasantville, New York (¶) Send dates of employment and evaluation of Kenneth Tom who is applicant for senior programmer position. Ben Byrom General Manager

LESSON 98

98A   Preparatory Practice ⑤ *each line three or more times*

Alphabet

Jim Flack was required to pay the tax on the zinc souvenirs he bought.

Figure-symbol

Terms of the May 6 invoice for $497.85 are 2/10, n/30. Pay it May 15.

Long words

Secretary Newenhall's noncommittal responses delighted his detractors.

Fluency

When you can type 60 words a minute with but a few errors, try for 65.

| 1 | 2 | 3 | 4 | 5 | 6 | 7 | 8 | 9 | 10 | 11 | 12 | 13 | 14 |

98B   Communication Aid: Semicolon and Colon ⑮

Full sheet; 1½" top margin; SS with DS between items; 70-space line

Type the following material as directed in 97B, page 170, except that you will use the heading SEMICOLON AND COLON.

	Words
SEMICOLON AND COLON	4
Rules	6
(1) Use a semicolon between the clauses of a compound sentence when no conjunction is used.	20 / 24
(2) Use a semicolon between the clauses of a compound sentence that are joined by a conjunctive adverb (however, therefore, etc.).	39 / 51
(3) Use a semicolon to separate the clauses of a compound sentence when one or both members are punctuated with commas.	65 / 75
(4) Use a colon to introduce an enumeration or listing.	86

TS

Examples	89
(1) The statements did not come with his letter; they may come today.	104
(2) We had engine trouble; consequently, we could not arrive in time.	118
(3) You may take Fay, Helen, and John; and the others will go by bus.	132
(4) Please ship us the following parts: fuse box, light, and switch.	146

TS

Other Examples (*Compose four sentences, each sentence illustrating one rule.*)   151

135D Technique Improvement: Stroking ⑩ *three or more correct copies of each line*

Double letters	Bill Hubbard asked Gregg Mann about a funny old man from Apple Valley.
Long reaches	Many young people eat their lunch at Myron Brigg's Cafe in Huntsville.
Long words	Specialists can edit and continue developing programming instructions.
3d and 4th fingers	Opal was puzzled by the quaint antique pots she saw in the old piazza.
One hand	Brad was aware, as we were, that the trade union exaggerated its case.
Balanced hand	The man must give some thought to his work if he is to profit from it.

| 1 | 2 | 3 | 4 | 5 | 6 | 7 | 8 | 9 | 10 | 11 | 12 | 13 | 14 |

135E Guided Paragraph Writings for Speed and Control ⑮

1. Type a 2' writing to establish your base rate.
2. Type three 2' writings with the call of the ½' guides at exactly your base rate.
3. Set a goal that is about 10 words higher than your base rate. Type two 2' writings; try to reach your new goal on each writing.

	GWAM 2'	3'	

¶1
1.5 SI
5.6 AWL
80% HFW

Men who know how a skill is acquired do not deny the vital need for rapid finger action. It is wrong, however, to think that motions alone can develop typewriting speed. Smooth typing at a fast rate is an end result of many things done extremely well. A typing student will soon learn that reading habits, posture, and attitude are necessary parts of a total performance. Without them, rapid finger action has little effect on the rate of speed.

2'	3'	
6	4	64
13	9	69
20	14	73
27	18	78
34	23	83
41	28	87
45	30	90

¶2
1.5 SI
5.6 AWL
80% HFW

An expert typist will, for example, read copy very carefully. His eyes follow the lines at an even rate. Typists who look away from the copy frequently lack the requisite continuity in typing, and speed is reduced materially. Do not read too far ahead. Focus on just a word or two at a time. When you come to a long, difficult word, type as you read each letter or syllable. Good reading habits can help to produce better typewriting results.

2'	3'	
52	34	94
59	39	99
66	44	104
73	48	108
80	53	113
87	58	118
90	60	120

2' GWAM | 1 | 2 | 3 | 4 | 5 | 6 | 7 |
3' GWAM | 1 | 2 | 3 | 4 | 5 |

letter on letterhead or plain paper. There are 153 words in the body of the letter.

Problem 2: Block Letter

158 words; open punctuation; block style

Words

February 15, 19–– Mr. George Jefferson 3412   9
Litchfield Place Spokane, WA 99208 Dear   17
Mr. Jefferson (¶ 1) Just announce that you   24
are moving, and you may have to do a lot of   33
talking to convince your teen-ager that she   42
can find new friends in her new community.   51
(¶ 2) American understands deeply the per-   58
sonal problems of moving, because we have   66
moved more families from familiar old friends   75
to interesting new ones than any other van   84
line in the world. (¶ 3) We also understand   92
how to be most helpful at this trying time.   101
While you do what you can about personal   109
matters, we do our best to relieve you of con-   118
cerns about the move itself. We advise you   127
about all the details of moving, and we han-   136
dle your things as if we owned them. (¶ 4)   143
When the cares of moving start piling up on   152
you, dial your American agent. He knows   160
how to change your outlook on moving. We   169
move families, not just furniture. Yours very   178
truly Wilson T. Bryant Vice-President   186/199

Words

February 15, 19–– Hal E. Webb, Inc. 356   8
Alvarado Houston, TX   77035 Attention   16
Mr. Joel Rich Gentlemen (¶ 1) The all-   22
electric concept proves itself again, this time   32
in the beautiful Del Amo Financial Center.   40
This financial complex is one more important   49
addition to the long list of all-electric projects   59
owned and operated by major corporations.   68
(¶ 2) Electric space-conditioning systems can   76
save builders 30 to 50 percent in first-cost   85
installation. In most cases, expensive stacks,   95
flues, and vents are eliminated, often saving   104
the equivalent in space of whole floors. Be-   113
sides, there is more freedom of design in all-   122
electric buildings. Less room is required for   131
the main space-conditioning plant, resulting   141
in a low first-cost, minimum-maintenance   149
building with very competitive per square foot   158
operating costs. (¶ 3) Del Amo Financial   166
Center, Allen Boyd, Architect, is just one of   175
the hundreds of case histories of all-electric   184
buildings in Texas. We shall be glad to show   193
you how to apply the all-electric concept to   202
your commercial or industrial building project   212
for remarkable savings. Write for free book-   221
let containing sample plans. Very truly yours   230
SOUTHERN TEXAS COMPANY Glen V. Ritter,   239
Chief Engineer   242/256

LESSON 99

99A   Preparatory Practice (5) *each line three or more times*

Alphabet   Prometheus gave fire to man; he was quickly judged and exiled by Zeus.

Figure-symbol   *Whytt & Kane used a 1967 estimate of $32\frac{1}{2}$ percent (4,580 square feet).

Hand position   Could you balance two dimes on the backs of your hands while you type?

Fluency   A good idea is just a thought unless we change it to words and action.

| 1 | 2 | 3 | 4 | 5 | 6 | 7 | 8 | 9 | 10 | 11 | 12 | 13 | 14 |

Drill Copy: Full sheet; 70-space line, SS.
Paragraph Copy: Full sheet; 70-space line, DS.
Production Typing: When complete directions are not given, use your own judgment. Make your work as neat and attractive as possible. When you are asked

Special Materials: Executive-size stationary and large and small envelopes (you will decide which to use) are needed to complete the problems in this section.

LESSON 135

135A Preparatory Practice ⑤ *each line three or more times*

Alphabet   Using a sextant, Jeff quickly realized the big ship was slowly moving.

Figures   Operator 26 in Reno wants you to call Area Code 702, 463–8591 at once.

Capitals   The Senator from the state of Vermont, Carl O. McGee, spoke at 12 p.m.

Fluency   Do you agree with men who think that life will begin at the age of 40?

| 1 | 2 | 3 | 4 | 5 | 6 | 7 | 8 | 9 | 10 | 11 | 12 | 13 | 14 |

135B Communication Aid: Abbreviations ⑩ *as directed in 122C, page 212; type a heading*

Full sheet; 1½″ top margin; 70-space line; SS with DS between items

Words

Rules   3

                                              5

(1) Type in full names of states when they stand alone.   16
(2) Names of months should not be abbreviated.   26
(3) Names of cities should not be abbreviated.   35
(4) Do not space in abbreviations containing periods, but space between 49
    initials.   52

Examples   55

(1) We spent the fall in Minnesota (not Minn.) as originally planned.   69
(2) The meetings have been set for February 15, April 10, and June 2.   83
(3) Our representatives will be in Chicago, New York, and Washington.   97
(4) Mr. E. L. Bossart left for Minneapolis at 9:30 a.m. on Wednesday.   111

Other Examples   117

135C Skill-Transfer Typing ⑩ *two 1′ writings on each sentence; compare gwam*

Words

Goal   The star of a show sings one song too few, not one too many.   12

Rough draft   An idea is not responsable for the poeple whom believe in it.   12

Script   Counting time is not nearly so important as making it count.   12

Figures   Their check for $137 brought the total collected to $892.50.   12

Communications 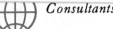 *Consultants*

2203 CEDAR DRIVE, E. / HICKSVILLE, NEW YORK 11804 / 212-869-2560

	Words in Parts	Total Words
February 12, 19--	4	4
Miss Margaret Lamson	8	8
62200 Beacon Hill Road	12	12
Waterbury, CT 06716	17	17
Dear Miss Lamson	20	20
Thank you for your letter of February 5 requesting a copy	32	32
of our Letter Writing Manual. I regret that this manual	44	44
is not yet in printed form. The mimeographed copies cur-	55	55
rently available are restricted to use in our offices.	67	67
We have adopted the block form illustrated in this letter.	12	79
You will observe that machine adjustments are simpler, re-	24	91
sulting in a saving of much time by the typist. The date,	36	103
address, salutation, and closing lines all begin at the	47	114
left margin. Paragraphs are blocked also. The form is	58	125
used in many business offices.	65	131
You should get a copy of our Letter Writing Manual in a	11	143
few weeks. There is no charge for the manual. We hope	22	154
you will find it useful. Please write me again if I can	34	165
send you any additional information.	41	173
Sincerely yours	45	176
S. James Whitmore		
S. James Whitmore	48	180
President	50	182
rsk	51	183

STYLE LETTER 4: *Block Style (Typed in Pica Type)*

CA   92504   **Terms** Net 30 days   **Date** September 20, 19--   **Our Order**
No. 5777   **Your Order No.** N14899   **Shipped By** Express

Quantity	Description	Cat. No.	Unit Price	Amount	
12	Regulation shuffleboard sets	1893-N	17.50	210.00	35
20	Master 6-ball croquet sets	1821-N	21.25	425.00	45
6	Big league archery sets	2106-E	24.70	148.20	54
10	Steel and aluminum golf carts	1956-G	23.60	236.00	65
3 doz.	League-style official baseballs	0056-B	18.20 doz.	54.60	78 80
Checked By (*Your Initials*)				1,073.80	82

Problem 3: Credit Memorandum

Type a credit memorandum from Harper Brothers Sports Equipment to William E. Lodge Company, 14932 Virginia Way, Ogden, UT   84403.   **Date:** September 28, 19--. **No.** 554. The entries are as follows:

Words
17

Quantity	Cat. No.	Description	Unit Price	Total	
2	1893-N	Regulation shuffleboard sets	17.50	35.00	27
3	1821-N	Master 6-ball croquet sets	21.25	63.75	36
1	1956-G	Steel and aluminum golf cart	23.60	23.60	46 48
				122.35	49

Problem 4: Statement of Account

Type a statement of account from Harper Brothers Sports Equipment to William E. Lodge Company, 14932 Virginia Way, Ogden, UT   84403. **Date:** September 30, 19--. The entries are as follows:

Words
16

Date	Items	Debits	Credits	Balance Due	
Sept. 1	Balance			425.50	21
8	Payment on account		425.50	00	28
12	Invoice #5215	829.30		829.30	34
20	Invoice #5777	122.35		951.65	40
28	Credit Memorandum #554		122.35	829.30	48

Rules   6

(1) Use a colon to introduce a question or long quotation.   17

(2) Two spaces follow a colon except when it is used to separate hours   32
and minutes or the initials in the reference line of a letter. As a   46
rule, use figures with a.m. and p.m.   54

(3) Use a hyphen in compound numerals from twenty-one to ninety-nine.   68

(4) Retain the hyphen in a series of hyphenations with the same ending.   83

Examples   86

(1) The question is this: What experience is necessary for the jobs?   100

(2) We finished the tour at 12:45 p.m. and left the city at 5:26 p.m.   114

(3) Approximately thirty-seven of the forty-eight delegates attended.   128

(4) All 15- and 20-day trips to Maine have been temporarily canceled.   142

Other Examples (*Compose four sentences, each sentence illustrating one rule.*) 148

99C Production Typing: AMS Simplified Letter (30)

Problem 1: Style Letter

Type the letter on page 176. There are 175 words in the body of the letter.

Problem 2: AMS Letter

178 words; AMS simplified style

Words

Mr. W. A. Lynn, Sales Manager Kerr Manu-   11
facturing Company 4715 Headford Avenue   19
Waterloo, IA 50701 PREPARATION OF A   26
MARKET SURVEY (¶1) Store owners, gen-   32
eral merchandise managers, and buyers need   41
to know every good furniture manufacturer   49
in the market. In order to be of service to   58
them, we are now preparing a MARKET SUR-   66
VEY that will be distributed to stores sub-   74
scribing to our service. (¶2) A similar survey   83
was sent to our subscribers two years ago.   92
Many furniture manufacturers also found this   101
survey to be instrumental in acquiring new   109
business. There is no expense involved on   118
your part; our services are paid for by the   127
stores we represent. (¶3) If your company   134
wishes to be listed in the MARKET SURVEY,   143
please give us the following information: 151

Words

1. A complete description of furniture manu-   160
factured. 2. Patterns and designs recently de-   170
veloped. 3. Dates and terms of delivery;   178
services rendered. (¶4) We should like to   186
have this information soon, as we intend to   195
go to press in six weeks. Your cooperation   203
in this matter will be deeply appreciated.   212
ROBERT ADAIR – PRESIDENT   218/237

Problem 3: AMS Letter

77 words; capitalize and punctuate

march 12, 19–– mr lawrence l crawford busi-   9
ness education department university of mary-   18
land college park md 20742 condensation of   27
your excellent article (¶1) I think you will   35
be pleased to know, Mr. Crawford, that we   43
have selected your excellent article, "Revo-   52
lutionary Changes in Our Schools," which   60
appeared in the January issue of Business   70
Education Forum, for condensation in a com-   81
ing issue of The School Digest. (¶2) Full   92
credit will be given to you and to the Forum.   103
I am sure that our readers will find your arti- 112
cle most worthwhile. jerome c peterson man-   121
aging editor   124/144

2   mr william raymond jr of ames iowa will address the camera club

3   we left fort worth texas however on saturday january 10 at 8 a m

4   when john goodmans report arrived we studied its contents carefully

5   we received the bird guide but its too expensive may we use yours

6   if we go to europe in january we shall visit london paris and rome

7   we ordered a 12 foot case a 10 foot case is too narrow for the study

8   ted morris car has been parked near the grand hotel for several days

134C   Growth Index   ⑩ *5-minute writing on 127B, page 219*

134D   Production Measurement   ㉚ *errors corrected; figure n-pram*

Type the following problems for 20 minutes. Make one carbon copy of each problem. You will be scored on the number of problems finished.

Problem 1: Purchase Order

					Words
To Harper Brothers Sports Equipment, 38908 Washington Street, Jersey					13
City, NJ 07302 **Order No.** N14899 **Date** September 12, 19–– **Terms**					21
Net 30 days **Ship Via** Express					25

Quantity	Cat. No.	Description	Price	Total	
12	1893-N	Regulation shuffleboard sets	17.50	210.00	36
20	1821-N	Master 6-ball croquet sets	21.25	425.00	46
6	2106-E	Big league archery sets	24.70	148.20	55
10	1956-G	Steel and aluminum golf carts	23.60	236.00	66
3 doz.	0056-B	League-style official baseballs	18.20 doz.	54.60	79 80
				1,073.80	82

	Words in Parts	Total Words

October 5, 19-- → 3 3

Begin all lines
at left margin

Mr. S. W. Jackson, Manager → 9 9
North American Cement Corp. → 14 14
39501 Bartlett Avenue → 19 19
Boston, MA 02129 → 22 22

Address at least
3 blank line
spaces below
date

Salutation omitted

Subject line in all
capital letters
with a triple
space before and
after it

AMS SIMPLIFIED STYLE → 26 26

This letter is typed in the timesaving simplified style → 38 38
recommended by the Administrative Management Society. → 49 49
To type a letter in the AMS style, follow these steps: → 60 60

1. Use block format with blocked paragraphs. → 9 69

2. Omit the salutation and complimentary close. → 19 79

3. Include a subject heading and type it in ALL CAPS a → 30 90
    triple space below the address; triple-space from → 41 101
    the subject line to the first line of the body. → 51 111

4. Type enumerated items at the left margin; indent → 61 121
    unnumbered listed items five spaces. → 69 129

5. Type the writer's name and title in ALL CAPS at least → 80 140
    four line spaces below the letter body. → 89 149

6. Type the reference initials (typist's only) a double → 100 160
    space below the writer's name. → 107 167

Enumerated items at
left margin; if
items are not num-
bered, indent 5
spaces

Correspondents in your company will like the AMS simpli- → 11 178
fied letter style not only for the "eye appeal" it gives → 23 190
letters but also because it reduces letter-writing costs. → 35 201

S. James Whitmore

S. JAMES WHITMORE - PRESIDENT → 41 207

akb → 41 208

Complimentary close
omitted

Writer's name and
title in all
capital letters
at least 3 blank
line spaces below
letter body

STYLE LETTER 5: *AMS Simplified Letter Style (Typed in Pica Type)*

The Administrative Management Society (formerly known as the National Office Management Association or NOMA) has adopted a simplified letter for use in business correspondence. Style Letter 5, above, is an example of the recommended form. Study the features of this style carefully. (This letter is typed in pica type.)

133B Skill-Comparison Typing (5) *1′ writings on each line of 133A, page 230; compare* gwam

133C Communication Aid: Capitalization (10) *as directed in 122C, page 212; type a heading*

Full sheet; 1½″ top margin; 70-space line; SS with DS between items

Words
3

Rules 5

(1) As a rule, capitalize nouns preceding a figure. The word page is 20
usually not capitalized, however, unless it begins a sentence. 33
(2) Capitalize only the first word of a complimentary close. 45
(3) All titles appearing in the address and closing lines of business 59
letters should be capitalized. 65
(4) Capitalize a title that precedes a name or that is used to refer to 80
a specific person. Titles appearing elsewhere may be written with- 94
out a capital, unless the title is one of high distinction. 105

Examples 109

(1) Each case is fully explained in Volume III, Chapter 12, page 207. 123
(2) Capitalize first words of complimentary closes: Sincerely yours. 137
(3) Capitalize titles in letter addresses: Mr. John Lowe, Treasurer. 151
(4) On Monday, President Fred Barnes had lunch with the club manager. 165

Other Examples 170

133D Production Skill Building (30) *errors corrected; figure* n-pram

Make a pencil notation of the problems at the right to be typed as a 20-minute writing. Make one carbon copy of each form. Finish as many of the problems as you can. Compute *n-pram.*

Page 223, 129D, Problem 2
Page 226, 130D, Problem 3
Page 227, 131D, Problem 3
Page 230, 132D, Problem 3

LESSON 134

134A Preparatory Practice (5) *each line at least three times*

Alphabet	Frankly, it would be an amazing experience just to visit with a queen.
Figure-symbol	In 1957, our profits were $37,461.05; this year, they are $189,227.13.
Outside keys	Professor Lopez' quiz in law was two hours long; still, we all passed.
Fluency	The man who wants to be a leader would do well to learn how to follow.

| 1 | 2 | 3 | 4 | 5 | 6 | 7 | 8 | 9 | 10 | 11 | 12 | 13 | 14 |

		Words
Figure-symbol	Type on Line 49, "137 pens @ $26.80 ea., less 5½%. <u>Ship immediately.</u>"	
Double letters	Ann Lee's well-written letters will soon arrive in the committee room.	
Fluency	To type rapidly, hold the arms quiet and make the fingers do the work.	

| 1 | 2 | 3 | 4 | 5 | 6 | 7 | 8 | 9 | 10 | 11 | 12 | 13 | 14 |

100B **Communication Aid:** Hyphen and Dash ⑮ *as directed in 97B, page 170*

Full sheet; 1½" top mar-gin; SS with DS be-tween items; 70-space line

HYPHEN AND DASH

<u>Rules</u>

(1) Use a hyphen to join compound adjectives preceding a noun.

(2) Use a dash (––) to indicate a sudden change in thought.

(3) Use a dash (––) for emphasis to set off an appositive.

(4) Use a dash (––) to introduce the name of an author when it follows a direct quotation.

<u>Examples</u>

(1) The well-known statesman has been appointed for a four-year term.

(2) The best way––perhaps the only way––to have friends is to be one.

(3) Your stars––freedom, opportunity, faith––are bright and constant.

(4) "The Road to Freedom, while narrow, is a two-way street."––Gross.

<u>Other Examples</u> (*Compose four sentences, each sentence illustrating one rule.*)

Words
3
5
18
30
42
56
60
64
78
92
106
120
125

100C **Manipulative Drill:** Aligning Columns at the Right ⑤ *repeat if time permits*

Full sheet; 2" top margin

1. Type the first column, aligning the items at the right 2 inches from the extreme left of the sheet according to the explanatory material at the right.
2. Type the second and third columns in the same way at the positions indicated. Do not tabulate from column to column.

ALIGNING COLUMNS AT THE RIGHT

1. Type the first listed item in its desired position.
2. On the next line, position the carriage one space to the right of the last letter (or mark of punctuation) of the item above.
3. Backspace once for each stroke in the second item (including any marks of punctuation).
4. Type the second item. Repeat procedure for any subsequent items.

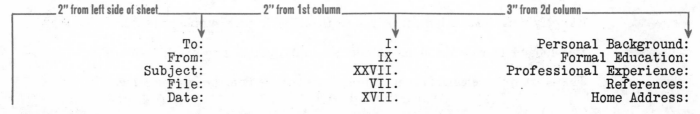

2" from left side of sheet	2" from 1st column	3" from 2d column
To:	I.	Personal Background:
From:	IX.	Formal Education:
Subject:	XXVII.	Professional Experience:
File:	VII.	References:
Date:	XVII.	Home Address:

Date	Items	Debits	Credits	Balance Due	
June 1	Balance			3,571.60	22
10	Payment on account		3,571.60	00	30
15	Invoice #47221	952.17		952.17	37
20	Invoice #47592	1,181.40		2,133.57	44
24	Credit Memorandum #524		181.40	1,952.17	53

Problem 4: Voucher Check

Type in duplicate the following voucher check. Use the variable line spacer to bring the ruled lines on the check into proper typing position.

16–310
1219

PACIFIC BUILDERS SUPPLY CO.
31553 Gladstone Blvd.
Riverside, California 92504

July 2 19 -- No. 4982   3

PAY to the order of _Burdett Building Corporation_ $ 952.17   13

Nine hundred fifty-two and 17/100------------------------------------ Dollars   27

WEST COAST NATIONAL BANK
LOS ANGELES, CALIFORNIA 90006

⑈1219⑈0320⑈ 143 0602 46⑈

Treasurer, PACIFIC BUILDERS SUPPLY CO.

Detach This Stub Before
Cashing This Check

TO Burdett Building Corporation
1348 Cactus Road, East
Phoenix, AZ 85022

PACIFIC BUILDERS SUPPLY CO.
31553 Gladstone Blvd.
Riverside, California 92504

IN PAYMENT OF THE FOLLOWING INVOICES: 33 38 41

Date	Invoice	Amount	
6/15/--	#47221	952.17	46

LESSON 133

133A   Preparatory Practice ⑤ *each line at least three times*

Alphabet   Medical experts frequently view smoking as a major hazard to the body.

Figure-symbol   Its weight is 36#; height, 2′ 8″; Length, 27′ 9″; code number, 14–10 *.

Direct reaches   Dee longed to troll for muskellunge, so Polly swerved to deeper water.

Fluency   There are many elements that combine to produce finer typing outcomes.

| 1 | 2 | 3 | 4 | 5 | 6 | 7 | 8 | 9 | 10 | 11 | 12 | 13 | 14 |

If an interoffice memorandum form is not available, use a full sheet of plain paper and type headings for the special sections as shown on the illustration on page 179.

Problem 2: Interoffice Memorandum

Interoffice memorandum form or plain sheet; SS; 1" left and right margins; no carbon copy; company mail envelope

Words

TO: Wilbur B. Maxwell, Regional Manager   7
FROM: George H. Hannah, Sales Manager   14
DATE: May 10, 19–– **SUBJECT:** Automobiles   19
(¶ 1) In assigning water systems specialists   26
to the various districts on the East Coast, we   36
will need very soon two new automobiles.   44
One of them is for W. R. Nelson, District #3;   53
the other for John Burns, District #5. I sug-   62
gest that we obtain authorization to buy the   71
two automobiles needed. (¶ 2) Tudor sedans   79
will be satisfactory for these men. I believe   88
authorization should cover the purchase of   97
one of the lighter makes. We can then take   106
whatever make is available in the small car   115
class. (¶ 3) The two men will be ready to go   123
into their territories about the middle of June.   133
We should have the cars by that time.   141/150

Problem 3: Interoffice Memorandum

Interoffice memorandum form or plain sheet; SS; 1" left and right margins; 3 carbon copies

vin Kahn **FROM:** John A. Rohr, Regional   13
Manager **DATE:** May 15, 19–– **SUBJECT:** Sale   18
of Overstocked Materials (¶ 1) It has come   25
to my attention that with the current high   34
levels of inventories, some of our divisional   43
offices are disposing of overstocked materials   53
to local customers at greatly reduced prices.   62
Perhaps it would be well for a divisional office   72
to circularize other divisional offices before   81
disposing of usable stock. In this way we can   91
take care of the needs of our offices before   100
disposing of our stock. (¶ 2) I am eager to   107
have your inventories balanced as rapidly as   116
possible and do not wish to slow down the   125
sale or disposal of surplus materials. I shall,   135
however, appreciate your sending a circular   143
letter to other divisions before surplus mate-   153
rials are sold.   156

Problem 4: Postal Card

48-space line; block style; SS; address the card to yourself; add salutation with your name

A message placed on a postal card must be brief, and the sender may find it necessary to omit any "extras" that fail to contribute directly to his main thought. He will usually include, however, the date, his typed name (except when writing to a friend), and a return address, printed or typed on the address side of the card. S. James Whitmore, President

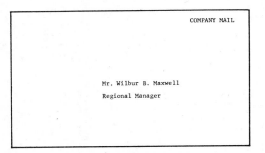

Company Mail Envelope

Postal Card—Address Side

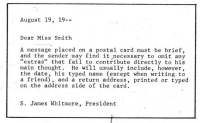

Postal Card—Message Side

Credit Memorandum

BB Burdett Building Corporation

1348 Cactus Road, East
Phoenix, Arizona 85022
Telephone 322-1960

No. 359

Date May 15, 19--

To Pacific Builders Supply Co.
31553 Gladstone Blvd.
Riverside, CA 92504

YOUR ACCOUNT HAS BEEN CREDITED FOR:

Quantity	Description	Cat.No.	Unit Price	Amount	
2	Radiant wall heaters	9352	9.95	19.90	25
1 ctn.	Embossed wood vinyl asbestos tile	1200	11.15	11.15	37
1	Oven wood-fan	3280	17.45	17.45	44
					46
				48.50	47

Statement of Account

Date May 31, 19--

To   Pacific Builders Supply Co.
31553 Gladstone Blvd.
Riverside, CA 92504

BB Burdett Building Corporation

1348 Cactus Road, East
Phoenix, Arizona 85022
Telephone 322-1960

Date	Items	Debits	Credits	Balance Due	
May 1	Balance			130.00	22
1	Invoice #45172	3,272.00		3,402.00	29
10	Invoice #45340	718.10		4,120.10	36
15	Credit Memorandum #359		48.50	4,071.60	45
20	Payment on account		500.00	3,571.60	52

Printed
headings

TO: Conrad V. Tilton, Sales Department

FROM: Eva L. Burnside, Training Supervisor

DATE: July 27, 19--

SUBJECT: Company Correspondence

Salutation
omitted

Correspondence within our company is typed on this special interoffice form. The general purpose of this form is to provide a
rapid, convenient means of preparing the communications that are
exchanged by the various members of this organization. As you
can see from the printed headings, information can be set up
quickly. Only essential information is included.

1-inch side
margins

Observe that titles, full addresses, the salutation, the complimentary close, and the signature are omitted. The inclusion of
a subject heading is highly recommended. It will immediately tell
the reader what subject is treated in the memorandum. The subject
heading is also an aid in filing the communication.

All interoffice messages, regardless of length, should be typed
with one-inch left and right margins. Generally, messages should
be single-spaced, with double spacing between paragraphs. Short
messages may be double-spaced if desired. The message should be
typed in block form with blocked paragraphs. A triple space
should separate the first line of the message from the subject
heading.

The initials of only the typist should be typed a double space
below the last line of the message. Notations regarding enclosures and carbon copy distribution should be included; and if
included, they should be typed in the same position they occupy
in regular correspondence.

When an envelope is needed, the notation COMPANY MAIL is typed in
the space normally used for the postage stamp. The address is
then typed on the envelope in the position normally occupied by
the address. The recipient's name and his departmental designa-
tion should be given.

Closing lines
omitted
Typist's
initials

cy

cc Ethel Bergman, Administrative Assistant
   Sales Department

Words
7
14
17
22
35
47
61
73
86
96
109
122
135
148
159
172
185
198
212
224
236
238
251
264
276
289
294
308
320
333
346
350
351
360
363

STYLE LETTER 6: *Interoffice Communication Style (Typed in Pica Type)*

They may deduct a discount of 3 1/3% ($124.80) from our Invoice #9567.
Sherry's committee passed coffee and cocoa at the Mississippi meeting.
Remember that very few men are experts in more than one or two fields.

| 1 | 2 | 3 | 4 | 5 | 6 | 7 | 8 | 9 | 10 | 11 | 12 | 13 | 14 |

132B Skill-Comparison Typing ⑤ *two 1' writings on each of Lines 1 and 4 of 132A; compare* gwam

132C Communication Aid: Capitalization ⑩ *as directed in 122C, page 212; type a heading*

Full sheet; 1½" top margin; 70-space line; SS with DS between items

Words

Rules

3

5

(1) Capitalize the first word of a complete quotation. Do not capital- 19
ize a quotation resumed within a sentence. 28
(2) Capitalize the first word following a colon if that word begins a 42
sentence. 44
(3) Capitalize adjectives or common nouns that are used as a part of 58
proper names. Do not capitalize geographic terms if they are used 72
in the plural. 75
(4) Capitalize words derived from proper nouns unless these words have 89
acquired independent, common meanings. 97

Examples 101

(1) "He is suffering," the critic said, "from paralysis of analysis." 115
(2) Use this rule: Capitalize principal words in titles of articles. 129
(3) We camped on Cedar and June lakes on our way to Ellis State Park. 143
(4) He had their lovely oriental rug cleaned by Tim Lee, an Oriental. 157

Other Examples 162

Production Typing Information

WINDOW ENVELOPES

Window envelopes have transparent or cut-out openings in the lower center, through which the address typed on a letter, an invoice, or other business forms can be seen.

FOLDING A HALF-SIZE SHEET FOR A WINDOW ENVELOPE

Keep in mind that the complete address must show through the window in the envelope. Fold a full-page form from the top down fully two thirds the length of the paper; then fold back the required distance to make the address come to the correct position. Fold a half sheet through the center, keeping the typewritten side on the outside. Insert the paper into the envelope with the address side toward the front.

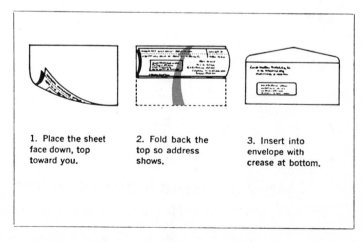

1. Place the sheet face down, top toward you.

2. Fold back the top so address shows.

3. Insert into envelope with crease at bottom.

Folding a Half-Size Form for a Window Envelope

Mr. Black's quizzical expression ...

Figure-symbol   Dan's note read, "On May 29, we will pay (at 6% interest) $13,784.50."

Adjacent reaches   We were excited and frightened; we looked like three dreaded warriors.

Fluency   Some people feel it is easier to be critical than it is to be helpful.
| 1 | 2 | 3 | 4 | 5 | 6 | 7 | 8 | 9 | 10 | 11 | 12 | 13 | 14 |

101B   Communication Aid: Spelling ⑤

1. Type these commonly misspelled words twice; study the words as you type them.

2. Close your book; type the words from your instructor's dictation; check your work.

concensus cylinder deferred deficient dissatisfied embarrass erroneous

gratuity guarantee haphazard height imitation inaugurate issuing suing

exaggerate exorbitant facsimile fiend fluorescent foreign fulfill lien

101C   Technique Improvement: Stroking ⑩ *two 1' writings on each line*

Long reaches   This is a very effective symbol; we have been using it for many years.

Double letters   It will be unnecessary to pay Mr. Tratt a commission in the beginning.

One hand   Face the facts; you can win an award only if you exceed Jim's average.

Balanced hand   Our neighbor and his visitor may take a dirigible to the ancient city.
| 1 | 2 | 3 | 4 | 5 | 6 | 7 | 8 | 9 | 10 | 11 | 12 | 13 | 14 |

101D   Production Skill Building: Special Communication Forms ㉚ *20' timing; errors corrected; figure n-pram*

Make a pencil notation of the problems listed at the right. Follow the directions indicated for each problem. Repeat the problems if time permits.

Page 173,   98C, Problem 2
Page 175,   99C, Problem 2
Page 178, 100D, Problem 3
Page 178, 100D, Problem 4

LESSON 102

102A   Preparatory Practice ⑤ *each line three or more times*

Alphabet   The buzzing, jumping insects quieted, for it was exactly five o'clock.

Figure-symbol   Compute: 640 pairs @ $38\frac{1}{2}$¢ and 975 sets @ $12\frac{1}{2}$¢; allow a $14\frac{1}{2}$% discount.

Hand position   All of us need to study and understand our economic system thoroughly.

Fluency   Fix your eyes on the book; trust your mind and fingers to do the work.
| 1 | 2 | 3 | 4 | 5 | 6 | 7 | 8 | 9 | 10 | 11 | 12 | 13 | 14 |

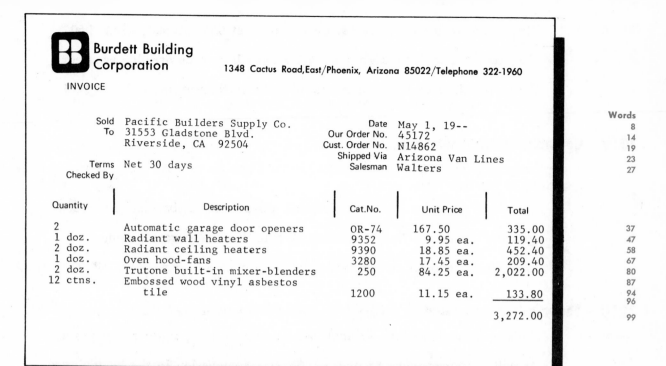

Burdett Building Corporation

1348 Cactus Road, East/Phoenix, Arizona 85022/Telephone 322-1960

INVOICE

						Words
Sold To	Pacific Builders Supply Co.		Date	May 1, 19--		8
	31553 Gladstone Blvd.		Our Order No.	45172		14
	Riverside, CA 92504		Cust. Order No.	N14862		19
			Shipped Via	Arizona Van Lines		23
Terms	Net 30 days		Salesman	Walters		27
Checked By						

Quantity	Description	Cat.No.	Unit Price	Total	Words
2	Automatic garage door openers	OR-74	167.50	335.00	37
1 doz.	Radiant wall heaters	9352	9.95 ea.	119.40	47
2 doz.	Radiant ceiling heaters	9390	18.85 ea.	452.40	58
1 doz.	Oven hood-fans	3280	17.45 ea.	209.40	67
2 doz.	Trutone built-in mixer-blenders	250	84.25 ea.	2,022.00	80
12 ctns.	Embossed wood vinyl asbestos				87
	tile	1200	11.15 ea.	133.80	94
					96
				3,272.00	99

Problem 2: Confirmation Letter

1. Compose and type a letter to Pacific Builders Supply Co. Thank them for their Order No. N14888, of April 25 (Problem 3, p. 226). Indicate that there will be a very brief delay due to a temporary shortage of some of the items. The number of the invoice for this order is given in Problem 3 below.

2. Type the letter on a full sheet; select the letter and punctuation style. Date the letter May 4.

Problem 3: Invoice

Type in duplicate

		Words
Sold To Pacific Builders Supply Co. 31553 Gladstone Blvd. Riverside,		12
CA 92504 **Terms** Net 30 days **Date** May 10, 19-- **Our Order No.** 45340		20
Your Order No. N14888 **Shipped By** Redman Van Lines		25

Quantity	Description	Cat. No.	Unit Price	Amount	
6 rolls	Asphalt felt, 30 lb.	1311	3.15 ea.	18.90	35
12 gals.	Wood preservative		2.50 ea.	30.00	44
8 rolls	Rosin sized sheathing, 20 lb.		2.50 ea.	20.00	55
6	Ceiling exhaust fans	8310	27.95 ea.	167.70	64
6	Wall exhaust fans	8510	32.75 ea.	196.50	73
1 doz.	Outdoor lights, brass	M-153	23.75 ea.	285.00	83
					84
Checked By (Your Initials) **Salesman** Walters				718.10	88

3	fifty one of the men had first or second class cabins for the cruise
4	a chemist in fact any scientist could analyze these strange fluids
5	joe who owns an old bus drives to tucson and it takes him 15 hours

| 1 | 2 | 3 | 4 | 5 | 6 | 7 | 8 | 9 | 10 | 11 | 12 | 13 | 14 |

102C Growth Index ⑩ *one 1' and one 5' writing; figure* gwam

All letters are used.

		GWAM	
		1'	5'

¶1
1.5 SI
5.6 AWL
80% HFW

You must remember that success is not achieved by lying awake at night, but by being awake in the daytime. Generally, the men who get ahead in any calling analyze their working methods. They compare them with the techniques used by celebrated experts in their chosen fields. So it must be with you in typewriting or any other course you may be taking. Study the methods you are using; be quick to perfect the techniques that may improve your work.

13	3	58
27	5	60
41	8	63
56	11	66
70	14	69
84	17	72
91	18	73

¶2
1.5 SI
5.6 AWL
80% HFW

The space bar is used very frequently in typewriting. One in every five strokes is handled by your right thumb. Strike the bar with very quick down-and-in movements. Keep your wrist steady as you control the bar. Ideally, the stroke is associated with the word just completed, not as a separate operation. Give very careful attention to operating the various other parts of your machine. Sooner or later, you will discover that you do more as you learn to do less.

14	21	76
28	24	79
42	27	82
57	30	85
71	32	87
86	35	90
94	37	92

¶3
1.5 SI
5.6 AWL
80% HFW

If you use a manual typewriter, study very carefully the way you return the carriage. Obviously, you must return it with adequate energy to get it back to the left margin. Keep the fingers of your right hand in position over the home keys. Quickly move the left hand to the return lever. Move it forward far enough to take up the slack; then throw the carriage with a very quick movement of the wrist. Return the left hand; resume typing immediately.

13	40	95
28	42	97
42	45	100
57	48	103
71	51	106
85	54	109
90	55	110

1' GWAM | 1 | 2 | 3 | 4 | 5 | 6 | 7 | 8 | 9 | 10 | 11 | 12 | 13 | 14 |
5 GWAM | 1 | 2 | 3 |

Problem 3: Purchase Order

Type in duplicate

To Burdett Building Corporation, 1348 Cactus Road, East, Phoenix, AZ 13
85022 **Order No.** N14888 **Date** April 25, 19--- **Terms** n/30 **Ship Via** Red- 21
man Van Lines 23

Quantity	Cat. No.	Description	Price	Total	
6 rolls	1311	Asphalt felt, 30 lb.	3.15 ea.	18.90	34
12 gals.		Wood preservative	2.50 ea.	30.00	43
8 rolls		Rosin sized sheathing, 20 lb.	2.50 ea.	20.00	54
6	8310	Ceiling exhaust fans	27.95 ea.	167.70	63
6	8510	Wall exhaust fans	32.75 ea.	196.50	71
1 doz.	M-153	Outdoor lights, brass	23.75 ea.	285.00	81
					83
				718.10	84

LESSON 131

131A Preparatory Practice ⑤ *each line at least three times*

Alphabet	Next, we quickly moved the jig-saw puzzle to a large table near a fan.
Figure-symbol	In Footnote (*) say, "Our bid of 3½¢ more in 1967 has paid $4,680.52."
Long words	The nonadaptive organization was often insensitive to its environment.
Fluency	We all make mistakes; they will help us if we try to profit from them.

| 1 | 2 | 3 | 4 | 5 | 6 | 7 | 8 | 9 | 10 | 11 | 12 | 13 | 14 |

131B Skill-Comparison Typing ⑤ *two 1' writings on each of Lines 1 and 4 of 131A; compare gwam*

131C Communication Aid: Capitalization ⑩ *as directed in 122C, page 212; type a heading*

Full sheet; 1½" top margin; 70-space line; SS with DS between items

3

Rules 5

(1) Capitalize names of the days of the week, months, and holidays; do 19
not capitalize names of seasons unless they are personified. 32
(2) Capitalize names of regions; do not capitalize nouns or adjectives 46
indicating direction. 51
(3) Capitalize names of organizations, clubs, and their derivatives. 65
Capitalize names of things with specific individuality that are used 79
as proper names. 82
(4) Capitalize names of specific courses; do not capitalize such names 96
when they are used to denote common divisions of knowledge. 109

Examples 112

(1) I can arrange for a showing of fall styles on Tuesday, August 28. 126
(2) I landed in eastern France after I had crossed the Arctic Circle. 140
(3) The Rotary Club met in the Jeffrey Room of the Continental Hotel. 154
(4) You must write shorthand well, so please enroll for Shorthand II. 168

Other Examples 174

Words

January 10, 19-- Mr. Harry M. Bing, Man- 8
ager Continental Supply Company 3331 Sher- 16
wood Street Boise, ID 83706 Dear Mr. 24
Bing (¶ 1) We never upset the balance of 31
nature. When we cut the drawer facing for 39
an IDEAL desk pedestal, we cut from the same 48
piece of walnut or teak. In that way, the 57
beauty of the grain pattern doesn't get lost. 66
(¶ 2) Most desk manufacturers run the grain 74
across. They get more drawers out of a piece 83
of wood, but they lose nature's design. (¶ 3) 91
At IDEAL, we pay so much attention to the 100
little things that the big ones take care of 109
themselves--like smoothly gliding drawers, 117
flawless finishes, and rattleproof construction. 127
(¶ 4) Why not see what we mean at your 134
IDEAL branch or dealer showroom? He is 142
listed in the Yellow Pages. Very truly yours 151
Sanford Thurber, Sales Manager 158/176

Problem 2: AMS Letter

123 words; open punctuation; AMS simplified letter
style; model on page 176; capitalize and punctuate

Words

january 10, 19-- mr d c vasquez vice-president 10
orient importers inc 3151½ livingston avenue 20
niagara falls ny 14303 the choice is yours 29
(¶ 1) There are two kinds of belt dictating 36
machines--magnetic and visible. We are the 45
only company that offers both. Since we 53
make both, we are perfectly content to let 62
you make your own choice. It is easy to 70
be objective when you have no axe to grind. 79
(¶ 2) You can choose our DICTATION-MASTER 86
Magnetic and get a reusable dictation belt that 96
lets you erase and correct your own mistakes. 105
Or you can choose our DICTATION-MASTER 113
Visible that lets you find your place instantly 123
and makes a permanent record of your dicta- 131
tion. (¶ 3) A telephone call will get a 138
DICTATION-MASTER representative right over 147
to help you make your choice. lawrence wood- 155
side sales manager 160/181

Words

TO: Henry O. McGraw, Personnel Director 7
FROM: H. B. Layne, Training Supervisor 14
DATE: July 30, 19-- SUBJECT: Placement of 19
Trainees (¶) On August 1, two trainees 26
(presently working in the Duplicating Depart- 35
ment) will have satisfactorily completed their 45
training with a sufficient amount of skill in 54
order to be eligible for jobs on our regular 63
staff as soon as suitable vacancies occur. 72
These trainees are Lynn Roget, a clerk-typist 81
who speaks French fluently, and Donna Far- 89
num, a stenographer. 94/103

Problem 4: File Copy of Telegram

Full sheet; 2" top margin;
60-space line; DS message

Words

TELEGRAM Telegram January 12, 19--, 11:30 8
a.m. Herman Brode, President National 16
Dynamics, Inc. 3119 Monroe Street Ports- 24
mouth, Virginia (¶) Inventories at capacity 32
or over. Confident we can furnish supplies as 41
needed for Gulf Bridge structure. Sufficient 50
cable for two bridges. Marvin Hunter, Man- 59
ager National Cable Corporation (*your initials* 66
as typist)

Problem 5: Postal Card

48-space line; block style; SS; address
card to Harry M. Bing (Problem 1)

Words

January 20, 19-- Dear Mr. Bing (¶) You are 8
very cordially invited to a demonstration of 17
IDEAL'S new "feed itself" Copier. You just set 26
the dial for the number of copies you want. 35
When all copies are made, the IDEAL shuts 44
itself off. It has many other new features. 53
You will want to see them. Sanford Thurber, 62
Sales Manager *Return address on card:* Ideal 65/83
Office Equipment Co. 4114 Rose Street, Boise,
ID 83703

130D Production Typing: Purchase Orders; Confirmation Card (25)

Problem 1: Purchase Order

Type in duplicate

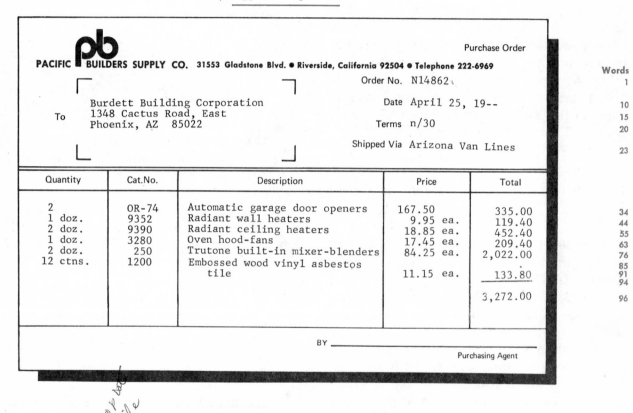

PACIFIC BUILDERS SUPPLY CO. 31553 Gladstone Blvd. ● Riverside, California 92504 ● Telephone 222-6969

Purchase Order

		Words
Order No. N14862		1
To Burdett Building Corporation 1348 Cactus Road, East Phoenix, AZ 85022	Date April 25, 19--	10
	Terms n/30	15
		20
	Shipped Via Arizona Van Lines	23

Quantity	Cat.No.	Description	Price	Total	Words
2	OR-74	Automatic garage door openers	167.50	335.00	34
1 doz.	9352	Radiant wall heaters	9.95 ea.	119.40	44
2 doz.	9390	Radiant ceiling heaters	18.85 ea.	452.40	55
1 doz.	3280	Oven hood-fans	17.45 ea.	209.40	63
2 doz.	250	Trutone built-in mixer-blenders	84.25 ea.	2,022.00	76
12 ctns.	1200	Embossed wood vinyl asbestos tile	11.15 ea.	133.80	85 91 94
				3,272.00	96

BY _____

Purchasing Agent

Problem 2: Confirmation Card

Type the confirmation message on a postal card; see p. 178 for placement directions

Words

April 28, 19-- Gentlemen (¶) Thank you for 8
your Order No. N14862 of April 25, 19--. 16
This order will be shipped immediately. If 25
you should need to write or call us about it, 34
please refer to our Invoice No. 45172. BUR- 43
DETT BUILDING CORPORATION *Address on* 48
card: Pacific Builders Supply Co. 31553 Glad- 56
stone Blvd. Riverside, CA 92504 62

Drill Copy: Full sheet; 70-space line; SS.
Paragraph Copy: Full sheet; 70-space line; DS; 5-space
¶ indention.

problems. Erase and correct errors.

LESSON 103

103A Preparatory Practice ⑤ *each line three or more times*

Alphabet	James Forrest's proxy quickly voted to recognize the required bylaws.
Figure-symbol	Felt & Blane's address is 7290 East 356th Street (Telephone 452–8134).
Quiet hands	Popular Queen Paula saw the purple azaleas on display at my dormitory.
Fluency	We should learn to spell, because we will have to do it all our lives.

| 1 | 2 | 3 | 4 | 5 | 6 | 7 | 8 | 9 | 10 | 11 | 12 | 13 | 14 |

103B Building Control ⑮ *two 1' control level writings on each ¶; then two 3' writings on all ¶s*

All letters are used.

		GWAM		
		1'	3'	

¶ 1
1.5 SI
5.6 AWL
80% HFW

The adage, "Give credit when credit is due," means that credit can | 13 | 4 | 72
be granted to deserving customers; if not merited, it must be denied. | 28 | 9 | 77
Another policy can mean financial loss. A man's character is crucial in | 42 | 14 | 81
credit matters, as is his power to pay. Can he pay? There is no sure | 57 | 19 | 86
answer, but business ability and honor must be weighed. | 68 | 23 | 90

¶ 2
1.5 SI
5.6 AWL
80% HFW

In addition to character and power to pay, the resources of the | 13 | 27 | 94
man must be examined. If he has adequate assets available, you can | 26 | 31 | 98
expect him to pay all his bills when they become due. If the capital | 40 | 36 | 103
in the owner's name comes primarily from earnings, he is usually a good | 55 | 41 | 108
charge risk. Earning reports must be analyzed with caution. | 67 | 45 | 112

¶ 3
1.5 SI
5.6 AWL
80% HFW

Finally, the general condition of the industry in which a man is | 13 | 49 | 116
engaged must be weighed. It is not enough to judge a man's credit | 26 | 54 | 121
potential by the three C's of credit: character, capacity, and capital. | 41 | 59 | 126
All factors must be looked at in the light of the economic conditions | 55 | 63 | 131
that prevail, for many elements are part of the total picture. | 68 | 67 | 135

| 1' GWAM | 1 | 2 | 3 | 4 | 5 | 6 | 7 | 8 | 9 | 10 | 11 | 12 | 13 | 14 |
| 3' GWAM | | 1 | | 2 | | 3 | | 4 | | 5 | |

Deliver to: Leonard B. Murphy **Location:** Department #47 **Job. No.:** 95

Quantity	Description	
6 rolls	Asphalt felt, 30 lb., No. 1311	22
12 gals.	Wood preservative	27
8 rolls	Rosin sized sheathing, 20 lb.	35
6	Ceiling exhaust fans, Model 8310	42
6	Wall exhaust fans, Model 8510	48
1 doz.	Outdoor lights, brass, Model M-153	57

LESSON 130

130A Preparatory Practice ⑤ *each line at least three times*

Alphabet

Six cold, quivering monkeys from the jungle had been put in warm zoos.

Figure-symbol

Bond #7365024 will not be called until 1978, and it pays $5\frac{1}{4}\%$ interest.

First row

Mr. Newman discovered zinc, bauxite, and miscellaneous minerals there.

Fluency

A good criticism is the kind that makes you feel you have been helped.

| 1 | 2 | 3 | 4 | 5 | 6 | 7 | 8 | 9 | 10 | 11 | 12 | 13 | 14 |

130B Paragraph Guided Writings for Rate Control ⑩

1. Type 128D, page 221, for three 1' writings at 40 words a minute.

2. Type three 1' writings at 60 words a minute. Try to hit your goal on the exact letter as time is called. The quarter or half minutes may be called to guide you.

130C Communication Aid: Quotation Marks ⑩ *as directed in 122C, page 212; type a heading*

Full sheet; 1½″ top margin; 70-space line; SS with DS between items

Words

3

Rules

5

(1) Place question marks or exclamation points inside quotation marks when they are part of the quotation; place them outside when they refer to the entire sentence, of which the quotation is but a part. — 19 33 47

(2) Use quotation marks to enclose the titles of magazine articles, reports, and lectures. — 60 65

(3) Use quotation marks to enclose subdivisions of published work. — 78

(4) Underline or type in all capitals titles of books, booklets, newspapers, magazines, and theses. — 92 99

(Continued on page 225)

1   Use two hyphens to type the dash--without space before and after them.

2   Either you or I can go. Neither of us has a session during that hour.

3   "We shall go tomorrow," said John. "We will go right now!" I shouted.

4   As I rode farther up the trail, I tried to analyze my problem further.

5   I am anxious about the last test, but I am eager to take the next one.
     | 1 | 2 | 3 | 4 | 5 | 6 | 7 | 8 | 9 | 10 | 11 | 12 | 13 | 14 |

103D   Skill-Comparison and Transfer Typing ⑮ *two 1' writings on each sentence*

Try reaching the rates set on the goal sentence in typing succeeding sentences. Type additional writings on the sentence on which you need to make the most improvement.

Words

1   Goal sentence   Just initial and return the enclosed order form to us today.   12

2   Weak fingers   I was puzzled by his apparent lack of aptitude for this job.   12

3   Direct reaches   Trudy hummed a hymn on the great stage and had fun doing so.   12

4   Rough draft   Please write if you have any questions about the operations.   12

5   Script   *We appreciate the confidence you have placed in our company.*   12

LESSON 104

104A   Preparatory Practice ⑤ *each line three or more times*

Alphabet   In a truly amazing way, John's books quickly verified his tax reports.

Figure-symbol   The tags marked * say: "Sell @ $17.89 each or @ $5,326.40 a carload."

Drill on **a, u**   Thousands of us order sauerkraut to inaugurate an auspicious New Year.

Fluency   Finish the job; in most cases it is the final half that really counts.
     | 1 | 2 | 3 | 4 | 5 | 6 | 7 | 8 | 9 | 10 | 11 | 12 | 13 | 14 |

104B   Skill-Comparison and Transfer Typing ⑮ *two 1' writings on each sentence in 103D, above; compare gwam*

104C   Production Typing: Outline ㉚

2 full sheets; 6" writing line; 2" top margin

1. Type the outline on page 185. As a reminder to leave about a 1" bottom margin on the first page, make a light pencil mark about 1½" from the bottom edge. (Erase the mark later.) Center the page number on the first page ½" from the bottom of the page.

2. On the second page, type the page number, 2, in the upper right corner even with the right margin ½" from the top of the page. Begin typing the copy for the second page on Line 7.

Two spaces follow the period after lettered or numbered divisions in an outline.

be omitted in columnar tabulations of figures 119
where the ruling separates the dollars from 128
the cents. It is customary to use abbrevia- 136
tions such as gal., ft., ea., %, # for No., and 148
other similar special abbreviations. Names of 157
months may be abbreviated when limited 165
space on the form makes this desirable. (¶ 4) 173
Single-space invoices, statements, and similar 183
forms (such as credit memorandums, purchase 192
requisitions, purchase orders, etc.) unless you 201
have three or fewer lines, in which case use 210
double spacing. (¶ 5) When more than one 217

line is required for the description on a form, 227
type the description on successive lines (single- 237
space and indent the second line 3 spaces). 246
(¶ 6) There is no hard-and-fast rule on spac- 253
ing data in columns. Generally, the longest 262
line in each column, except the one in which 271
the items are listed or described, is centered 281
by eye measurement under the column head- 289
ing. Centering by exact methods is not re- 297
quired or recommended. Begin the description 306
items about 2 spaces to the right of the ruled 316
line. 317

Problem 2: Purchase Requisition

Type in duplicate

Words

PURCHASE REQUISITION

pb

PACIFIC BUILDERS SUPPLY CO. 31553 Gladstone Blvd. ● Riverside, California 92504 ● Telephone 222-6969

leave 1 space

Deliver To Lee Bolden   Requisition No. 1012   3

Location Department #42   Date April 20, 19--   9

Job No. 72   Date Required May 10, 19--   12

Quantity	Description	
2	Automatic garage door openers, Model OR-74	21
1 doz.	Radiant wall heaters, Model 9352	38
2 doz.	Radiant ceiling heaters, Model 9390	45
1 doz.	Oven hood-fans, Model 3280	55
2 doz.	Trutone built-in mixer-blenders, Model 205	29
12 ctns.	Embossed wood vinyl asbestos tile, Model 1200	66

↑
Approximate center

↑
Tab 2 spaces from rule

Purchasing Agent

A. Unbound Manuscripts and Reports   16

1st tab stop ⟶   1. Top: first page, $1\frac{1}{2}$ or 2 inches; other pages, 1 inch   28

       2. Sides and bottom: 1 inch   34

B. Manuscripts and Reports Bound at the Left   43

       1. Top: first page, $1\frac{1}{2}$ or 2 inches; other pages, 1 inch   55

       2. Sides: $1\frac{1}{2}$ inches at the left; 1 inch at the right   66

       3. Bottom: 1 inch   70

C. Manuscripts and Reports Bound at the Top   79

       1. Top: first page, 2 or $2\frac{1}{2}$ inches; other pages, $1\frac{1}{2}$ inches   92

       2. Sides and bottom: 1 inch   98

⟶ Backspace   DS

II. SPACING   101

A. Body   103

       1. Double-spaced with 5-, 7-, or 10-space paragraph indentions   116

       2. Quoted material of 4 or more lines single-spaced and indented 5 spaces   131

2nd tab stop ⟶   from both margins; quotation marks permissible but not required   145

       3. Tabulated material: single-spaced   153

B. Footnotes   155

       1. Numbered consecutively throughout report, or in books numbering   169

         started anew with each chapter   176

       2. Identified by superior figures typed $\frac{1}{2}$ space above the line of writing   191

       3. Separated from the last line of manuscript by a divider line, approxi-   206

         mately $1\frac{1}{2}$ inches in length; divider line preceded by a single vertical   221

         space and followed by a double space   229

       4. Indented and single-spaced with a double space between footnotes   243

Determine ⟶ **III. HEADINGS AND SUBHEADINGS**   250
when to
begin the
next page

A. Main Heading   254

       1. Centered in all capital letters over the writing line   265

       2. Followed by a triple space   272

B. First-Order Subheadings (Side Headings)   281

       1. Typed at left margin on separate line and underlined   292

       2. Main words started with capital letters   301

       3. Preceded by triple space and followed by double space   313

C. Second-Order Subheadings (Paragraph Headings)   323

       1. Indented as first line of paragraph and underlined   334

       2. Usually, only first word capitalized   342

       3. Preceded by a double space   349

IV. PAGINATION (PAGE NUMBERING)   356

A. Unbound and Leftbound Manuscripts and Reports   366

       1. First page: centered $\frac{1}{2}$ inch from bottom of page   377

       2. Other pages: on the fourth line even with right margin   389

B. Topbound Manuscripts and Reports   397

       1. All pages: centered $\frac{1}{2}$ inch from bottom edge of paper   409

       2. Page number separated from text or footnote by at least a triple space   424

         (A partially filled page will require more than a triple space.)   437

Figure-symbol	The item was numbered 749/830/12 **. The simplified number is 749–56 *.
One hand	The greatest act we ever saw was the Savage Lion of Sweetwater, Texas.
Fluency	Any man has difficulty guiding another further than he himself can go.

| 1 | 2 | 3 | 4 | 5 | 6 | 7 | 8 | 9 | 10 | 11 | 12 | 13 | 14 |

129B Paragraph Guided Writings for Control ⑩

1. Type 128D, page 221, for 1' to establish your base rate.
2. Set a goal 8 to 10 words lower than your base rate.
3. On five 1' writings, type no faster than your goal. Try for errorless copies. The quarter or half minutes may be called to guide you.

129C Communication Aid: Quotation Marks ⑩ *as directed in 122C, page 212; type a heading*

Full sheet; 1½" top margin; SS with DS between items; 70-space line

Words

3

Rules

5

(1) Use quotation marks to enclose a direct quotation. — 16
(2) When a quotation is broken by such expressions as <u>he said</u>, enclose both parts of the quotation with quotation marks. — 32 / 42
(3) Place periods or commas inside the ending quotation mark. — 55
(4) Place semicolons or colons outside the quotation mark. — 66

Examples

70

(1) This man wrote, "Happiness is not the end of life; character is." — 84
(2) "Great minds," Irving wrote, "have purposes; others have wishes." — 98
(3) "What we need," Harry said, "is dirtier hands and cleaner minds." — 112
(4) She said, "I listen for facts"; I know she concentrates on ideas. — 126

Other Examples

132

129D Production Typing: Interoffice Memorandum; Purchase Requisition ㉕

Problem 1: Interoffice Memorandum

Full sheet; 1" side margins; SS

Words

TO: My Vacation Replacement **FROM:** The (5) Secretary to the Purchasing Agent **DATE:** (12) (*Current*) **FILE:** AOO **SUBJECT:** Business (18) Forms (¶ 1) As I shall not have an opportu-(25) nity to meet and talk with you before you (34) begin working in Mr. Frank's office during (42) my vacation, I think it will be helpful if I (51) explain briefly how business forms are to be (60) typed. (¶ 2) Make full use of the tabulator (68) mechanism to insure proper alignment of fig-(77) ures in the columns and to speed up your (85) work. Space forward for short amounts; back-(93) space for long amounts. (¶ 3) Periods may (101) be omitted after abbreviations, and they may (110)

After a week's pro..,

Models #823–7 and #495–1 are available at discounts of from 6% to 10%.

Polly Young and Jon Cassavetes were dressed for the "Lollipop Minuet."

Just one ounce of appreciation is often worth many pounds of pressure.

| 1 | 2 | 3 | 4 | 5 | 6 | 7 | 8 | 9 | 10 | 11 | 12 | 13 | 14 |

105B   Sentence Guided Writings ⑩

Type two or more 1' writings on each sentence with the guide called each 15, 12, or 10 seconds. Try completing a sentence and returning your carriage as the guide is called.

GWAM

	15"	12"	10"
1 If they agree to this proposal, we can send them a corrected contract.	56	70	84
2 Anyone who works in this company must be skillful as well as pleasant.	56	70	84
3 To erase an error near the end of a page, roll the paper down, not up.	56	70	84
4 The talent of success is nothing more than doing what you can do well.	56	70	84

| 1 | 2 | 3 | 4 | 5 | 6 | 7 | 8 | 9 | 10 | 11 | 12 | 13 | 14 |

105C   Production Typing: Topbound Manuscript with Footnotes ㉟

1. Before you type the manuscript on pages 187-188, read the material carefully so that you will understand its content.

2. Type the manuscript in topbound form (see page 185) with a 2" top margin for the first page and a 1½" top margin for succeeding pages. Use a 5-space paragraph indention. Number the pages.

3. Type each footnote on the page on which the reference appears even though all footnotes are given at the end of the report in the problem. Be sure to leave enough space at the bottom of a page for the 1-inch margin and footnotes. Number the footnotes from 1 up throughout the manuscript.

4. The illustration at the right shows the second page of the manuscript (typed in pica type).

   Note. You will not complete this problem in this lesson; additional time is given in Lessons 106 and 107.

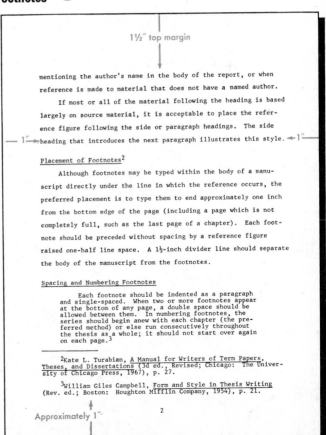

Drill Copy: Full sheet; 70-space line; SS.
Paragraph Copy: Full sheet; 70-space line; DS; 5-space ¶ indention.
Production Copy: Follow carefully the directions given with each problem; erase and correct errors.

Special Materials: Use printed forms if they are available, or half sheets of paper with the typewritten material arranged as it would be on printed forms. *Do not type headings that would be printed on the forms.*

LESSON 128

128A Preparatory Practice ⑤ *each line at least three times*

Alphabet   Would John Knox have kept Mary, Queen of Scots, from Elizabeth's grip?

Figure-symbol   How can B/O & H, Inc., meet accounts of $217,463 and $58,900 by May 1?

Long words   If an additional air-conditioning duct is needed, it can be installed.

Fluency   Hard luck is composed of equal portions of laziness and poor judgment.

| 1 | 2 | 3 | 4 | 5 | 6 | 7 | 8 | 9 | 10 | 11 | 12 | 13 | 14 |

128B Skill-Comparison Typing ⑩ *type each line of 128A for two 1' writings; compare gwam*

128C Technique Improvement: Stroking ⑩ *type each line of 121B, page 210, as directed*

128D Paragraph Guided Writings for Speed ⑩

1. Type for 1' to establish your base rate.
2. Set a goal 8 to 10 words higher than your base rate.

3. Type five 1' writings. Try to reach your new goal in each minute. Quarter or half minutes may be called to guide you.

1.5 SI
5.6 AWL
80% HFW

Another grand old product is being threatened with obsolescence. This time it is thread. Because of higher labor costs, many of the makers of garments are increasing their use of "fusing" or other adhesive techniques. A leader in the field reports that within a very few years, almost all the garments made will be partially or wholly fused. In a short time, thus, when anyone says he feels as if he is coming unglued, he may really mean it.

| 1 | 2 | 3 | 4 | 5 | 6 | 7 | 8 | 9 | 10 | 11 | 12 | 13 | 14 |

128E Building Control ⑮

Use the ¶s of 127B, page 219. Type two 1' *control-level* writings on each ¶; then a 5' writing on all three ¶s combined.

(1) The guides for handling footnotes and footnote references in this report are based on a careful study of standard reference works, such as those by the University of Chicago Press, Turabian, Campbell, Harbrace, and Perrin. While these authorities do not agree with one another on all points of style, the guides recommended in this report are based on majority practice.

TS

Placement of Footnote Reference Figures

DS

(¶ 2) Footnote reference figures (superscripts) should be placed in a manuscript so that the least interruption in thought results. Four placements of footnote reference figures are in common use. They are described below. (¶ 3) The preferred practice is to place the reference figure at the end of material that is directly or indirectly quoted or paraphrased.[1] An almost equally acceptable practice is to place the reference figure at the end of the statement that introduces directly quoted material. (4) A less acceptable practice, but one enjoying considerable use, is to place the reference figure after the name of the author of the reference. A major disadvantage of this practice is the inconsistency that results if references are made to materials without mentioning the author's name in the body of the report, or when reference is made to material that does not have a named author. (5) If most or all of the material following the heading is based largely on source material, it is acceptable to place the reference figure following the side or paragraph headings. The side heading that introduces the next paragraph illustrates this style.

the line in which the ....
preferred placement is to type them to end approximately one inch from the bottom edge of the page (including a page which is not completely full, such as the last page of a chapter). Each footnote should be preceded without spacing by a reference figure raised one-half line space. A 1½-inch divider line should separate the body of the manuscript from the footnotes.

Spacing and Numbering Footnotes

DS; SS the ¶

(¶ 7) Each footnote should be indented as a paragraph and single-spaced. When two or more footnotes appear at the bottom of any page, a double space should be allowed between them. In numbering footnotes, the series should begin anew with each chapter (the preferred method) or else run consecutively throughout the thesis as a whole; it should not start over again on each page.[3]

(¶ 8) Two or more short footnotes may be typed on one line if they are separated by at least two blank spaces. In no instance, however, may a footnote so begun be continued on a second line. (¶ 9) Lengthy footnotes containing explanatory material may be continued to the foot of the next page, above any footnotes for that page. They should be broken in the middle of a sentence to make it obvious that the footnote is incomplete.

Form of Footnotes

(¶ 10) The footnotes that follow represent the consensus of authorities for basic style and defensible compromise of differences on points on which some authorities disagree. (¶ 11) There is a generally accepted, brief form of footnote that can be used when a complete

mr marvin s hardwick 310 national avenue montgomery al 36105 dear marvin (¶ 1) The following list shows the shipments of Chemtox made to Kingway & Company last year. All invoices were paid by them within the 30-day discount period.

Order No.	Date	Amount
LA-517032-M	April 7	$3,605.22
LA-517099-M	April 9	814.79
LA-517322-M	June 6	40.00
LA-517846-M	August 1	175.23
Total		$4,635.24

(¶ 2) I suggest you call on Mr. Chambers, the Kingway & Company purchasing officer. Find out, if you can, why we have not had an order from them since last August. sincerely harold brookings sales manager

Problem 2: Interoffice Memorandum

Full sheet: SS: current date

TO: Clark Yardley FROM: Norbert L. Peoples DATE: *Current* SUBJECT: Commissions Earned by Salesmen (¶ 1) As you know, the Company pays a 5 percent commission on all sales exceeding the quota set for each salesman. Commissions earned during the last month are as follows:

Salesmen	Commissions
Brooks, Harvey	$250
Casady, F. A.	425
Diamond, George	130
Flowers, Hunter	325
Moody, Charles A.	250
Willis, Bernard	325

(¶ 2) The commissions are paid on net sales. The amounts included do not include amounts added for sales taxes, and discounts are deducted.

(¶ 1) The Borough of Alden has the most highly developed business district in its trading area. The following tabulation shows the type and number of services it offers:

TYPE AND NUMBER OF SERVICES IN ALDEN AREA	
Food stores	11
Eating places	14
General merchandise	2
Apparel	12
Furniture, appliances	8
Gasoline stations	12
Lumber, building, hardware stores	6
Drugstores	4
Other retail stores	12
Personal services	23
Auto repair shops	8
Merchant wholesalers	6
Other wholesalers	1
Photography studios	2
Paint stores	3

(¶ 2) Included in the above establishments are several large wholesale, retail, and service chains that have located in and around Alden. A new One-Trip Market is located in a plaza that has recently been built about two miles east of town.

(¶ 3) There are other businesses in the Alden area which, although they employ fewer people, are important because of their diversity. There are (1) the Federal Bakery, (2) Davidson Wood Products, (3) the Alden Gazette, (4) the Alden Concrete Company, (5) Selectron Metal Products Company, (6) Mills Technical Institute, (7) Leads Manufacturing Company, and (8) Preston Builders, Inc. These companies are now working at 75 percent of capacity.

in Footnote 4 below.⁴ (¶ 12) The complete footnote for a book reference is given in Footnote 1. Observe the footnote style used when reference is made to a work for which no author is given.⁵ (¶ 13) When reference must be made to an article appearing in a magazine, the form illustrated in Footnote 6 is recommended.⁶ When no author is given for a magazine article and when the volume and issue number are not known or given, the form illustrated in Footnote 7 is preferred.⁷ (¶ 14) Governmental agencies acting as authors are listed with the largest body first, followed by its division and subdivision in order. For printed works available from the U.S. Government Printing Office, the facts of publication are as shown.⁸ (¶ 15) For references to lectures and speeches, the pertinent available facts are placed in parentheses after the name of the speaker and the title of the lecture or speech.⁹ Unpublished reports, minutes, letters, and the like, are credited informally by showing the available facts in logical order without parentheses.¹⁰ (¶ 16) When two footnotes contain references to the same work and one follows the other without intervening footnotes, use Ibid., the abbreviation for ibidem (in the same place), and the exact page number for the second footnote if it differs from the first one.¹¹ (¶ 17) When a footnote refers to a different page in a work already cited and one or two footnotes separate it from the first one, use the author's name and the notation op. cit., the abbreviation for opere citato (meaning in the work cited), with the page number, instead of repeating the name of the publication and other identifying data.¹² (¶ 18) If the footnote reference is to precisely the same matter covered by a reference not immediately preceding, use cited). Page numbers ... ... loc. cit. for the simple reason that they are unnecessary.¹³

SS and type divider line
DS to footnotes

¹ Peyton Hurt, Bibliography and Footnotes (Rev. ed.; Berkeley: University of California Press, 1963), p. 61. (*30 words*)

² Kate L. Turabian, A Manual for Writers of Term Papers, Theses, and Dissertations (3d ed., Revised; Chicago: The University of Chicago Press, 1967), p. 27. (*46 words*)

³ William Giles Campbell, Form and Style in Thesis Writing (Rev. ed.; Boston: Houghton Mifflin Company, 1954), p. 21. (*26 words*)

⁴ Bruce Bliven, Jr., The Wonderful Writing Machine, p. 25. (*21 words*)

⁵ Life Insurance Fact Book (New York: Institute of Life Insurance, 1957), p. 30. (*21 words*)

⁶ George A. W. Boehm, "How They Predict the Economic Future," Think, Vol. XXXIII, No. 4 (July-August, 1967), p. 8. (*24 words*)

⁷ "Office Services in an Age of Sophistication," Administrative Management (November, 1967), pp. 20-26. (*25 words*)

⁸ U.S. Bureau of the Census, Statistical Abstract of the United States: 1966 (87th ed.; Washington: U.S. Government Printing Office, 1966), p. 66. (*38 words*)

⁹ Lainie Koslyn, "Profile of a Secretary" (From a lecture to the National Secretaries Association, Honolulu, March 18, 1968). (*29 words*)

¹⁰ From a letter written by Margaret MacMillan to Judy Bennett, April 5, 1967. (*15 words*)

¹¹ Ibid., p. 2. (*4 words*)

¹² Bruce Bliven, op. cit., p. 52. (*8 words*)

¹³ William Giles Campbell, loc . cit. (*9 words*)

Alphabet	Six big jet planes flew over the Azores and quickly landed in Morocco.
Figures	She traveled about 726,894 miles, logging 1,530¼ hours of flying time.
Drill on vowels	Every trainee receives a special certificate at graduation ceremonies.
Fluency	Discuss business in the office; outside it, talk about something else.

| 1 | 2 | 3 | 4 | 5 | 6 | 7 | 8 | 9 | 10 | 11 | 12 | 13 | 14 |

127B Growth Index ⑮ *type one 5' control level writing on each ¶*

All letters are included.

	GWAM		
	1'	5'	

¶ 1
1.5 SI
5.6 AWL
80% HFW

Literally, dozens of studies have been made of the reasons that office workers fail in their jobs. With but very few exceptions, the reports we have show that failure is due to a lack of personal qualities needed for a job. Weak office skills are an infrequent cause of dismissal. The case is very clear. Loyalty, good work habits, and the ability to work well with others are essential for success in an office job.

13	3	58
27	5	61
41	8	64
55	11	66
69	14	69
83	16	72
84	17	73

¶ 2
1.5 SI
5.6 AWL
80% HFW

Efficiency in the basic office skills is fundamental. Let there be no doubt on this point. A person, for example, who is unable to type, spell, proofread, or solve simple arithmetic problems would likely not get a typing job in the first place. The idea that is being presented here, however, is that the ability to type is not enough. A typist is expected to bring to the job a number of impeccable personal qualities that permit him to use his skill in typing to best advantage.

13	19	75
27	22	78
40	25	80
54	28	83
68	31	86
83	33	89
97	36	92

¶ 3
1.5 SI
5.6 AWL
80% HFW

Courtesy is a superb example of a quality that is essential in office work. It determines just how well we can get along with the people with whom we work. Reflect on your own experiences for a moment. Is it not true that the people to whom you have been sincerely courteous have been courteous to you? Is it not true, too, that your success is measured by what others think of you? Courtesy has many satisfying rewards. Everyone agrees that it is indispensable in office work.

13	39	94
26	41	97
39	44	100
54	47	103
69	50	106
83	53	108
97	56	111

1' GWAM | 1 | 2 | 3 | 4 | 5 | 6 | 7 | 8 | 9 | 10 | 11 | 12 | 13 | 14 |
5' GWAM | 1 | 2 | 3 |

127C Production Measurement ㉚ *errors corrected; figure n-pram*

Type as many of the problems as you can in 20 minutes. Correct all errors. Do not make carbon copies.

Alphabet	Equip the tug Zyma B for work and expect her to be judged serviceable.
Figure-symbol	In 1925, A & E Company's net sales were $283,490; in 1968, $6,708,351.
One hand	The sea breezes were piling up the waves into great rolling mountains.
Fluency	We can always do more good by being good than we can in any other way.

`| 1 | 2 | 3 | 4 | 5 | 6 | 7 | 8 | 9 | 10 | 11 | 12 | 13 | 14 |`

106B   Building Control ⑮ (*12′ timing*)

Working for 12 minutes, type as many errorless copies of ¶ 1, page 183, as you can. Type from the textbook. Score 1 point for each errorless copy of the paragraph. A score of 2 is *acceptable*; 3, *good*; 4, *very good*; 5 or above, *excellent*.

106C   Production Typing: Topbound Manuscript with Footnotes ㉚ *continue typing 105C, pages 186-188*

LESSON 107

107A   Preparatory Practice ⑤ *each line three or more times*

Alphabet	Subsequently, Jack wouldn't have a copy of my magazine, The Executive.
Figure-symbol	King & Wynn collected $6,582, plus $4\frac{1}{2}\%$ interest, less $137.90 in fees.
Long words	Vehicular traffic commenced utilizing the enormous structure Thursday.
Fluency	The trouble with a temper is that it can be lost when we need it most.

`| 1 | 2 | 3 | 4 | 5 | 6 | 7 | 8 | 9 | 10 | 11 | 12 | 13 | 14 |`

107B   Building Control ⑮ (*12′ timing*)

Working for 12 minutes, type as many errorless copies of ¶ 2, page 183, as you can. Type from the textbook. Score 1 point for each errorless copy of the paragraph. A score of 2 is *acceptable*; 3, *good*; 4, *very good*; 5 or above, *excellent*.

107C   Production Typing: Topbound Manuscript with Footnotes ㉚ *continue typing 105C, pages 186-188*

LESSON 108

108A   Preparatory Practice ⑤ *each line three or more times*

Alphabet	Excessive assignments will often quickly jeopardize both joy and zeal.
Figure-symbol	The * before the A & Z firm name denotes 1968 sales exceeded $234,750.
Inside keys	Janet has just finished tying over fifty bright ribbons on your gifts.
Fluency	It should be reward enough just to know you have done the right thing.

`| 1 | 2 | 3 | 4 | 5 | 6 | 7 | 8 | 9 | 10 | 11 | 12 | 13 | 14 |`

Alphabet
Figure-symbol
Adjacent keys
Fluency

Don forgot to cover Kay's jonquil; he expected below-zero temperature.
About 17 2/3 percent of the 16,450 men have read George Orwell's <u>1984</u>.
Fred tried to decide just how much of the old junk might be destroyed.
Do not use a long word when there is a short one you know you can use.

| 1 | 2 | 3 | 4 | 5 | 6 | 7 | 8 | 9 | 10 | 11 | 12 | 13 | 14 |

126B Communication Aid: Numbers ⑩ *as directed in 122C, page 212*

Full sheet; 1½" top margin; SS with DS between items; 70-space line

	Words
NUMBERS	2

Rules | 4

(1) Numbers preceded by nouns are usually expressed in figures. | 17
(2) Express measures, weights, and dimensions in figures. | 28
(3) In business letters, the percent sign (%) is preferred when it is | 42
preceded by definite figures. With approximations and in most | 55
formal writings, <u>percent</u> is preferred. | 63
(4) Spell names of small-numbered avenues and streets (ten and under). | 77
Type house numbers in figures, except for house number <u>One</u>. | 90

Examples | 93

(1) We found the exact quotation in Volume VIII, Section 4, page 191. | 107
(2) The box Ralph sent measured 7 ft. 6 in. and weighed 45 lbs. 3 oz. | 121
(3) About 85 percent of all loans will bring a return of 6% interest. | 135
(4) They have moved from One 125th Street to 1830 North First Street. | 149

Other Examples | 155

126C Tabulation Skill Builder ⑤

Type two 2' writings on the following short table. Allow 10 spaces between the columns. You need not center the table vertically. Type the two writings on one page. Compute *gwam* by dividing words by 2.

		Words
LIFETIME ANNUAL MEAN INCOME--1963		7
Males 25-64 Years Old		11
Elementary school dropout	$ 3,641	18
Elementary school graduate	4,921	25
High school dropout	5,592	30
High school graduate	6,693	36
College dropout	7,839	40
College graduate	10,062	45

126D Production Skill Building ㉚ *errors corrected; figure n-pram*

Make pencil notations of the problems at the right to be typed for a 20' writing. Figure your *n-pram*.

Page 214, 123D, Problem 1
Page 216, 124D, Problem 1
Page 217, 125C, Production Typing

copies of ¶ 3, 103B, page 183, as you can. Type the textbook. Score 1 point for each errorless copy of

108C   Production Typing: Bibliography and Title Page ㉚

Problem 1: Bibliography

Topbound manuscript form; same margins as on p. 1; SS with DS between entries

Type the bibliography below to accompany the manuscript typed as 105C, pages 186-188. Start the first line of each entry at the left margin; set a tab stop to indent the second and succeeding lines 5 spaces. Remember to type the appropriate manuscript page number.

		Words
	BIBLIOGRAPHY	3
	TS	
One-author book	Bliven, Bruce, Jr. The Wonderful Writing Machine. New York: Random House, 1954.	23 / 25
Magazine article	Boehm, George A. W. "How They Predict the Economic Future," Think. Vol. XXXIII, No. 4 (July-August, 1967), pp. 8-11.	40 / 50
One-author book	Campbell, William Giles. Form and Style in Thesis Writing, Rev. ed. Boston: Houghton Mifflin Company, 1954.	71 / 79
Two-author book	Erlich, Eugene, and Daniel Murphy. Writing and Researching Term Papers and Reports. New York: Bantam Books, 1964.	97 / 108
One-author book	Hurt, Peyton. Bibliography and Footnotes, Rev. ed. Berkeley: University of California Press, 1963.	127 / 133
Lecture notes	Koslyn, Lainie. "Profile of a Secretary." From a lecture to the National Secretaries Association, Honolulu, March 18, 1968.	148 / 158
No author listed	Life Insurance Fact Book. New York: Institute of Life Insurance, 1957.	177 / 178
Letter reference	MacMillan, Margaret. Letter written to Judy Bennett, April 5, 1967.	192
Ignore a, an, or the in alphabetizing	A Manual of Style, 12th ed. Chicago: The University of Chicago Press, 1969.	210 / 211
Magazine article	"Office Services in an Age of Sophistication," Administrative Management. (November, 1967), pp. 20-26.	229 / 237
Author and editors cited	Perrin, Porter G. Writer's Guide and Index to English, 4th ed., prepared and edited by Karl W. Dykema and Wilma R. Ebbitt. Chicago: Scott, Foresman and Company, 1965.	259 / 273 / 278
Government publication	Style Manual. Washington: U.S. Government Printing Office, 1967.	294
One-author book	Turabian, Kate L. A Manual for Writers of Term Papers, Theses, and Dissertations, 3d ed., rev. Chicago: The University of Chicago Press, 1967.	319 / 335 / 336
Government publication	U.S. Bureau of the Census. Statistical Abstract of the United States: 1966, 87th ed. Washington: U.S. Government Printing Office, 1966.	358 / 373

is page 4 (or pages 4 and 5) of the manuscript. Type the page number in the proper position. Double-space . . . . single space the table copy. Decide on number of spaces between columns.

Note. The center point of the paper will be about 3 spaces to the right of the point normally used.

	Words
A typical NSA (National Secretaries Association) member must be	13
proficient in a great many areas. Of the 15 duties listed in the 1966	27
study in which 291 members responded, a majority of NSA members do	40
8 duties daily. On only 1 of the 15 duties did a majority of the members indicate they never perform the task. This task is maintaining	54
	68
the employer's personal financial records.	77
The following table lists in rank order the percentage of NSA members	91
who daily do each of the tasks. Also shown is the percentage of members who never do them. For example, 93 percent of the secretaries in this	104
	120
study place and receive telephone calls on a daily basis. One percent never	135
use it. The duty ranks first in the list of duties performed daily by NSA	150
members.	152

FREQUENCIES OF SECRETARIAL DUTIES   TS — 159

DS

Figures Represent Percent of NSA Members Responding — 169

TS

Duty	Daily	Never	
			176
		DS	
Place and receive telephone calls	93	1	184
Read, sort, and route mail	85	3	190
Organize and maintain files	81	–	197
Compose letters, instructions, notes	78	–	205
Make appointments	74	2	210
Receive customers and meet public	71	2	217
Take and transcribe dictation	60	2	224
Duplicate materials	52	8	229
Perform accounting duties	38	16	236
Make travel arrangements	29	8	242
Supervise other workers	29	29	248
Organize and type reports, speeches, publications	25	10	260
Transcribe from voice recording machines	19	38	269
Maintain employer's personal financial records	11	56	280
Take minutes of meetings	4	36	286

TS

	Words
The foregoing data, which are fully reported in the December, 1966,	300
issue of THE SECRETARY, permitted the investigator to determine within	314
the 95 percent confidence limits that the findings would be no more than	329
5.64 percent in error.	333

1. Center and sp...
   as directed.

2. When you have finished typing the title page, arrange all your papers in this order:

   Title page (this problem)
   Manuscript pages (105C, pages 187 and 188)
   Bibliography page (Problem 1, page 190)

3. Fasten all the sheets together at the top.

2½″

2½″

Name of Student

Name of School

Current Date

LESSON 109

109A Preparatory Practice ⑤ *each line three or more times*

Alphabet   I know that an extreme Quebec blizzard may be jeopardizing four lives.

Figure-symbol   Corley & Wellman sent us Check #723 (dated November 19) for $4,867.50.

Long words   The audio-visual environment offers unique opportunities for research.

Fluency   The more they leave to chance the less chance they have of getting it.

| 1 | 2 | 3 | 4 | 5 | 6 | 7 | 8 | 9 | 10 | 11 | 12 | 13 | 14 |

109B Sentence Guided Writings ⑩ *type 105B, page 186, as directed there*

109C Building Speed ⑮

1. Type two ½′ writings; reach for 30 or more words in that time.
2. Type two 1′ writings; reach for 60 or more words.
3. Type two 1½′ writings; reach for 90 or more words.

4. Type two 2′ writings; try to complete the paragraph.
5. If you complete the paragraph, begin it again. The goals are marked in the copy.

All letters are included.

	Words
Men who hold jobs with high salaries and who enjoy greater social	13
prestige appear to have a common attribute. They can express a thought,	28
an idea, or a concept in exact words. They know how to create vivid	42
effects with the words they use. They have an adequate vocabulary, and	56
they know how to use it to obtain the results they want. In addition,	71
they must have something more than a hazy notion of their subject. The	85
blunt truth is that recognition and prosperity seem to come more easily	99
to the men who have sufficient word power to express their ideas in	113
clear, accurate, and convincing ways.	120

1.5 SI
5.6 AWL
80% HFW

CS17 REVISED TEST SCHEDULE

Full sheet; 1" side margins; DS; indent ¶s;
SS quotation in ¶ 2; SS tabulated report

TS

Test	Day	Director	
Stress	Monday	Dr. Carlson	209
Thermal	Tuesday	Dr. Koontz	214
Flexibility	Wednesday	Mr. Kunselman	221
Tension	Thursday	Mr. Joseph	227
Corrosion	Friday	Mr. Recupero	233

197 — CS17 REVISED TEST SCHEDULE
203 — Director (DS)

Words

TO: Henry Wagner, Director of Research — 7
FROM: John D. Neff, Production Manager — 14
DATE: (*Current*) — 17
SUBJECT: Retesting Copper Alloy #17 — 22

(¶ 1) According to Dr. Maetinson's report, — 29
the failure of our tests on CS17 was due to — 38
a mistake in formula application. Dr. Maetin- — 47
son says that the correct formula for use in — 56
our basic procedure (Step 6) should have been — 65
the Benzloff formula: $M^2/M + 14_s = P_s$. — 74
The thermal exposure should have been 1900° — 82
F. instead of 1750° F. Dr. Maetinson — 90
explains: — 92

(¶ 2) An attempt to apply the Craig– — 98
Towne formula [the one we used] in tests — 107
such as this is understandable; but the differ- — 116
ence between the formulas [the Benzloff and — 125
the Craig–Towne], although small, was criti- — 133
cal in the CS17 tests. (¶ 3) The complete — 141
Maetinson report is in my office, and copies — 150
of it will be sent to you as soon as they can — 159
be made. (¶ 4) Will you please review all — 166
computations for CS17 promptly and have — 174
materials and staff ready for new tests at 9:30 — 184
on the following mornings next week. — 191

TS

Problem 2: Letter with Tabulated Report

Decide on letter and punctuation style; estimate length of letter.

Words

mr theodore m byers 331 fernwood avenue — 11
trenton nj 08610 dear mr byers reference — 21
escrow #768 (¶ 1) The Lexington Guarantee — 28
Building & Loan Association has deposited — 36
with us in escrow Deed of Reconveyance and — 45
Stanford Fire Insurance Policy No. 44380, — 53
subject to the payment of the following: — 62

Principal balance	$2,663.49	67
Interest	4.14	71
Trustee's fee on reconveyance	3.00	77
		81
Total	$2,670.63	85

(¶ 2) Additional interest is to be paid at the — 94
rate of 52 cents per diem from July 1, 19––, — 103
to date of receipt of a final settlement. yours — 112
very truly frank d hill real estate department — 123/135

LESSON 125

125A Preparatory Practice ⑤ *each line three or more times*

Alphabet

Jack now realizes that his brusque expletives often frightened my dog.

Figure-symbol

L/P, Inc., 7521½ Hone Road, grossed 2¼% more ($2,348.60) than in 1968.

Double letters

Miss Capp occasionally allows Babbette a banana for dessert at dinner.

Fluency

If a thing is right, stand up for it; if it is wrong, try changing it.

| 1 | 2 | 3 | 4 | 5 | 6 | 7 | 8 | 9 | 10 | 11 | 12 | 13 | 14 |

125B Building Speed ⑮ *type two 1' writings on each ¶ of 121D, page 211;*
compute gwam on the better writing of each pair

Type a 10' writing on 104C, pages 184 and 185.
Correct errors; figure *g-pram*.

~~Type a~~ errors; figure *g-pram*.

LESSON 110

110A   Preparatory Practice ⑤ *each line three or more times*

Alphabet   We were quickly exhausted, proving no match for zebra in wild jungles.

Figure-symbol   Our $1,906.47 payment saved us 37¼ cents (.3725) on each of 138 items.

Drill on a, e   Kathleen Allen has read "The Faerie Queen"; maybe she is rereading it.

Fluency   Our education starts before age 6; it should not end until we pass 96.
| 1 | 2 | 3 | 4 | 5 | 6 | 7 | 8 | 9 | 10 | 11 | 12 | 13 | 14 |

110B   Growth Index ⑮ *type two 5' control-level writings on ¶s of 102C, page 181; compute gwam on the better writing*

110C   Production Measurement: Rough Draft of a Leftbound Manuscript ㉚ *20' timing; figure n-pram; repeat if time permits*

Leftbound manuscript form; 2" top margin (see p. 185 for correct form)

Words

The Machine-Age Office) center   5

¶ What highly-sophisticated machines are being used in ~~in~~ this coun-   13

try's offices? What ~~questions~~ problems are ~~this~~ these machines presenting   29

and ~~who~~ how are these problems being solved? These are the ques-   41

tions with which this paper deals. The ~~findings~~ answers to these questions are based on a na-   58

tional survey of 500 administrative managers.[1]   68

Triple-space
Computers   71

[All those taking part in this study assert that computers will ~~surely~~   84

become an indispensable part of the office in the 1970's. Com-   97

puters are now in their ~~3d~~ third generation, and ~~the 4th~~ fourth generation ma-   110

chines are just merging. the ~~third~~ fourth generation computers will be   124

characterized by "firmware," a term denoting packaged programs.   137

138 words; mixed punctuation; decide on spaces between columns

		Words
mcarthur furniture store 23141 rock island		12
road ft. lauderdale fl 33311 Gentlemen (¶1)		20
In accordance with your order No. 990, we are		29
shipping to you today the following rugs:		38

12	9' x 12' Wiltons	42
7	9' x 12' Broadlooms	46
1	6' x 14' Axminster	51
10	8' x 14' Wiltons	55

(¶2) Each rug is separately wrapped; and, following your special instructions, the Broadloom rugs bear the following tag: — 62 / 71 / 78

		Words
Weight	86#	81
Size	9' x 12'	83
Fringe	4"	85
Type	Broadloom	88
Color	(Gray, blue, or coral)	94

(¶3) We hope these rugs will be entirely satisfactory. Our company has been weaving fine carpets for over 75 years, and to our knowledge we have not lost a customer because of unsatisfactory workmanship or poor service. (¶4) Accept our sincere thanks for this first order. We promise you the best of service in the years ahead. Very truly yours sanders rug company wendell e baines president — 101 / 110 / 119 / 126 / 135 / 143 / 152 / 162 / 169

172/187

LESSON 124

124A Preparatory Practice (5) *each line three or more times*

Alphabet Examine Herb's work; judge for quality; recognize needed improvements.

Figure-symbol Type: "Buy 2,850 pins @ 43½¢ each for the 1969 and 1970 conventions."

One hand We referred only a minimum number of monopoly cases to my legal staff.

Fluency Do not hesitate to say, "I don't know"; it can save many explanations.

| 1 | 2 | 3 | 4 | 5 | 6 | 7 | 8 | 9 | 10 | 11 | 12 | 13 | 14 |

124B Communication Aid: Symbols (10)

Full sheet; DS; 14 spaces between columns; center in reading position

OTHER MEANINGS FOR PRESENT CHARACTERS

		his
Caret (insert)	Diagonal	for/pictures
Times	x (lower case)	62 x 18
Minus	Hyphen	25 - 15
Signed	Diagonals, s	/s/ J. R. Stout
Pounds	Number sign	100# of coal
Feet	Apostrophe	9' x 12'
Minute	Apostrophe	5' writing
Inch or inches	Quotation mark	8½" x 11"
Second	Quotation mark	3" warning
Ditto	Quotation mark	John Bellen, Erie
		E. S. Brior, "

124C Technique Improvement: Stroking (5) *type a 1' writing on each of the first four lines of 121B, page 210*

time-sharing plans by which for a [...]

to use a computers 25 hours a month. Packaged programs covering for ac- 176

counting procedures for a variety of industries will be # available at relatively small 195

cost. Virtually everyone in the office will be expected to know how to use the a 207

computer. 209

Copying Duplication Machines 220

Machines using the electrostatic copying process will continue to dominate 235
the field. An offset duplication machine has been developed, 248
however, that can print on both sides of a sheet in one opera- 260
tion. In addition, a new mimeograph stencil has been developed 273
that can be inserted with the original copy into a copier. 285
No ¶ The copier cuts the stencil in a matter of seconds. Costs 297
of copying equipment, now quite high, will go down. Plans are 309
currently under way to market a "family copier" very shortly 321
for less than $30. The books and magazines of the future may 334
not be prepared on big presses, bound, and mailed the way they 346
are today. According to Kleinschrod: 354

¶ Page images may be stored on super-miniaturized 364
microfiche--some catalog publishers are doing this 374
already--to be mailed far less expensively in small 384
thin envelopes. You then ask the system for en- 394
larged hard copies of only those pages that inter- 404
est you.[2] 406

Triple-space

Problems Created by Machinery 418

The most pressing two problems reported by administrative managers 431
in connection with the advent of the Office Machine age are break- 444
downs and inadequately trained operators. people. Office machines equipment of 457
the 1970's will be more complex. Extensive training will be needed 470
to operate them, many and skilled technicians will be needed 482
to maintain them. keep them in repair. 487

_____

[1] Kleinschrod, Walter, "Office Services in an Age of Sophis-
tication," *Administrative Management* (November, 1967), pp. 20-26. *(34 words)*

[2] *Ibid.*, p. 24. *(7 words)*

Full sheet; DS; 8 spaces between columns; center in reading position

CONSTRUCTING SPECIAL SYMBOLS

triple-space

Plus	*8 spaces*	Diagonal; backspace; hyphen	+
Divided by		Hyphen; backspace; colon	÷
Left bracket		Diagonal; backspace; underline; roll cylinder back one line; underline	[
Right bracket		Underline; diagonal; backspace; roll cylinder back one line; underline	]
Exponent		Ratchet release, number	*8 spaces* 25^4
Degrees / Superior		Ratchet release, o (lower case) / Ratchet release, figure or letter	$75°$ / be seen.[1]
Inferior		Ratchet release, figure or letter	H_2O
Equals		Ratchet release, hyphens	=

123D Production Typing: Letters with Tabulated Reports (30)

Problem 1: Modified Block Letter

214 words; open punctuation; decide on spaces between columns

Words

March 12, 19-- Mr. George Stanton 104 — 8
Logan Crescent West | Yorkton Saskatche- — 15
wan | CANADA Dear Mr. Stanton (¶ 1) You — 22
will be glad to know that Bond–Handley's re- — 30
turn on net shipments for the year just past — 39
was about 11 percent. This figure compares — 48
very favorably with about 10 percent for the — 57
previous year. Included in net earnings of the — 66
year is a nonrecurring net gain of $821,200 — 75
from forward sales of pound sterling to pro- — 83
tect our interest in Bond–Lanham, Limited. — 92
(¶ 2) In November, the Board of Directors — 99
declared a 3-for-2 stock split and increased — 108
the regular quarterly dividend from an ad- — 116
justed 26 cents to 30 cents per share after the — 126
split. The financial highlights of the year are — 136
as follows: — 138

DS

		Words
Net shipments	$108,449,883.00	145
Net earnings	11,449,948.00	150
Earnings per share	2.01	157
Dividends per share	1.20	164
Book value per share	13.38	171
Working capital	58,290,766.00	177
Shareholders' investment	76,373,015.00	184

DS

(¶ 3) The Company continues to make a major — 192
commitment to its expanded product develop- — 200
ment program, which accounts for an increas- — 209
ingly large percentage of new business and — 218
backlog. The rate of incoming orders in the — 227
past several months indicates that improved — 235
shipments and earnings may be expected dur- — 244
ing the coming year. (¶ 4) On behalf of the — 252
directors, I extend thanks to all the share- — 260
holders for their support. Sincerely yours — 269
Benjamin V. Hornsberger Chairman and — 276
President — 279/293

Production Measurement

You will be directed to type representative problems from prior lessons. Follow the original directions for each problem. Since these problems are timed, get ready to type quickly. Use the current date if none is given; your reference initials; appropriate envelope; erase and correct errors. Unless otherwise directed, follow this procedure:

Drill Copy: Full sheet; 70-space line; SS.
Paragraph Copy: Full sheet, 70-space line; DS; 5-space ¶ indention.

Materials Needed

Letterheads (or full sheets); carbon sheets; file copy sheets; interoffice communication forms (if available); envelopes of appropriate size.

$$\text{N-PRAM} = \frac{\text{Gross (total) words} - \text{Penalties}}{\text{Length (in minutes) of writing}}$$

Penalties for Errors: Deduct 10 words for each error not erased on an original copy; deduct 5 words for each error not erased on a carbon copy.

LESSON 111

111A   Preparatory Practice ⑤ *each line three or more times*

Alphabet — We quickly proved the existence of the glazed lamp you just described.

Figure-symbol — Cox & Conan's office, 3450 Cord Street, opened May 12, 1967, at 8 a.m.

Drill on i, o — Ohio's position as a contributor to this nation's growth is improving.

Fluency — Each of us will steer his ship by the star he has chosen to guide him.

| 1 | 2 | 3 | 4 | 5 | 6 | 7 | 8 | 9 | 10 | 11 | 12 | 13 | 14 |

111B   Building Speed ⑮ *type 109C, page 191, as directed there*

111C   Production Measurement: Business Letters ㉚ *20' timing; errors corrected; figure n-pram*

Problem 1: Block Style Letter with Subject Line, Enclosure Notation, and Postscript

116 words; open punctuation; blocked subject line; carbon copy

Words
miss sue fremont lowell–grant agency 7751   12
highland drive salt lake city ut 84121   20
dear miss fremont subject susan longlade con-   29
cert (¶ 1) The contract you sent us for the   37
Susan Longlade concert was signed this morn-   45
ing. We are retaining one copy for our files;   55
the original is enclosed. (¶ 2) The Arts Board   63
has asked me to express to you its sincere   72

Words
gratitude for obtaining this engagement for   81
us. We are most pleased to add Mlle. Long-   89
lade's program to our list of winter perform-   98
ances, which now includes Alfred Stone, the   107
McKinley Dancers, Fern Madison, and Do-   115
menica Leschenko. (¶ 3) If there is anything   123
I can do to help with the local arrangements   132
for the Longlade concert, please let me know.   141
I shall be glad to help. Sincerely yours martin 151
v kenton chairman arts board enclosure: 160
signed contract (*Postscript*) Please send photo- 167
graphs and publicity on Susan Longlade for   175
use in our promotion of the concert.   183/199

	Words	
	Prob. 1	Prob. 3

March 20, 19—— Mr. Thomas B. Washington 2200 Franklin Road Newport News, VA 23601 Dear Mr. Washington

	Prob. 1	Prob. 3
	13	13
	21	21

(¶ 1) Of the 68 wells drilled last year in which we had full or part interest, 18 were exploratory. We found 4 oil and gas-distillate pools, 1 gas field, and 3 additional oil and gas zones under established producing fields. (¶ 2) The attached table shows you the number of acres in which we have an interest in various oil fields or regions.

	Prob. 1	Prob. 3
	35	35
	49	49
	63	63
	76	76
	88	88
		130

(¶ 3) In addition to our interest in the foregoing regions, we hold leases, options, or operating rights on 15,000 acres in Alaska. On the Kenai Peninsula, where Alaska's first major oil discovery was made, we hold 5,000 acres, some within six miles of the discovery well. (¶ 4) Inquiries and comments about our activities are always welcome from our stockholders.

	Prob. 1	Prob. 3
	102	144
	116	158
	130	172
	143	185
	157	199
	159	201

Very truly yours AMERICAN PETROLEUM COMPANY Donald A. Barret Executive Vice-President

	Prob. 1	Prob. 3
	172	214
	177/193	219/235

Problem 2: Table

SS; 6 spaces between columns; type timed writings on one sheet

Type the table at the left below for two 1' writings. No erasures. Compute *gwam*.

		Words
Ship Shoal	10,100	4
Southeast Timbalier	1,200	9
Bay Marchand	2,500	13
Bastian Bay	1,725	16
Azalea	12,700	19
Eugene Island, Dome	3,200	25
Eugene Island, Shark	1,200	30
North Henderson	250	34
Wolfe Creek	1,400	38
North Hitchcook	950	42

Problem 3: Letter with Table

1. Insert the table at the left after ¶ 2 of the letter in Problem 1. Make the necessary change in the wording of ¶ 2.
2. Type two 5' writings on the combined problems. Compute *gwam*.

Note: Adjust, by judgment, the margins and the spacing between the top of the paper and the date for this problem to center the letter attractively.

LESSON 123

123A Preparatory Practice ⑤ *each line at least three times*

Alphabet	Explain quietly how Dickens vilified Ebenezer Scrooge or Jacob Marley.
Figure-symbol	Your memo #83-40 (dated May 25) mistakenly cites "16 prs. @ 79¢ a pr."
Capitals	Mary, Jack, and Sarah Jane visited St. Paul, Minnesota, last November.
Fluency	I will give most of my time to work; it must be a worthy contribution.

| 1 | 2 | 3 | 4 | 5 | 6 | 7 | 8 | 9 | 10 | 11 | 12 | 13 | 14 |

Words

mr louis la croix, chief engineer south bend — 12
building corporation 22100 bernice street south — 22
bend in 46637 dear mr la croix reference con- — 31
tract #1322 (¶ 1) You may begin work on the — 39
property at 5522 Berkley Place, South Bend. — 48
Please notify us when trenches have been dug — 57
and forms have been placed so that we may — 65
inspect them before the foundation is poured. — 75
(¶ 2) At least 24 hours before requesting pay- — 83
ment under the building loan agreement, — 91
please call for an inspection. The expense of — 100
a second inspection, if one is necessary, must — 109
be borne by the contractor. (¶ 3) It will be — 117
necessary for you to obtain, at this office, — 126
receipt forms which must be signed by sub- — 135
contractors and material dealers as payments — 144
are made. If you wish, call us; and we shall — 153
send the forms to you by mail. yours very — 161
truly roy l calhoun chief architect cc mr — 171
thomas best — 173/195

Problem 3: AMS Simplified Letter with Mailing and Enclosure Notations

114 words; open punctuation; airmail notation; 1 carbon copy

Words

mr mason brown president brown–scranton — 13
advertising agency 3412 longfellow street — 22

---

no tapes, no discs to adjust. You just pick up
the simple handset and dictate. (¶ 2) A light — 64
comes on at your secretary's desk. To tran- — 72
scribe, she slips on a tiny headset and types–– — 82
even as you dictate––if she wishes. If she is — 91
busy, Foremost will store the recorded mate- — 100
rial until later, automatically. Result? You — 109
get less confusion, less frustration, more at- — 118
tention, and more accomplished. (¶ 3) Read — 127
the enclosed folder; then ask your Foremost — 135
dealer to install a set for a week's free trial. — 145
charles b whitcomb sales manager enclosure — 154/175

Problem 4: Interoffice Memorandum

Full sheet; SS message

Words

TO: All Division Managers **FROM:** Avril — 6
Burnstein, Controller **DATE:** (*current*) **SUB-** — 13
JECT: Foremost Dictation Sets Available — 20
(¶ 1) Foremost Dictation Sets are now avail- — 27
able to all division managers. This system has — 37
been checked out in my office and found to be — 46
very efficient. I suggest that you see the set — 56
in my office before you decide to order one. — 65
The attached folder gives you details. (¶ 2) — 73
If you wish, we can install a dictation set in — 82
your office for a trial period. Installation of a — 93
set takes but a few minutes. Enclosure — 101

LESSON 112

112A Preparatory Practice ⑤ *each line three or more times*

Alphabet   The Jazz Quintet will play excellent background music for a new movie.

Figure-symbol The problems are 276 ÷ 13 and 845 ÷ 90; set them up this way: 13)276.

Double letters My committee addressed letters to Miss Barbara Serere, 77 Hill Street.

Fluency   The things at which men laugh often tell you the kind of men they are.

| 1 | 2 | 3 | 4 | 5 | 6 | 7 | 8 | 9 | 10 | 11 | 12 | 13 | 14 |

... (with numbers); underline the side headings.

...sentence illustrating one rule. Number these sentences to correspond with the rules.

NUMBERS

Rules

Words

(1) Numbers ten and under are generally spelled out; numbers eleven and above are written in figures.

(2) When several numbers are used in the same context, all numbers should be typed the same way, either in figures or spelled, except that any number that begins a sentence must be spelled.

(3) As a general rule, spell the shorter of two numbers used together.

(4) Isolated fractions are usually spelled, but a series of fractions is written in figures.

Examples

(1) He bought six bananas and two pints of cream to make the dessert.

(2) Sixty-five people (57 men, 5 boys, and 3 women) climbed Mt. Hood.

(3) Order No. 135 was for two 50-gallon drums and 27 ten-gallon cans.

(4) Almost one fourth of the job is finished. Add 1/2, 3/7, and 5/8.

Other Examples

(Words column: 2, 4, 17, 24, 38, 51, 65, 77, 92, 96, 99, 113, 127, 141, 155, 161)

Production Typing Information

TABULATED REPORTS IN WRITTEN COMMUNICATIONS

When space permits, indent a table from both margins. Single-space the tabulated material. For a table with a centered heading, triple-space before the heading and after the last line. For a table without a centered heading, double-space before the first and after the last lines.

For letters up to 200 words (containing a report), use 1½-inch side margins; for letters over 200 words, use 1-inch side margins. In addition, reduce the space between the top edge of the paper and the date line by one or two lines for each line in the table. This is a rough guide; your judgment should prevail.

As a rule, use the backspacing method for deciding on the placement of columns.

Shortcut for Placement of Simple Two-Column Tables. For simple two-column tabulations, set a tab stop for the first column 5 to 10 spaces to the right of the left margin. For the second column, backspace 5 to 10 spaces for the indention from the right margin and 1 space for each letter and space in the longest columnar entry; then set a tab stop for the right column. Be careful, however, not to have columns too far apart for easy reading.

ADJUSTMENTS IN VERTICAL PLACEMENT OF LETTERS

You may occasionally find that you have misjudged the length of a letter and that it is going to be either too high or too low on the page. The following suggestions for condensing or expanding letters may be used to help you solve such letter-placement problems.

Condensing. To condense a letter that is extremely long:

1. Reduce the space allowed for a signature.
2. Omit the company name (if one is used) in the closing lines.
3. Type the reference initials on the same line as the writer's typewritten name.

Expanding. To expand letters that are extremely short:

1. Allow 2 blank lines between the letter body and the complimentary close.
2. Type the reference initials 4 to 6 spaces below the dictator's name.
3. Allow more blank lines for the penwritten signature.

¶ 1
1.5 SI
5.6 AWL
80% HFW

The goal of a methods modernization is to accomplish the required tasks. The theoretical objective is to find the best way to do a particular job. Many tasks have been studied again and again, and some really significant improvements have been developed. As job requirements change and new tools and goods are produced with which to do a task, new methods will be found by modern man that will ultimately lead to a better way.

¶ 2
1.5 SI
5.6 AWL
80% HFW

Most large companies hire or train analysts to do methods improvement work. When this is not done, enthusiasm in improvement lags because no one has been designated to inject interest in it. In large firms, the selection of a methods analyst is justified. The person must not only direct methods studies of his own, but he must train the workers how to simplify their jobs. As a rule, this plan leads to a better way.

¶ 3
1.5 SI
5.6 AWL
80% HFW

One special tool that methods experts use to study work procedures is the flow chart. It is simply nothing more than a picture of each step through which a paper goes in order to process the particular data. Every step is shown by a symbol. A symbol indicates what operation takes place and what machine, if any, is needed to handle it. With a chart before them, analysts can visualize the total job and discover better ways of doing it.

43	9	61
57	11	64
71	14	67
85	17	70
92	18	71
13	21	74
28	24	77
42	27	80
56	30	82
70	32	85
84	35	88
13	38	91
27	41	93
41	43	96
55	46	99
68	49	102
82	52	104
88	53	106

1' GWAM | 1 | 2 | 3 | 4 | 5 | 6 | 7 | 8 | 9 | 10 | 11 | 12 | 13 | 14 |
5' GWAM | 1 | 2 | 3 |

112C Production Measurement: Rough Draft; Leftbound Manuscript; Outline ⓪

20' for typing; errors corrected; compute n-pram

Problem 1: Rough Draft

Leftbound manuscript form; 2" top margin (see p. 185 for correct form)

Words

TS The Dictionary   3

A good dictionary contains all of the principal words in a   14
language. Such a book, sometimes called a lexicon, is equipped   28
with words that are currently acceptable as good usage. Those   41
words are called the standard words; that is, they are words   56
that a speaker or writer would normally use. These are several   69
hundred thousand standard words; and consequently, a good many   80
dictionary contains many words that the typical person sees   93

or heard rarely. It is a recognized fact that most people have   104

[only an "average" vocabulary with "understandable" pronunciation.   118

In fact, and average college student might be embarrassed to discover   130

he is familiar with the meaning and pronunciation of less thd fewer   142

then one tenth of all the works in his language.   151

... you make an error.

4. Type three times the line in which you made the error; continue until you complete the three ¶s.

Compute *gwam*. Compare rates on the two writings.

All letters are used.

	GWAM	
	1'	5'

¶ 1
1.5 SI
5.6 AWL
80% HFW

The words a business writer uses must be active and alive. A letter that contains ordinary, dated words gets little attention. Such letters make us feel that we have been cheated. Strong, forceful words give an impression of a lively, vital writer with an important message on his mind. He utilizes short words and on occasion a unique word to drive home a unique point. No one expects a letter writer to be a novelist, but he can be interesting.

1'		5'
12	2	59
27	5	62
41	8	65
55	11	68
69	14	70
83	17	73
90	18	75

¶ 2
1.5 SI
5.6 AWL
80% HFW

When you compose technical papers, you will discover that the initial writing is rarely your best one. Your papers may be readable all right, but usually there are several areas that lack polish. An excellent first step, therefore, is to record your opinions on paper as quickly as possible. You can then edit and revise as needed. Read your paper aloud; if it sounds good to you, it will probably sound good to your reader. Time will not permit you to be overly fussy. Know when to polish––and when to finish.

1'		5'
12	21	77
26	23	80
40	26	83
54	29	85
67	31	88
82	34	91
96	37	94
103	39	95

¶ 3
1.5 SI
5.6 AWL
80% HFW

A man should have some special qualities to be an effective business writer. He should be adjustable; he should know how to size up people; he must be courteous and sincere; and he should have at his command an adequate supply of words that he can utilize to get across his ideas. If he can explain complex technical problems and provide sensible solutions to them in a sincere, direct way, he will be equal to the demands of business writing.

1'		5'
13	41	98
27	44	101
40	47	103
54	50	106
68	52	109
82	55	112
89	57	113

1' GWAM | 1 | 2 | 3 | 4 | 5 | 6 | 7 | 8 | 9 | 10 | 11 | 12 | 13 | 14 |
5' GWAM | 1 | 2 | 3 |

LESSON 122

122A Preparatory Practice ⑤ *each line three or more times*

Alphabet Jerry will exchange zinc for quicksilver because of price adjustments.
Figure-symbol That policy, #7639–858–42–RJ* (issued February 16, 1960), has expired.
Outside keys The six dazed, weary antelopes walked slowly down the westward slopes.
Fluency Learn what you can today; experience will be a most demanding teacher.

| 1 | 2 | 3 | 4 | 5 | 6 | 7 | 8 | 9 | 10 | 11 | 12 | 13 | 14 |

122B Skill-Comparison Typing ⑩ *two 1' writings on each line of 122A; compare gwam*

Classification Systems

Words

	Words
Classification Systems	9

(¶ 1) The orderly classification of books in a library constitutes an interesting study. The clay tablets discovered in the Assyrian library of Ashurbanipal, 688 to 626 B.C., were grouped under two headings: those dealing with the earth and those dealing with the heavens. Early Jesuit libraries classified their collections under two headings also. On the shelves of one side of the library were the beautifully bound books of the conformists. On the shelves of the other side were the black bound books of the heretics. These early systems had one thing in common: they were based on the contents of the books. This is the way books are classified today.[6] (¶ 2) To avoid confusion, libraries use one of the standard

17 27 36 46 54 63 72 82 91 99 109 117 126 135 143 152

classification systems that have been developed. There are three such systems in use today. They are the Dewey Decimal System, the Cutter System, and the Library of Congress System. (¶ 3) According to Johnson, a classification system has three major functions: (1) to provide a uniform "shorthand" system for indicating the contents of a book, (2) to group books treating similar subjects under the same headings, and (3) to facilitate the physical organization of books on library shelves.[7]

161 169 178 186 194 202 211 220 229 239 248 250

Footnote Information: The material for both footnotes was paraphrased from page 6 of H. Webster Johnson's book, *How To Use the Business Library*, Third Edition, 1964, published by the South-Western Publishing Company, Cincinnati. (*35 words*)

Problem 3: Outline

Full sheet; 2" top and left margins (see p. 185 for correct form)

Add outline designations; indent, space, capitalize, and punctuate the outline correctly.

	Words
how to use the library	5
I. locating books	8
library card catalog	13
information on card	18
author's name	22
title of reference	27
subject of book	32
call number	35
organization of cards	41
cumulative book index	50
list of books in print	56
information included	61
publisher's weekly	69
list of books by week of issue	76
description of subject treated	83

	Words
II. classification systems	90
dewey decimal system	95
most widely used	99
based on progressive use of numbers	108
major groupings	112
000--general works	117
100--philosophy	121
200--religion	125
300--social sciences; sociology	133
400--philology	137
500--pure science	142
600--useful arts	147
700--fine arts; recreation	153
800--literature	158
900--history	161
library of congress system	168
cutter system	171

Unless otherwise directed, proceed as follows:

Drill Copy: Full sheet; 70-space line; SS.

Paragraph Copy: Full sheet; 70-space line; DS; 5-space ¶ indention.

Production Copy: For letters, use the current date (unless one is given); your reference initials. Carbon copies are optional; correct all errors. Capitalize, space, and punctuate opening and closing lines.
Materials Needed: Letterheads or full sheets; inter-office communication forms.

LESSON 121

121A   Preparatory Practice ⑤ *each line three or more times*

Alphabet	I realized the heavily boxed "junk" from a shipwreck was antique gold.
Figure-symbol	B & B, Inc.'s orders (#189K to 207K) for ½ and ¼ lots total $4,536.63.
First row	Ancient, wizened men circled the bubbling mixture, exorcising a demon.
Fluency	It is the things you do, not yourself, that you should take seriously.

| 1 | 2 | 3 | 4 | 5 | 6 | 7 | 8 | 9 | 10 | 11 | 12 | 13 | 14 |

121B   Technique Improvement: Stroking ⑩

Type each line three times on the *control level*. Hold your arms and hands quiet. Center the stroking action in your fingers.

1	awa	The police are aware of this unpopular policy. They await your reply.
2	pol	The politician is away. He won the popularity award in this district.
3	Long reaches	Under this new system, all their employees receive annuities annually.
4	Long reaches	I may prepare a summary of my lumber and linoleum purchases this year.
5	Double letters	It occurred to the committee that a fall meeting would be unnecessary.
6	Double letters	Lowell succeeded in getting the proof, although the fee was excessive.
7	One hand	Fred saw John in Honolulu. He agreed to charge only the minimum rate.
8	One hand	We referred Rex Vetter to your address on West Union Street in Joplin.

| 1 | 2 | 3 | 4 | 5 | 6 | 7 | 8 | 9 | 10 | 11 | 12 | 13 | 14 |

121C   Communication Aid: Spelling ⑩

1. Type each line twice.
2. Close your book; type the words from your instructor's dictation.
3. Check your work.
4. Retype any words in which you made an error.

overrun pronunciation parallel recede tiring usage weird safety liable

omissions neither perseverance persistent paralysis pageant occurrence

forty nineteen fifty miniature marries optimism persuade replies occur

temperament statement studying shining similar familiar humorous chord

Unless otherwise directed, proceed as follows:
Drill Copy: Full sheet; 70-space line; SS.
Paragraph Copy: Full sheet; 70-space line; DS; 5-space
¶ indention.

Production Copy: Follow directions for each problem. You need not make carbon copies of the problems in this section.

LESSON 113

113A Preparatory Practice ⑤ *each line three or more times*

Alphabet Howard Long paid the tax on five quarts of gray paint for Jack Bozman.
Figure-symbol The footnote (*) refers to p. 230 of Vol. 45, the May 27, 1968, issue.
Outside keys Paul X. Wazo passed the quiz; he knew (at last) "Vox populi, vox Dei."
Fluency The busy worker knows that 60 minutes in an hour is never enough time.

| 1 | 2 | 3 | 4 | 5 | 6 | 7 | 8 | 9 | 10 | 11 | 12 | 13 | 14 |

113B Building Speed ⑮

1. Type three ½′ writings; reach for 30 or more words in that time.
2. Type three 1′ writings; reach for 60 or more words.

3. Type three 1½′ writings; reach for 90 or more words.
The goals are marked in the copy.

	1′ GWAM
As you begin to type, make very certain you are sitting in a	12
proper position. Sit well back in the chair; keep your feet flat on	26
the floor for good equilibrium. Position the copy so that you can read	41
it easily. Adjust the typewriter, the desk, and the chair until they	55
are in a suitable position in accordance with your height. Be alert,	69
but be comfortable. In conclusion, approach each task with a positive	83
attitude. You can improve your typing ability by adding to the cer-	96
tainty with which you work.	102

1.5 SI
5.6 AWL
80% HFW

1′ GWAM | 1 | 2 | 3 | 4 | 5 | 6 | 7 | 8 | 9 | 10 | 11 | 12 | 13 | 14 |

113C Technique Improvement: Tabulating ⑮ *type the drill three times on one sheet*

Full sheet; 3″ top margin; SS; decide spaces between columns

			Words
31,730	53,108	45,041	4
16,235	27,372	13,132	8
52,546	25,153	75,784	13
76,317	42,768	47,465	17
98,900	68,985	38,479	21
17,480	10,356	47,925	25

ADVERTISING EXPENDITURES: 1950 and 1966

(Figures in Millions)

Medium	1950	1966
Newspapers	$2,076	$ 4,895
Radio	605	1,001
Television	171	2,784
Magazines	515	1,291
Farm Papers	21	34
Direct Mail	803	2,454
Business Papers	251	712
Outdoor	143	178
Miscellaneous	1,125	3,253
Totals	$5,710	$16,602

Source: Reader's Digest Almanac, 1968.

Problem 2

Words

U.S. PRESIDENTS AND THEIR TERMS

Since 1900

Theodore Roosevelt	1901 – 1909
William Howard Taft	1909 – 1913
Thomas Woodrow Wilson	1913 – 1921
Warren Gamaliel Harding	1921 – 1923
John Calvin Coolidge	1923 – 1929
Herbert Clark Hoover	1929 – 1933
Franklin Delano Roosevelt	1933 – 1945
Harry S Truman	1945 – 1953
Dwight David Eisenhower	1953 – 1961
John Fitzgerald Kennedy	1961 – 1963
Lyndon Baines Johnson	1963 – 1969
Richard Milhous Nixon	1969 –

PROJECTED CHANGES IN DISTRIBUTION OF EMPLOYMENT

Major Occupational Groups

Group	1964	1975	Change
Farm	6.3	3.9	—21.0%
Service	13.2	14.1	35.0
White Collar	44.2	48.3	38.0
Blue Collar	36.3	33.7	17.0

Source: U.S. Department of Labor, America's Industrial and Occupational Manpower Requirements, 1964-1975.

Problem 4

Arrange in columns; add $ sign where needed

Words

PERSONAL EXPENDITURES

(Figures in Millions)

Group	Amount
Food and Tobacco	115,446
Clothing; Accessories; Jewelry	48,406
Personal Care	8,215
Housing	67,135
Household Operation	66,658
Medical Care	31,250
Personal Business	23,992
Transportation	55,607
Recreation	28,673
Private Education and Research	6,667
Religious and Welfare Activities	6,475
Foreign Travel and Remittances	3,384
Total Personal Outlay	461,908

Source: The World Almanac, 1968.

Stroke	Most profits...
Word	What is done is done—we learn from the past, but we cannot change.
Combination	Desire for personal growth can lead a man to the books he should read.
Combination	A young man who wants to go to the top learns to express himself well.
Combination	Although it may seem longer, it pays to do a job right the first time.

| 1 | 2 | 3 | 4 | 5 | 6 | 7 | 8 | 9 | 10 | 11 | 12 | 13 | 14 |

LESSON 114

114A Preparatory Practice ⑤ *each line three or more times*

Alphabet	Fred McBee's organization works hard extirpating juvenile delinquency.
Figure-symbol	The invoice cited "24 doz. prs. #5083 shoes @ $17.39 (less 65¢) a pr."
Adjacent keys	We were assured Polk Power Saws were proper saws to cut sides 32 x 45.
Fluency	Your personality might get you a job, but skills must hold it for you.

| 1 | 2 | 3 | 4 | 5 | 6 | 7 | 8 | 9 | 10 | 11 | 12 | 13 | 14 |

114B Skill-Comparison Typing ⑤ *each line for 1'; compare rates*

Goal sentence	He is sure to say that you can gain ability by meeting difficult jobs.
Hyphen	The well-to-do manager solicited the funds in a door-to-door campaign.
Weak finger	Only I was quite puzzled by his apparent lack of aptitude for the job.

| 1 | 2 | 3 | 4 | 5 | 6 | 7 | 8 | 9 | 10 | 11 | 12 | 13 | 14 |

114C Communication Aid: Apostrophe ⑩

Full sheet; 1½" top margin; 70-space line; SS with DS between items

1. For the heading, type APOSTROPHE.
2. Type the rules and examples given below (with numbers); underline the side headings.
3. Compose and type four sentences, each sentence illustrating one rule. Number these sentences to correspond with the rules.

	Words
APOSTROPHE	2
Rules	4
(1) The singular possessive is usually formed by adding 's; but for words	19
having more than one syllable and ending in s, only the apostrophe	33
is added.	35
(2) When plural nouns do not end in s, add 's to form the possessive.	50
(3) Add only the apostrophe to form the possessive of plural nouns ending	65
in s.	66
(4) The possessive of initials, abbreviations, etc., is formed with 's.	81
Examples	84
(1) The Countess' son (my boss's uncle) financed all his boy's trips.	98
(2) Children's shoes and women's robes are on sale at the local shop.	112
(3) The girls' shoes and boys' coats will be shipped by fast express.	126
(4) William Wright, Jr.'s signature must appear on the YMCA's checks.	140
Other Examples	146

119A Preparatory Practice ⑤ *each line three or more times*

Alphabet Dank fog hid unlit objects; expressway driving became quite hazardous.

Figure-symbol *List does not include Day & Company's Policy #87–6230–WE–1954 (paid).

Third row We were there two weeks earlier; point out where you were living then.

Fluency A man who is just minutes late each day loses hours of work in a year.

| 1 | 2 | 3 | 4 | 5 | 6 | 7 | 8 | 9 | 10 | 11 | 12 | 13 | 14 |

119B Technique Improvement: Response Patterns ⑮ *each line at least three times*

1 Word-recognition A plan will help you do the things you should when you should do them.

2 Stroke Several important inventions and discoveries changed their operations.

3 Combination There is nothing dangerous about the great movement that is under way.

4 Word-recognition Who can know the great things he can do until he tries to do his best?

5 Stroke Of all the major forms of mass transportation, the pipeline is unique.

6 Combination A pipeline merely stands still and lets the freight do all the moving.

7 Word-recognition The will to win is a big aid to all the men who want to do big things.

8 Stroke Mt. Blanc tunnel represents an engineering feat of heroic proportions.

9 Combination No one is so futile as he who will not or cannot control his thoughts.

| 1 | 2 | 3 | 4 | 5 | 6 | 7 | 8 | 9 | 10 | 11 | 12 | 13 | 14 |

119C Production Skill Building ㉚

Make a notation of the problems listed at the right to be typed for a 20′ writing. Type them until time is called. Compute your *n-pram*.

Page 202, 115D, Problem 1
Page 205, 116D, Problem 2
Page 206, 117C, Problem 1

LESSON 120

120A Preparatory Practice ⑤ *each line three or more times*

Alphabet Mary Turner quickly ate the extra pizza we had saved for Jane Boering.

Figure-symbol Lee & Cowl's 14¼% discount applies to your $27,630 and $58,909 orders.

Adjacent keys We were pleased to allow her to point out her real reasons for asking.

Fluency A man who makes many mistakes in his work can be a very costly worker.

| 1 | 2 | 3 | 4 | 5 | 6 | 7 | 8 | 9 | 10 | 11 | 12 | 13 | 14 |

120B Growth Index ⑮ *two 5′ writings on 112B, page 196; figure* nwam *(net words a minute) on the better writing.*

To figure NWAM—
1. Determine *gwam*.
2. Deduct from *gwam* 2 for each error.

120C Production Measurement ㉚ *type for 20 minutes; compute n-pram*

1. Use a full sheet, reading position, and double spacing for each problem.

2. Decide on spaces between columns.
3. Erase and correct all errors.

Exact. Count total lines to be used, including spaces between lines; subtract total from lines available; divide remainder by 2 (ignore fractions). Leave this number of blank lines at the top of the sheet.

Reading Position. Type material two lines above what has been computed as exact center.

Alternate Method. Insert the paper; roll it to the vertical center. Roll the cylinder back (toward you) once for every two lines in the copy to be typed. This will place the copy in exact vertical center. To type a problem in reading position, roll the cylinder back two additional lines.

Spacing after Headings. Leave one blank line between a main and a secondary heading and between a columnar heading and its column. Leave two blank lines after a main heading if a secondary heading is not used, or after a secondary heading when a main heading and a secondary heading are both used.

Headings. After spacing down to allow for the top margin as determined by vertical placement computations, center the main heading; double-space and center the secondary heading (if one is used); then triple-space.

Columns. Note the longest item in each column (if a columnar heading is the longest item, count it as such unless judgment indicates otherwise). Decide the number of spaces to leave between columns.

Backspace from the center of the page once for every two spaces tween all the columns. At the point where you finish backspacing, set the left margin stop for the first column.

From the left margin, space forward once for every stroke in the longest item of the first column and once for each space between the first and second columns. Set the first tab stop. Follow this same procedure for setting tab stops for the remaining columns.

Columnar Headings. Center columnar headings over the columns. When a heading has been counted as the longest item in a column, it may be necessary to reset the tab stop in order to center the column under the heading.

There are several methods of centering columnar headings over a column, but probably the easiest way is to add the figures from the cylinder scale for the first and last strokes in the column. Dividing this sum by 2 will result in the center point of the column.

Columnar headings are usually underlined.

HORIZONTAL RULINGS

Horizontal lines are often used in tabulated reports to set off the columnar headings. A double line is usually placed above columnar headings and a single line below them. A single line is also placed under the last line of the report. These lines can be the exact width of the report, or they can extend several spaces on each side of it.

To type rulings the exact width of the report, first determine the placement of columns. When you set the tab stop for the last column, continue spacing forward one space for each stroke in the longest item in that column. Immediately after stroking for the ings can then be typed across the page until the carriage locks.

Double Lines. Double-space from the last line of the heading; type the first of the double lines; then operate the variable line spacer; move the cylinder forward slightly; type the second line. Double-space between this double line and the columnar headings.

Single Lines. Single-space from columnar headings; type a single line. Double-space after this line before typing columnar entries.

Single-space after typing the last columnar entries and type a single line.

Source Note (If Used). Double-space from the single line; type the source note at the left margin or indent 3 to 5 spaces.

TABULATOR STOPS FOR UNEVEN COLUMNS

Uneven Columns. When columns contain amounts of figures of uneven length, set the tab stop at a point that will take care of the greatest number of entries. After tabulating, backspace for longer items or space forward for shorter ones.

Dollar Signs. In a money column, type a dollar sign before the first amount in the column and before the total (if one is shown). Place the dollar sign before the first amount and the total, typed so that it will be one space to the left of the longest amount in the column.

Totals. Totals are treated as a part of the column. To make them easier to read, totals are usually separated by a double space from the column.

Alphabet	Max Jackson left the quiz show early to give Mable a prize he had won.
Figures	Of the 1,670 dispensers made by Employee #8492, 158 could not be OK'd.
Double letters	The officers will meet with the committee to discuss the class dinner.
Fluency	Even though your rate varies, try to strike all keys with equal force.

| 1 | 2 | 3 | 4 | 5 | 6 | 7 | 8 | 9 | 10 | 11 | 12 | 13 | 14 |

118B Building Speed ⑮ *type 113B, page 198, as directed there*

118C Production Typing: Tabulated Reports ㉚

Problem 1: Multiline Columnar Headings

Full sheet; DS; reading position; decide on spaces between columns

To center the heading over the second and third columns: (1) Move the carriage to the first stroke in the second column; note the number on the scale. (2) Move the carriage to the last stroke in the third column; note the number on the scale. (3) Add the two numbers; divide by 2 to find the center of the column, the point from which the backspacing begins.

			Words
SUNFLOWER TRANSPORTATION COMPANY			7
Long-Term Debt			10
		December	13
First Mortgage Bonds	1968	1969 SS	25
3 1/8% series due 1976	$50,000	$50,000	33
3 7/8% series due 1976	45,000	47,000	40
4 1/8% series due 1980	70,000	82,500	48
4 3/8% series due 1982	60,500	68,000	55
5 1/2% series due 1982	55,000	57,000	63
5 1/8% series due 1984	90,000	94,500	70
5 1/4% series due 1984	82,500	84,000	77
5 3/4% series due 1988	77,500	85,000	85
5 7/8% series due 1988	55,500	64,500	92
6 1/4% series due 1990	63,000	72,500	100
6 1/2% series due 1990	92,000	91,500	107

Problem 2: Multiline Headings

Full sheet; DS; reading position; decide on spaces between columns; SS 2-line main heading; do not abbreviate any words

Job Title	Established Ranges		Words
	Average Low	Average High	
NATIONWIDE WEEKLY SALARY DATA FOR SELECTED EDP JOBS			6 / 10
			18 / 28
		SS	31
Lead Systems Analyst	$201	$273	37
Senior Systems Analyst	180	249	44
Junior Systems Analyst	149	207	50
Lead Programmer	176	242	55
Senior Programmer	154	210	60
Junior Programmer	126	173	65
Lead Computer Operator	138	186	71
Senior Computer Operator	138	186	78
Junior Computer Operator	100	134	84
Tab Equip. Manager	144	194	90
Lead Tab Equip. Operator	114	150	98
Senior Tab Equip. Operator	99	131	105
Junior Tab Equip. Operator	89	116	113
Keypunch Supervisor	110	148	118
Lead Keypunch Operator	95	124	125
Senior Keypunch Operator	85	111	131
Junior Keypunch Operator	77	99	138

			142
Source: "EDP Salary Study--1968," Business			152
Automation (June, 1968), pp. 40-41.			161

←——Main heading——→ **FORMADEX DISTRIBUTORS**
DS

←——Secondary heading——→ Video Tapes
TS

←——Columnar headings——→ <u>Company</u>   <u>Location</u>
DS

Company	Location	Words in Columns	Total Words
			4
			7
			13
Electronics Service Company	Phoenix	7	20
Evenview Television Systems	Hollywood	15	28
AVF Communications, Inc.	Santa Barbara	23	36
Elsco Colorado, Inc.	Denver	28	41
Audio Video Industries, Inc.	Miami	35	48
Lock Audio Associates	Atlanta	41	54
Electronic Equipment, Inc.	Chicago	48	61
Lake Systems Corporation	Boston	55	68
General TV Network	Detroit	60	73
Dayton Communications	Dayton	66	79

KEY | 28 | 14 | 13 |

114D   Production Typing: Two-Column Tabulated Report ㉚

Problem 1

Problem 2

Half sheet; exact center; SS; 14 spaces between columns

After studying the information on page 200, type the tabulated report shown above.

If time remains, type the problem again. Omit the secondary heading and leave 10 spaces between columns. (*76 words*)

LESSON 115

115A   Preparatory Practice ⑤   *each line three or more times*

Alphabet   The bold Viking queen came for her topaz, aquamarine, and onyx jewels.

Figure-symbol   Invoice #46–891 lists credit terms of $2\frac{1}{2}/15$, n/30. We can save $7.49.

Long words   We can outline the economic implications and technical specifications.

Fluency   Learning to live with others might be as hard on them as it is on you.

| 1 | 2 | 3 | 4 | 5 | 6 | 7 | 8 | 9 | 10 | 11 | 12 | 13 | 14 |

117C Production Typing: Tabulated Reports ㉟

Problem 1: Report with Uneven Columns and Totals

Full sheet; DS; reading position; decide spaces between columns

Words

BERNARD LUSKIN WEAR

First Quarter Departmental Sales

Department	January	February	March	Words
				4
				11
				23
Shoes	$ 840.12	$ 660.13	$ 489.90	32
Dresses and Lingerie	3,487.37	3,200.34	4,591.25	43
Hats	660.14	860.25	940.46	48
Coats	1,027.78	2,806.50	2,175.70	56
Jewelry	89.48	95.35	103.36	61
Gloves and Handbags	376.24	350.80	421.56	70
Sweaters and Blouses	385.67	435.78	497.90	78
Furs	816.57	730.69	500.89	83 / 91
Totals	$7,683.37	$9,139.84	$9,721.02	101

Type total line immediately under last amount; double-space and type total.

Problem 2: Tabulated Report from Corrected Script

Full sheet; DS; reading position; decide spaces between columns

Words

Item	1968	1969	Words
Midland Packaged Foods *all caps*			5
Sales Promotion Costs			9
			14
~~Books~~ Circulars	$10,472	$12,800	21
~~Letters~~ (Automatic)	830	750	26
Samples	11,~~450~~ 733	8,10[5]	32
Direct Mail	(3,489)	(5,400)	37
Exhibits *and* ~~&~~ Demonstrations	980	825	44
~~Awards~~ Prizes	279	370	47
Midland News *all caps*	3,48[6]3	4,762	53
(Misc.) Costs *spell out*	(552)	(418)	59 / 64
Totals	$33,598	$31,698	68

115B Communication Aid: Apostrophe ⑩ *as directed in 114C, page 199*

Full sheet; 1½″ top margin; 70-space line; SS with DS between items

Words

APOSTROPHE

2

Rules

4

(1) When common possession is to be shown for two or more persons, use 's with the last name only.

18
25

(2) Possessive pronouns do not take an apostrophe. It's is a contraction for it is. The apostrophe is used in contractions.

40
52

(3) When a proper name of one syllable ends in s, add 's for possession.

67

(4) Add only an apostrophe to a proper name of more than one syllable that ends in s to show possession.

81
88

Examples

92

(1) Van and Bert's mother is in England; Jane's mother is in Austria.

106

(2) The book is hers. Its cover is torn, so wrap the book with care.

120

(3) Bess's talk on antiques was better organized than James's report.

134

(4) Carl Williams' store is only one block from Vince Meadows' house.

148

Other Examples

154

115C Production Skill Building ⑤

Full sheet; DS; 16 spaces between columns

As you are timed for 4 minutes, make machine adjustments and type the columns of the tabulated report illustrated on page 201. Type on the *control level*.

115D Production Typing: Tabulated Reports ㉚

Full sheet; DS; reading position; 8 spaces between columns

Problem 1: Three-Column Report

Words

ALL-TIME BEST SELLERS
TS

4

Title	Author	No. Sold
Peyton Place	Metalious	9,919,785
In His Steps	Sheldon	8,065,000 *
God's Little Acre	Caldwell	8,061,812
Gone with the Wind	Mitchell	6,978,211
Lady Chatterley's Lover	Lawrence	6,326,470
The Carpetbaggers	Robbins	5,563,841
Exodus	Uris	5,473,710
I, the Jury	Spillane	5,390,105
To Kill a Mockingbird	Lee	5,363,909
The Wonderful Wizard of Oz	Baum	5,000,000 *

13
DS
19
26
33
41
49
56
61
67
74
83
87

SS ⟶
DS ⟶

Source: Alice Payne Hackett, 70 Years of Best Sellers, 1895–1965 (New York: R. R. Bowker Co., 1968).

108
114

* Estimated.

117

Problem 2: Report with Horizontal Rulings

Full sheet; DS; reading position; decide spaces between columns; add horizontal rulings as in Problem 1; put the source note below the bottom rule

DOMESTIC EXPORTS BY COMMODITY GROUPS

Figures in Millions of Dollars

Commodity	1960	1965
Food and Live Animals	2,662	4,004
Beverages and Tobacco	483	517
Crude Materials, Except Fuels	2,777	2,856
Mineral Fuels	814	947
Animal and Vegetable Oils and Fats	307	471
Chemicals	1,816	2,402
Machinery and Transport Equipment	7,011	10,016
Other Manufactured Goods	4,076	4,840
Other Transactions	450	952

Source: Statistical Abstract of the United States, 1966.

Words: 7, 14, 38, 42, 55, 62, 69, 77, 83, 92, 97, 106, 114, 120, 133, 153

LESSON 117

117A Preparatory Practice ⑤ *each line three or more times*

Alphabet Jealous of Banquo, MacBeth, vainly prizing a crown, executed the king.

Figure-symbol Clee & Gray's sales, $68,490.23, are 5/17 greater than five years ago.

Direct reaches I decided my funny brindle puppy, "Mimi," could jump on my TV program.

Fluency We can begin to worry if we discover our work is not worth our salary.

| 1 | 2 | 3 | 4 | 5 | 6 | 7 | 8 | 9 | 10 | 11 | 12 | 13 | 14 |

117B Communication Aid: Apostrophe ⑩ *as directed in 114C, page 199*

Full sheet; 1½" top margin; 70-space line; SS with DS between items

APOSTROPHE

Words: 2, 4

Rules

(1) Add 's to form the plural of numbers and letters (7's, five's).

(2) Use the apostrophe to show omission of figures (class of '65).

(3) Use the apostrophe to show omission of letters in abbreviations (Rob't, Marg't, Sec'y). No period follows such abbreviations.

(4) Use single quotation marks (apostrophe) for quotes within quotes.

Words: 18, 32, 45, 58, 72, 76

Examples

(1) The teacher gave 5 A's, 7 B's, and 30 C's to a class of 42 girls.

(2) The dinner meeting for the class of '66 will be held on Thursday.

(3) The minutes of the meeting were signed "Charles S. Clark, Sec'y."

(4) Mr. Kromer said, "I heard them say to your sister, 'It is time.'"

Words: 90, 104, 118, 132

Other Examples

Words: 137

Problem 2: Rough Draft of Tabulated Report

Full sheet; DS; reading position; decide spaces between columns

ALL-TIME BEST SELLERS ←DS   4
Nonfiction←   7
    TS

Title → Center over column	Date	Copies	13
#The pocket books of Baby And Child Crae *are*	1946	19,076,822	24
#Better Homes and Gardens Cook Book	1930	11,325,299	34
Pocket Atlas	~~1071~~ 1917	11,000,000	40
Betty Crocker's *Picture* CookBook	1950	7,000,000*	50
How To Win A friend and Influence People	19(7)3	6,578,314	61
101 Famous Poems	1917⁶	6,000,000*	68
English-Spanish, Spanish-English (Dictionary)	1948	~~4,567,000~~ 5,899,000	74 / 80
Profiles in Corage	19(65)	5,498,651	87
Roget's pocket Thesaurus	1923	5,416,857	95

     98
DS [Source: 70 Years of Best Sellers, 1895-1965 (1968).   126
DS *Estimated.   128
Alice Payne Hackett, (New York: R.R. Bowker Co.,

LESSON 116

116A Preparatory Practice ⑤ *each line three or more times*

Alphabet   Jim quickly played the exciting pizzicato movement from Boccio's work.
Figure-symbol   My new figures show a 1,235,780 increase, or 469½% more than expected.
Inside keys   The Ghurka rug was torn five times before Mr. Hunter finally fixed it.
Fluency   For a lazy man, each hour of each day seems to have 120 weary minutes.

| 1 | 2 | 3 | 4 | 5 | 6 | 7 | 8 | 9 | 10 | 11 | 12 | 13 | 14 |

116B Communication Aid: Apostrophe ⑩ *as directed in 114C, page 199*

Full sheet; 1½" top margin; 70-space line; SS with DS between items

APOSTROPHE   2

Rules   4

(1) Company and organization names sometimes omit the apostrophe.   18
(2) It is better not to use the possessive form for inanimate objects,   32
but business sanctions the possessive with <u>day</u>, <u>month</u>, <u>year</u>, etc.   45
(3) Use 'd to form the past and past participle of coined words.   58
(4) Do not use an apostrophe if a preposition follows a possessive noun.   73

Examples   76

(1) She walked from Wilson's Department Store to Citizens State Bank.   90
(2) It's true that eight years' work was destroyed in one day's time.   104
(3) The office manager X'd out the last line; then he OK'd the cable.   118
(4) Fred has had ten years of experience as manager of Eckert Studio.   132

Other Examples   138

116C   Production Skill Building ⑤

Type the report on page 202, as directed on that page. Plan and type as much of the problem as you can in 4 minutes.

Type on the *control level*. When time is called, compute *g-pram*. Good: 6 to 10 words.

116D   Production Typing: Report with Horizontal Rulings ㉚

Problem 1: Report with Horizontal Rulings

Full sheet; DS; reading position; decide spaces between columns

Guides for typing table can be found on page 200.

			Words
ORIENTATION SCHEDULE			4
February			6
			27
Topic	Leader	Date	30
			41
Customer Relations	Johnson	2	51
Personnel Policies	Endicott	4	57
Company History	Endicott	3	63
Employee Benefits	Endicott	5	68
Products We Make	Goodman	9	74
Company Social Programs	Sanchez	10	81
Company Organization	Taylor	11	87
Branch Operations	Taylor	12	93
Letter Writing Techniques	Perkins	13	100
File It and Find It	MacMillan	20	107
Questions and Answers	Staff	21	113
Suggestion System	Goodman	23	119
Training Programs	Endicott	24	125
The Computer Center	Wagner	25	131
Safety First	Serron	27	137
A Word from Our President	Fischer	28	144
			154

DS →
DS →
DS →
SS →
DS →
SS →

REFERENCE GUIDE

TYPEWRITER OPERATIVE PARTS

Typewriters have similar operative parts, the names of which vary somewhat from typewriter to typewriter even when the function is the same. These similar operative parts are identified in the four segments of a typewriter given below and on page ii. Each segment is a composite and not an exact segment of any one typewriter. For this reason, the exact location of a part identified in the segment may be slightly different from that on your typewriter; but the differences are, for the most part, few and slight.

Extra parts that are peculiar to the typewriter you operate can be identified by reference to the instructional booklet distributed by the manufacturer of the typewriter. This booklet can be very helpful to you because all its content is directed to the operation of one specific make of machine.

In using the illustrations, follow the line from the number to the part location. Know the function of each part, as explained in the textbook, and learn to operate it with maximum efficiency.

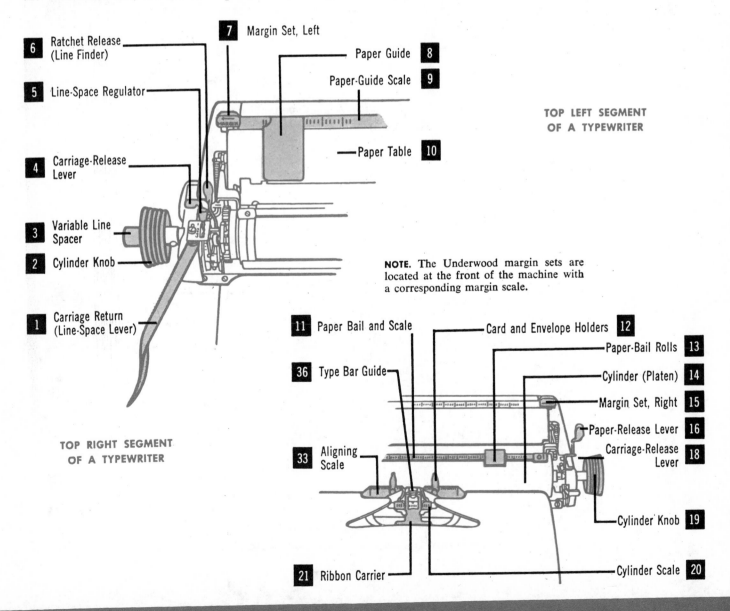

7 Margin Set, Left

6 Ratchet Release (Line Finder)

5 Line-Space Regulator

4 Carriage-Release Lever

3 Variable Line Spacer

2 Cylinder Knob

1 Carriage Return (Line-Space Lever)

Paper Guide **8**

Paper-Guide Scale **9**

Paper Table **10**

TOP LEFT SEGMENT OF A TYPEWRITER

NOTE. The Underwood margin sets are located at the front of the machine with a corresponding margin scale.

11 Paper Bail and Scale

36 Type Bar Guide

33 Aligning Scale

21 Ribbon Carrier

Card and Envelope Holders **12**

Paper-Bail Rolls **13**

Cylinder (Platen) **14**

Margin Set, Right **15**

Paper-Release Lever **16**

Carriage-Release Lever **18**

Cylinder Knob **19**

Cylinder Scale **20**

TOP RIGHT SEGMENT OF A TYPEWRITER

LOWER SEGMENT OF A MANUAL TYPEWRITER

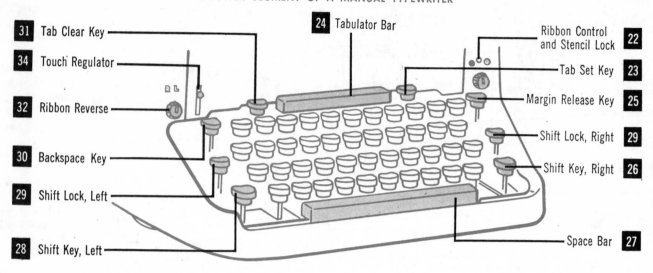

31 Tab Clear Key

34 Touch Regulator

32 Ribbon Reverse

30 Backspace Key

29 Shift Lock, Left

28 Shift Key, Left

24 Tabulator Bar

22 Ribbon Control and Stencil Lock

23 Tab Set Key

25 Margin Release Key

29 Shift Lock, Right

26 Shift Key, Right

27 Space Bar

LOWER SEGMENT OF AN ELECTRIC TYPEWRITER

> **CHECK YOUR TYPEWRITER TO SEE IF:**
> **1.** The position is different for: ¢ @ * _ (underline)
> **2.** These keys have "repeat" action: *backspace, space bar, carriage return, hyphen-underline*
> **3.** Extra keys are used: **+ = ! 1**

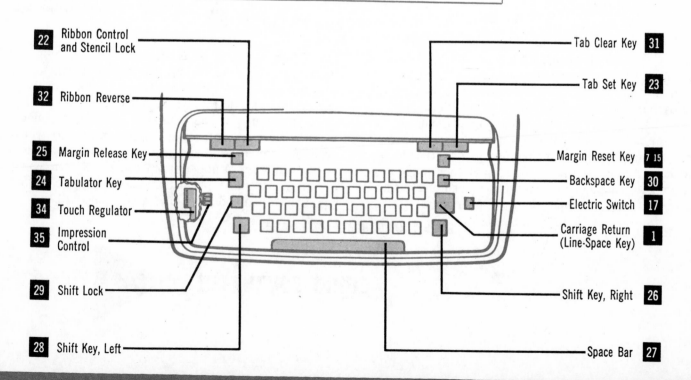

22 Ribbon Control and Stencil Lock

32 Ribbon Reverse

25 Margin Release Key

24 Tabulator Key

34 Touch Regulator

35 Impression Control

29 Shift Lock

28 Shift Key, Left

31 Tab Clear Key

23 Tab Set Key

7 15 Margin Reset Key

30 Backspace Key

17 Electric Switch

1 Carriage Return (Line-Space Key)

26 Shift Key, Right

27 Space Bar

PAPER GUIDE AND CENTERING POINT

Typewriters are of three types in regard to setting the paper guide and arriving at the center point.

Type 1: ROYAL, OLYMPIA, AND SMITH-CORONA "SECRETARIAL 250" ELECTRIC

Set the paper guide on 0 on the paper-guide scale. When 8½″ by 11″ paper is inserted with the left edge against the guide, the centering point will be 42 for pica and 51 (or 50 for convenience) for elite machines.

Type 2: IBM MODEL D, AND REMINGTON

The fixed centering point is 0 for both pica and elite machines. Marks on the paper-guide scale aid the typist in setting the paper guide to center paper correctly.

Type 3: SMITH-CORONA NON-ELECTRIC, R. C. ALLEN, IBM SELECTRIC, AND UNDERWOOD

A variety of marks appear on the paper table or copy-guide scale to aid the typist in setting the paper-guide scale for automatic centering of 8½″ by 11″ paper. Marks on the paper-bail scale indicate the center point of the paper.

If no marks appear on the paper-bail scale to indicate the center point of the paper, insert the paper after the paper guide has been set. Add the carriage scale reading on the left edge of the paper to the reading at the right edge. Divide this sum by 2 to arrive at the center point.

STANDARD DIRECTIONS APPLYING TO ALL TYPEWRITERS

On every typewriter, there is at least one scale, usually the cylinder scale (20), that reads from 0 at the left to 85 or more at the right, depending on the width of the carriage and style of type—either pica or elite. The spaces on this scale are matched to the spacing mechanism on the typewriter.

To simplify direction giving, your instructor may ask you to insert paper into your machine so that the left edge corresponds to 0 on the carriage scale. The center point on 8½″ by 11″ paper will then be 42 on the carriage scale for a pica machine or 51 (or 50 for convenience) on an elite machine.

If this procedure is adopted, adjust the paper guide to the left edge of your paper after it is inserted with the left edge at 0 on the carriage scale. Note the position of the paper guide. Move it to this point at the beginning of each class period.

SETTING THE MARGIN STOPS

PLANNING THE MARGIN STOPS (7, 15)

To center typed material horizontally, set stops for the left and right margins. Typewriters differ in their mechanical adjustments and the bell rings at different points on different typewriters; but the carriage locks at the point where the right margin stop is set. After the bell rings, there will be from 6 to 11 or more spaces before the carriage locks, some machines allowing more but none fewer than 6 spaces.

Test out your typewriter and determine the number of spaces the bell rings before the carriage locks. Take this into consideration when setting the right margin stop. Since the ringing of the bell is a cue to return the carriage, set the right stop 3 to 7 spaces beyond the desired line ending so the ringing will come at approximately 3 spaces before the point at which you want the line to end.

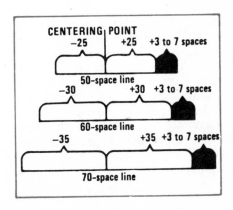

MECHANICS OF SETTING MARGIN STOPS

IBM "MODEL D" AND UNDERWOOD ELECTRIC

To Set Left Margin Stop: Move the carriage to the left margin stop by depressing the return key. Depress and hold down the margin reset key as you move the carriage to the desired new margin position; then release the margin reset key.

To Set Right Margin Stop: Move the carriage until it is against the right margin stop. Depress and hold down the margin reset key as you move the carriage to the desired new margin position; then release the margin reset key.

IBM "SELECTRIC"

To Set Left and Right Margin Stops: Push in on the appropriate stop and slide it to the correct position on the margin scale; release the stop. Use the space bar to move the carrier out of the way when setting a margin stop to the right of the carrier's present location.

(Continued on page iv)

SETTING MARGIN STOPS (Continued)

OLYMPIA AND UNDERWOOD NONELECTRIC

To Set Left and Right Margin Stops: Move the left and right margin stops to the desired position on the front scale for the Underwood typewriter and on the scale in back of the cylinder for the Olympia.

The Underwood typewriter has margin indicators (solid geometric shapes) on the front scale to indicate balanced margin set positions. The Olympia has an easy-to-see red line, on the upright plastic guide, to indicate exact position of setting.

REMINGTON ELECTRIC AND NONELECTRIC

To Set Left and Right Margin Stops: Move the left margin stop to the desired position to begin the line of writing. Move the stop for the right margin to the desired position to set the right margin stop.

ROYAL ELECTRIC AND NONELECTRIC

To Set the Left Margin Stop: Pull forward the left margin lever, move the carriage to the desired point, and release the lever. Set the right margin the same way, using the right margin lever.

SMITH-CORONA ELECTRIC

To Set Left and Right Margin Stops: Depress the left carriage-release button and the left margin button and move the carriage to the desired location for the left margin stop; release the two buttons simultaneously.

Use a similar operation to set the stop for the right margin.

SMITH-CORONA NONELECTRIC AND R. C. ALLEN

To Set the Left Margin Stop: Move the carriage to the desired point and touch the left margin button or key.

Set the right margin stop the same way, using the right margin button or key.

Another Method: While holding down the button or key, move the carriage to the point desired; then release the button or key.

KNOW YOUR TYPEWRITER

Your machine may have timesaving features not included in this discussion of operating parts. Learn these features from a study of the manufacturer's pamphlet which describes and illustrates the operating parts of the typewriter you are using. You can get this pamphlet without cost from the manufacturer of your typewriter. The pamphlet will have many ideas for your operative improvement.

CHANGING TYPEWRITER RIBBONS

Techniques for changing ribbons vary from machine to machine. The steps that follow are basic to all machines:

1. Wind the ribbon on one spool, usually the right one.

2. Raise and lock the ribbon carrier as follows: Depress the shift lock. Set the ribbon control for typing on the lower portion of the ribbon. Depress and lock any two central keys, such as *y* and *t*.

3. Remove the ribbon from the carrier. Remove both spools.

4. Hook the new ribbon on the empty spool and wind several inches of new ribbon on it. Be sure the ribbon winds and unwinds in the proper direction.

5. Place both spools on their holders. Thread the ribbon through the ribbon carrier.

6. Release the shift lock. Return the ribbon indicator to type on the upper portion of the ribbon. Unlock the two keys.

7. Clean the keys if necessary to make your work clear and sharp.

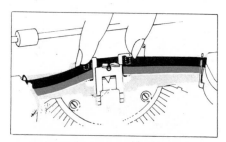

Ribbon Threaded Through the Ribbon-Carrier Mechanism

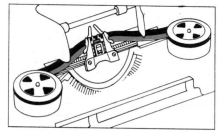

Nonelectric (Underwood)

Path of the Ribbon as It Winds and Unwinds on the Two Spools

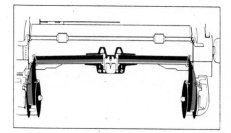

Electric

IBM Ribbon

office aides inc

suite 1045 carew tower one fifth street cincinnati, ohio 45202 telephone (513) 271-8811

October 20, 19--

Republic Supply Company
2670 Queen City Avenue
Cincinnati, OH 45238

Attention Miss Janet Wellington

Gentlemen:

The modified block style has some distinctive features, as
shown by this letter and described in the enclosed pamphlet.

The date, complimentary close, and name and official title of
the dictator are begun at the horizontal center of the page.
These can be placed correctly with one tabulator adjustment.

Special lines (reference, enclosure, and carbon copy notations)
are placed at the left margin, a double space below the last
of the closing lines. If the dictator's name is part of the
closing lines, only the typist's initials are required in the
reference. If the dictator's initials are used, they precede
those of the typist and are usually typed in capital letters.

The modified block style, about which you inquired yesterday,
is widely used by the clients for whom we prepare letters.
We think you will like it, too.

                    Sincerely yours,

                    Randall B. Parkhurst

                    Randall B. Parkhurst
                    Communications Director

lkd

Enclosure

cc Mr. John R. Rodgers, Jr.

Modified Block, Blocked ¶s, Mixed

PD Consultants in Business Practices
PERRY & DERRICK, INC.
111 Lincoln Park / Newark, New Jersey 07102 / Telephone 201-227-0453

                    February 15, 19--

AIRMAIL

Miss Evelyn Terry, Office Manager
Standard Steel Equipment Company
270 - 53d Street
Brooklyn, NY 11232

Dear Miss Terry

     The booklet you requested about letter format is en-
closed. The format features described are those adopted
by this company. This letter follows them.

     The first line of each paragraph is indented five
spaces. The date, complimentary close, company name,
and the dictator's name are started at the center point
of the paper. We use open punctuation. In this style,
punctuation marks are omitted after the date, address,
salutation, and closing lines unless an abbreviation is
used, in which case the period is typed as part of the
abbreviation.

     Although we do not usually show the company name
in the closing lines, we have done so here to illustrate
for you the correct handling of it. Since the dictator's
name is typed in the closing lines, only the typist's
initials are used in the reference notation.

     Special mailing notations are typed in all capital
letters at the left margin, a double space below the date.

     After you have had an opportunity to examine your
copy of Styling Business Letters, I shall appreciate
your sending us your impressions of it.

                    Sincerely yours

                    PERRY & DERRICK, INC.

                    Richard S. Perry

                    Richard S. Perry, Manager

mev

Enclosure

Modified Block, Indented ¶s, Open

BUSINESS WRITING, INCORPORATED
Communications Consultants

2203 CEDAR DRIVE, E. / HICKSVILLE, NEW YORK 11804 / 212-869-2560

          February 12, 19--

          Miss Margaret Lamson
          62200 Beacon Hill Road
          Waterbury, CT 06716

          Dear Miss Lamson

          SUBJECT: Letter Writing Manual

          Thank you for your letter of February 5 requesting a copy
          of our Letter Writing Manual. I regret that this manual
          is not yet in printed form. The mimeographed copies cur-
          rently available are restricted to use in our offices.

          We have adopted the block form illustrated in this letter.
          You will observe that machine adjustments are simpler, re-
          sulting in a saving of much time by the typist. The date,
          address, salutation, and closing lines all begin at the
          left margin. Paragraphs are blocked also. The form is
          used in many business offices.

          You should get a copy of our Letter Writing Manual in a
          few weeks. There is no charge for the manual. We hope
          you will find it useful. Please write me again if I can
          send you any additional information.

          Sincerely yours

          S. James Whitmore

          S. James Whitmore
          President

          rsk

Block, Open

BUSINESS WRITING, INCORPORATED
Communications Consultants

2203 CEDAR DRIVE, E. / HICKSVILLE, NEW YORK 11804 / 212-869-2560

          October 5, 19--

          Mr. S. W. Jackson, Manager
          North American Cement Corp.
          39501 Bartlett Avenue
          Boston, MA 02129

          AMS SIMPLIFIED STYLE

          This letter is typed in the timesaving simplified style
          recommended by the Administrative Management Society.
          To type a letter in the AMS style, follow these steps:

          1. Use block format with blocked paragraphs.

          2. Omit the salutation and complimentary close.

          3. Include a subject heading and type it in ALL CAPS a
             triple space below the address; triple-space from
             the subject line to the first line of the body.

          4. Type enumerated items at the left margin; indent
             unnumbered listed items five spaces.

          5. Type the writer's name and title in ALL CAPS at least
             four line spaces below the letter body.

          6. Type the reference initials (typist's only) a double
             space below the writer's name.

          Correspondents in your company will like the AMS simpli-
          fied letter style not only for the "eye appeal" it gives
          letters but also because it reduces letter-writing costs.

          S. James Whitmore

          S. JAMES WHITMORE - PRESIDENT

          akb

AMS Simplified

ADDRESSING ENVELOPES

Address Placement and Spacing. Block the address lines; use single spacing. Type the city and state names and ZIP Code in that sequence on the bottom line.

For a small envelope, start the address lines 2″ from the top and 2½″ from the left edge.

For a large envelope, start the address lines 2½″ from the top and 4″ from the left edge.

State Abbreviations. When the ZIP Code is known, use the 2-letter abbreviation (page viii) in all caps, without a period. Type the ZIP Code 2 spaces after the abbreviation. If the ZIP Code is not known, type the state name in full or use the standard abbreviation.

Notations. Type postal directions, such as AIRMAIL and SPECIAL DELIVERY, below the space required for the stamp. Type HOLD FOR ARRIVAL, PERSONAL, PLEASE FORWARD, etc., a triple space below the return address and 3 spaces from the left edge.

Return Address. Type the return address on the second line from the top and 3 spaces from the left edge.

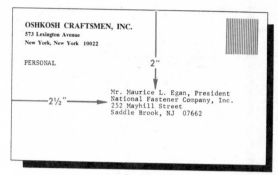

Small Envelope

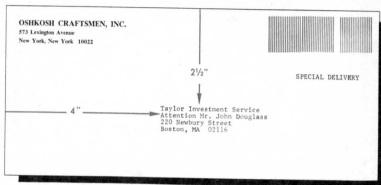

Large Envelope

FOLDING-AND-INSERTING PROCEDURE FOR ENVELOPES

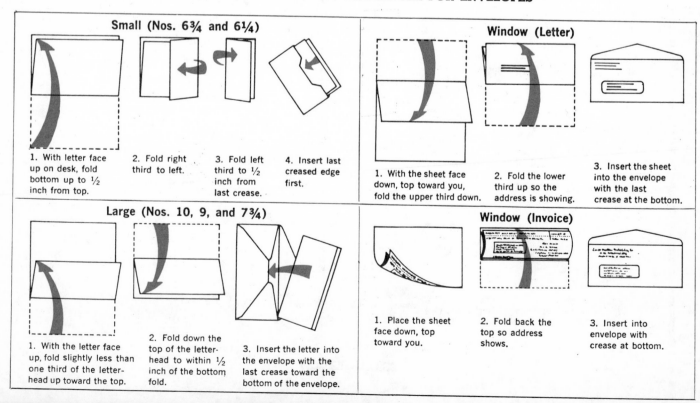

Small (Nos. 6¾ and 6¼)

1. With letter face up on desk, fold bottom up to ½ inch from top.
2. Fold right third to left.
3. Fold left third to ½ inch from last crease.
4. Insert last creased edge first.

Window (Letter)

1. With the sheet face down, top toward you, fold the upper third down.
2. Fold the lower third up so the address is showing.
3. Insert the sheet into the envelope with the last crease at the bottom.

Large (Nos. 10, 9, and 7¾)

1. With the letter face up, fold slightly less than one third of the letterhead up toward the top.
2. Fold down the top of the letterhead to within ½ inch of the bottom fold.
3. Insert the letter into the envelope with the last crease toward the bottom of the envelope.

Window (Invoice)

1. Place the sheet face down, top toward you.
2. Fold back the top so address shows.
3. Insert into envelope with crease at bottom.

LETTER-PLACEMENT POINTERS

Margins and Date Placement. Some offices use standard side margins for all letters. Others vary the side margins according to letter length, as is the case in the following guide:

5-Stroke Words in Letter Body	Side Margins	Date Line
Up to 100	2"	20
101 – 300	1½"	18–12*
Over 300	1"	12

*Date line is moved up 2 line spaces for each additional 50 words.

The horizontal placement of the date depends on the style of letter, design of the letterhead, or a combination of these factors.

Block and AMS Simplified Styles: Type the date at the left margin.

Modified Block Style: Begin date at center point or type it even with right margin.

Address. Type the first line of the address on the fourth line space below the date. Type an official title, when used, on either the first or second line, whichever gives better balance.

Attention Line. Type an attention line, when used, on the second line below the letter address and a double space above the salutation. Type it at the left margin (preferred), or center it.

Subject Line. Type a subject line on the second line below the salutation. In block or AMS Simplified styles, type the subject line even with the left margin. In other styles, type it even with the left margin, at paragraph point, or centered.

Type the word *Subject* in all capitals or with only the first letter capitalized, or omit it (as in the AMS Simplified style).

Company Name in Closing. When the company name is included in the closing, type it in all caps on the second line below the complimentary close.

Typewritten Name and Official Title. Type the name of the writer of a letter and his official title on the 4th line space below the complimentary close, or on the 4th line space below the company name when it is used. Type the writer's name and his official title on the same line, or type the title below the writer's name.

Enclosure Notation. Type an enclosure notation (*Enc.* or *Enclosure*) on the second line space below the reference initials.

Two-Page Letters. Include at least two lines of a paragraph at the bottom of the first page and at least two lines at the top of the second page of a two-page letter. Do the same for any letter of more than one page.

Begin the heading on continuation pages an inch from the top edge of the sheet. You may use either the block or horizontal form. Leave 2 or 3 blank lines between the heading and the first line of the resumed letter; use the same side margins as for the first page.

Second-Page Headings

```
Mr. A. C. Dow
Page 2
May 6, 19--
```
Block Form

Horizontal Form

```
Mr. A. C. Dow      2      May 6, 19--
```

GUIDES FOR WORD DIVISION

Divide—

1. Words between syllables only.

2. Hyphenated words and compounds at hyphens only.

3. Words so that *cial, tial, cion, sion,* or *tion* are retained as a unit.

4. A word of three or more syllables at a one-letter syllable. Type the one-letter syllable on the first line unless it is part of such terminations as *ible, able,* or *ical,* in which case carry it to the second line. If two one-letter syllables come together, divide between them.

5. A word in which the final consonant is doubled when a suffix is added between the double letters, as *control-ling.*

6. A word that ends in double letters after the double letters when a suffix is added, as *will-ing.*

Do not—

7. Divide a word of five or fewer letters.

8. Separate a one-letter syllable at the beginning or end of a word.

9. Separate a two-letter syllable at the end of a word.

10. Divide the last word on a page.

11. Separate a syllable without a vowel from the rest of a word, as *would-n't.*

Avoid if possible—

12. Separating a two-letter syllable at the beginning of a word.

13. Dividing words at the ends of more than two successive lines.

14. Dividing abbreviations, numbers, and proper names; but a surname may be separated from the initials or given name, when necessary.

TWO-LETTER ABBREVIATIONS FOR STATE, DISTRICT, AND TERRITORY NAMES

These two-letter abbreviations, recommended by the U.S. Post Office Department, should be used for business addresses for which ZIP Codes are known and used.

Alabama	AL	Illinois	IL	North Carolina	NC
Alaska	AK	Indiana	IN	North Dakota	ND
Arizona	AZ	Iowa	IA	Ohio	OH
Arkansas	AR	Kansas	KS	Oklahoma	OK
California	CA	Kentucky	KY	Oregon	OR
Canal Zone	CZ	Louisiana	LA	Pennsylvania	PA
Colorado	CO	Maine	ME	Puerto Rico	PR
Connecticut	CT	Maryland	MD	Rhode Island	RI
Delaware	DE	Massachusetts	MA	South Carolina	SC
District of Columbia	DC	Michigan	MI	South Dakota	SD
Florida	FL	Minnesota	MN	Tennessee	TN
Georgia	GA	Mississippi	MS	Texas	TX
Guam	GU	Missouri	MO	Utah	UT
Hawaii	HI	Montana	MT	Vermont	VT
Idaho	ID	Nebraska	NE	Virgin Islands	VI
		Nevada	NV	Virginia	VA
		New Hampshire	NH	Washington	WA
		New Jersey	NJ	West Virginia	WV
		New Mexico	NM	Wisconsin	WI
		New York	NY	Wyoming	WY

ASSEMBLING A CARBON PACK

METHOD 1 (Desk Assembly)

1. Place the sheet ("second" or "file copy sheet") on which the carbon copy is to be made flat on the desk; then place a carbon sheet, *carbon (glossy) side down*, on top of the sheet. Add the original sheet (letterhead or plain sheet) on top of the carbon sheet.

   Note. For each carbon copy desired, add one set (the "second" or "file copy sheet" and a carbon sheet).

2. Pick up the carbon pack and turn it so the second sheets and the glossy sides of the carbon sheets face you.

3. Straighten the pack by tapping the top of the sheets gently on the desk.

4. Insert the pack by holding it firmly in one hand while turning the cylinder slowly with the other.

METHOD 2 (Machine Assembly)

1. Assemble paper for insertion into the typewriter (original sheet on top; second sheets beneath).

2. Insert paper, turning the cylinder until the sheets are gripped slightly by the feed rolls; then lay all but the last sheet over the top of the machine.

Deck Assembly of a Carbon Pack

3. Place carbon sheets between the sheets of paper with the *glossy side toward you.* Flip each sheet back as you add each carbon.

4. Roll the pack into typing position.

REMOVING THE CARBON SHEETS

Because carbon sheets do not extend to the top edge of the paper in the machine assembly of a carbon pack, the sheets can be easily removed by pulling them out all at one time as you hold the left top edge of the paper.

GUIDES FOR INSERTING A CARBON PACK

1. *To keep sheets straight when feeding,* place pack under an envelope flap or in the fold of a plain sheet of paper.

2. *To "start" the carbon pack:*
   (a) Release the paper-release lever,
   (b) Feed the pack around the cylinder until sheets appear at the front; then
   (c) Reset the paper-release lever.
   (d) After the pack is inserted, remove the envelope or paper fold.

3. *To avoid wrinkling,* release and reset the paper-release lever after the pack has been partially inserted.

Machine Assembly of a Carbon Pack

SUMMARY OF MANUSCRIPT FORM

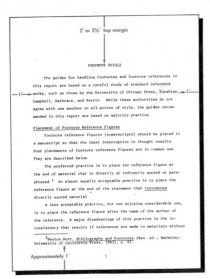

First Page, Topbound

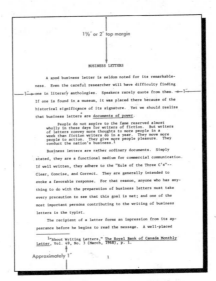

First Page, Unbound

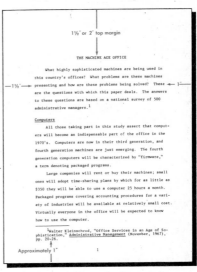

First Page, Leftbound

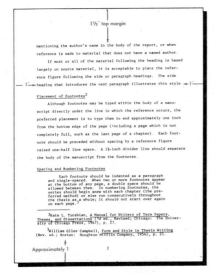

Second Page, Topbound

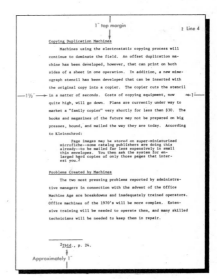

Second Page, Unbound

Second Page, Leftbound

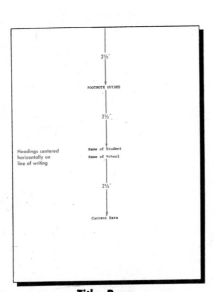

Title Page

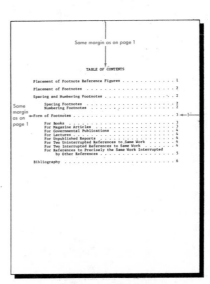

Table of Contents

Bibliography

CORRECTION SYMBOLS (PROOFREADERS' MARKS)

Sometimes typed or printed copy may be corrected with proofreaders' marks. The typist must be able to interpret correctly these marks in retyping the corrected copy or *rough draft* as it may be called. The most commonly used proofreaders' marks are shown below.

Mark	Meaning
‖	Align type
Cap or ≡	Capitalize
⌣	Close up
ℰ	Delete
ds	Double-space
=/	Hyphen
∧	Insert
✓	Insert apostrophe
⊙	Insert colon
⋋	Insert comma

Mark	Meaning
⊙	Insert period
?/	Insert question mark
ᵛ ᵛ	Insert quotation marks
; or ;/	Insert semicolon
# or #	Insert space
#>	Insert space between lines
Stet	Let it stand (ignore correction)
☐	Move to left
☐	Move to right

Mark	Meaning
no ¶ [	No new paragraph
¶	Paragraph
ss	Single-space
#	Space
SP	Spell out
═══	Straighten line
∼ or tr	Transpose
ts	Triple-space
───	Underline
l.c.	Use lower case

CENTERING SUMMARY

HORIZONTAL CENTERING

From the center, backspace once for each two letters, figures, spaces, and punctuation marks in the heading or line to be centered. (In backspacing, disregard an odd or leftover stroke.) Start typing where the backspacing ends.

HORIZONTAL CENTERING—SPREAD HEADINGS

1. From the center, backspace once for each letter except the last one in the heading and once for each space between words.
2. In typing the heading, space once after each letter or character and three times between words.

VERTICAL CENTERING
BACKSPACE-FROM-CENTER METHOD

1. Move the paper to vertical center: 34th line space for a full sheet; 17th line space for a half sheet.

2. Roll the platen back once for each two lines (including blank lines). Ignore an odd or leftover line. Start typing where the spacing ends.
3. For reading position on a full sheet, roll the platen back 2 additional line spaces.

VERTICAL CENTERING
MATHEMATICAL METHOD

1. Count lines and blank line spaces in problem.
2. Subtract lines used from lines on sheet.
3. Divide by 2 to get top and bottom margins. If a fraction results, disregard it.
4. For reading position, subtract 2 from the top margin.
5. Space down from top edge of paper 1 more than the number of lines to be left in top margin.

TABULATION SUMMARY

VERTICAL PLACEMENT

For vertical placement of tables, use either the backspace-from-center or the mathematical method explained on page x.

Spacing after Headings. Leave one blank line between a main and a secondary heading. Leave two blank lines after a secondary heading. If a secondary heading is not used, leave two blank lines after a main heading.

Leave one blank line between a columnar heading and its column.

HORIZONTAL PLACEMENT OF TABULATIONS

Columns. Note the longest item in each column. (If a columnar heading is the longest item, count it as such unless judgment indicates otherwise.) Decide the number of spaces to leave between columns, preferably an even number.

Backspace from the center of the paper once for every two spaces in the longest item in each column and once for every two spaces between all the columns. At the point where you finish backspacing, set the left margin stop for the first column.

From the left margin, space forward once for every stroke in the longest item of the first column and once for each space between the first and second columns. Set the first tab stop. Follow this same procedure for setting tab stops for the remaining columns.

Columnar Headings. Center the columnar headings over the columns.

When a heading has been counted as the longest item in a column, it will usually be necessary to reset the tab stop in order to center the column under the heading.

There are several methods of centering columnar headings over a column, but probably the easiest way is to add the first and last strokes in the column. Divide this sum by 2 to get the center point of the column. Columnar headings are usually underlined.

HORIZONTAL RULINGS

Horizontal lines are often used in a tabulated report to set off columnar headings. A double line is usually placed above columnar headings and a single line below them. A single line is also placed under the last line of the report. These lines can be the exact width of the report, or they can extend several spaces on each side of it.

To type rulings the exact width of the table, first determine the placement of columns. When you set the tab stop for the last column continue spacing forward one space for each stroke in the longest item in that column. Immediately after stroking for the last stroke in this item, move the right margin stop so that the typewriter will lock at this point. Rulings can then be typed across the page until the carriage locks.

Placement of Double Lines. After typing the secondary heading, double-space; type the first of the double lines; then operate the variable line spacer; move the cylinder forward slightly; type the second line. Double-space between this line and the columnar headings.

Placement of Single Lines. After typing the columnar headings, single-space; type a single line; then double-space to the first columnar entries. Single-space after typing the last columnar entries and type a single line.

Source Note (If Used). Double-space from the single line; type the source note at the left margin or indent 3 to 5 spaces.

TABULATOR STOPS FOR UNEVEN COLUMNS

Uneven Columns. When columns contain amounts of figures of uneven length, set the tab stop at a point that will take care of the greatest number of entries. After tabulating, backspace for longer items or space forward for shorter ones.

Dollar Signs. In a money column, type a dollar sign before the first amount in the column and before the total (if one is shown). Place the dollar sign before the first amount and the total, typed so that it will be one space to the left of the longest amount in the column (usually the total).

Totals. To make them easier to read, totals are usually separated by a double space from the column. Type the total line immediately under the last amount in the column. Do not space before typing the total line.

DRAWING RULED LINES

To Draw Horizontal Lines: Place the pencil point through the cardholder (or on the type bar guide above the ribbon); depress the carriage-release lever to draw the carriage across the line.

To Draw Vertical Lines: Operate the line finder. Place the pencil point or pen through the cardholder (or on the type bar guide above the ribbon). Roll the platen up the page until you have a line of the desired length. Remove the pen or pencil and reset the line finder.

HOW TO ERASE AND CORRECT ERRORS

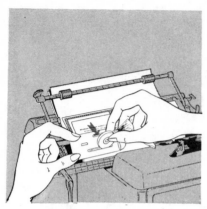

Using an Eraser Shield

1. Depress margin-release key and move carriage to extreme left or right to prevent eraser crumbs from falling into the typing mechanism.
2. To avoid disturbing the paper alignment of the type, turn the cylinder forward if the erasure is to be made on the upper two thirds of the paper; backward, on the lower third of the paper.
3. To erase on the original sheet, lift the paper bail out of the way, and place a 5″ x 3″ card *in front of* the first carbon sheet. Use an eraser shield to protect the writing that is not to be erased. Brush the eraser crumbs away from the typewriter.
4. Move the protective card in front of the second carbon, if more than one copy is being made. Erase the errors on the carbon copy with a soft (or pencil) eraser first, then with the hard typewriter eraser used in erasing on the original copy.
5. When the error has been erased on all copies, remove the protective card, position the carriage to the proper point, and type the necessary correction.

SQUEEZING AND SPREADING OF LETTERS

In correcting errors, it is often possible to "squeeze" omitted letters into half spaces or to "spread" letters to fill out spaces.

1. *An omitted letter at the beginning or end of a word:*

Error: an omitte letter
Correction: an omittedletter

Corrective steps:
1. Move carriage to the letter *e.*
2. Depress and hold down the space bar; strike the letter *d.*

Note. On an electric typewriter, it may be necessary to hold the carriage by hand at the half-space point.

2. *An omitted letter within a word:*

Error: a leter within
Correction: a letter within

Corrective steps:
1. Erase the incorrect word.
2. Position the carriage at the space after the letter *a.*
3. Press down and hold the space bar; strike the letter *l.*
4. Release the space bar, then press it down again and hold it; strike the next letter.
5. Repeat the process for any additional letters.

3. *Addition of a letter within a word:*

Error: a lettter within
Correction: a letter within

Corrective steps:
1. Erase the incorrect word.
2. Position the carriage as if you were going to type the letter *l* in its regular position following the space.
3. Press down and hold the space bar; strike the letter *l.*
4. Release the space bar; then repeat the process for each remaining letter.

IBM SELECTIC TYPEWRITER

When making corrections, you may locate the horizontal position of the typing element by using either the black line on the clear view card holder (circled at right) or the red arrow on the margin scale. If you use the card holder as your indicator, position the black line at the point on the paper at which you want to insert the new character. Then return to the line of type and insert the correction.

Crowding Letters

Error: the ordr today
Correction: the order today

To crowd the "e" into "ordr," erase the final "r." Backspace until the black line on the card holder is over the space formerly occupied by the final "r." Place the palm of the right hand on the top of the front cover. Reach under the cover and press LEFT against the carrier position post with your finger until the black line is moved back one-half space (as indicated in the illustration). Hold the carrier in this position and type the "e." Repeat the procedure for the "r."

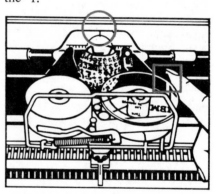

Spreading Letters

Error: He will send
Correction: He can send

To replace "will" with "can," first erase "will." Type "c" in place of "w" and type "n" in place of final "l."

Position the black line on the card holder over the position occupied by the first "l." Place the palm of the right hand on the top of the front cover. Reach under the cover and press left against the carrier position post with your finger until the black line of the card holder is directly between the "i" and "l." Type "a." Release the carrier and continue to type.